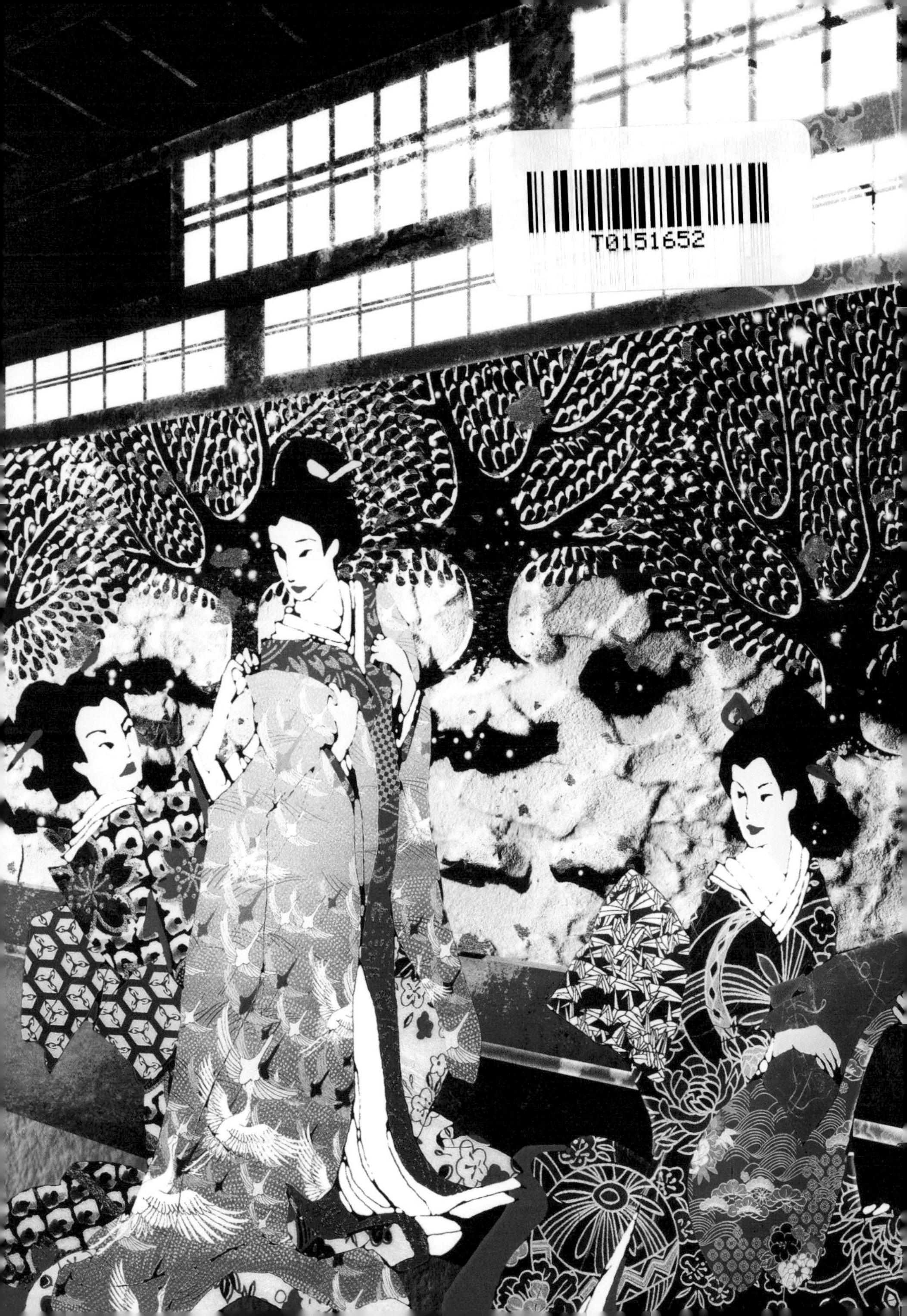

JAPAN
IN 100 WORDS

FROM ANIME TO ZEN
Discover the Essential
Elements of Japan

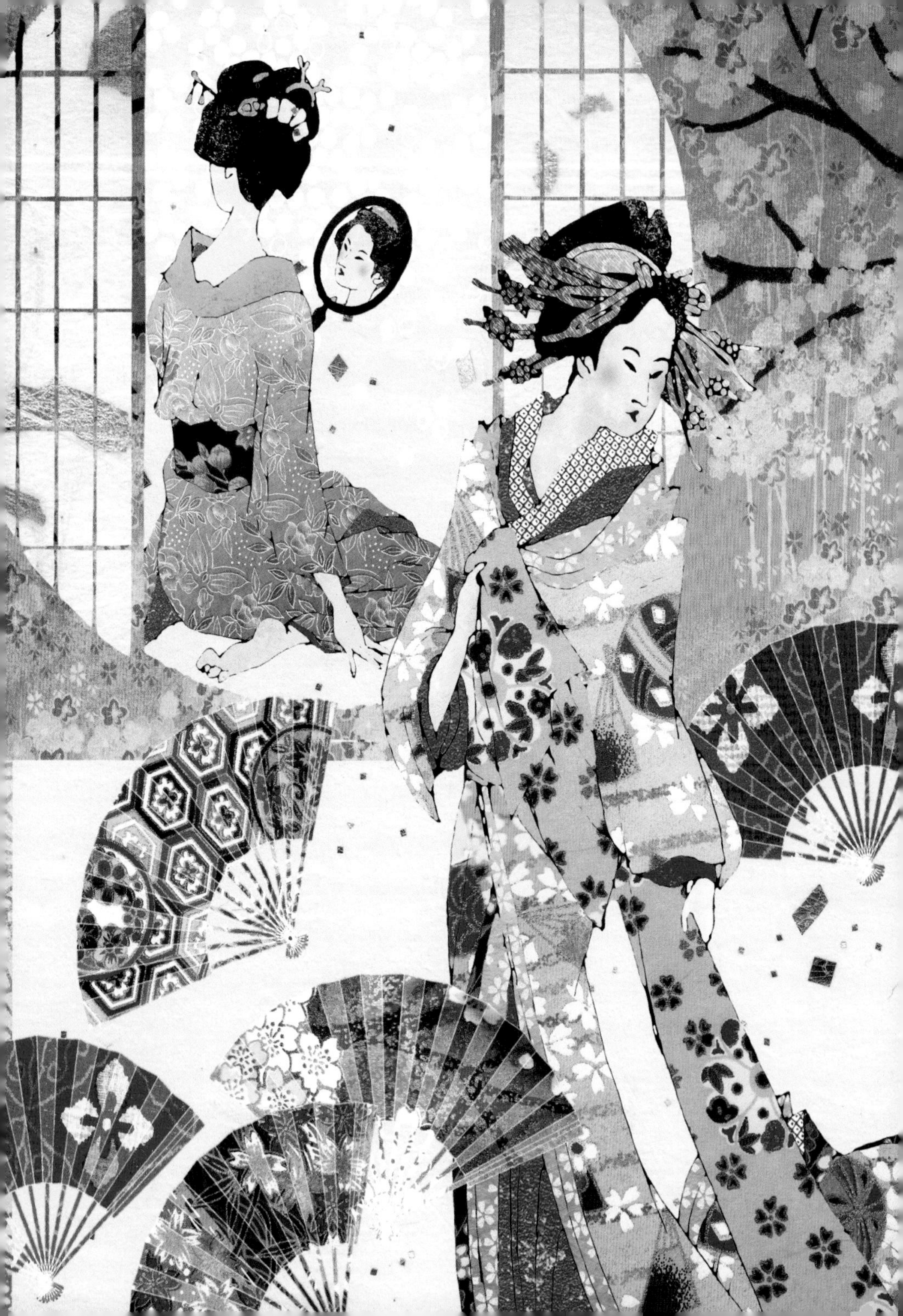

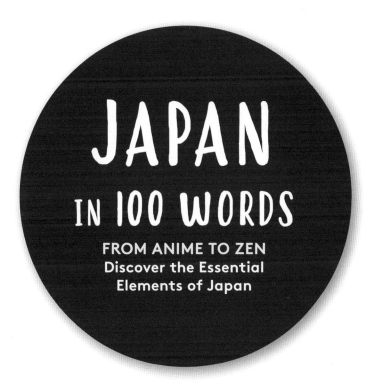

JAPAN
IN 100 WORDS

FROM ANIME TO ZEN
Discover the Essential
Elements of Japan

Ornella Civardi & Gavin Blair
Illustrations by **Ayano Otani**

TUTTLE Publishing

Tokyo | Rutland, Vermont | Singapore

ANIME

BONSAI

FUGU

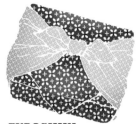

FUROSHIKI

4 **HASHI**

KABUKI

KIMONO

NINJA

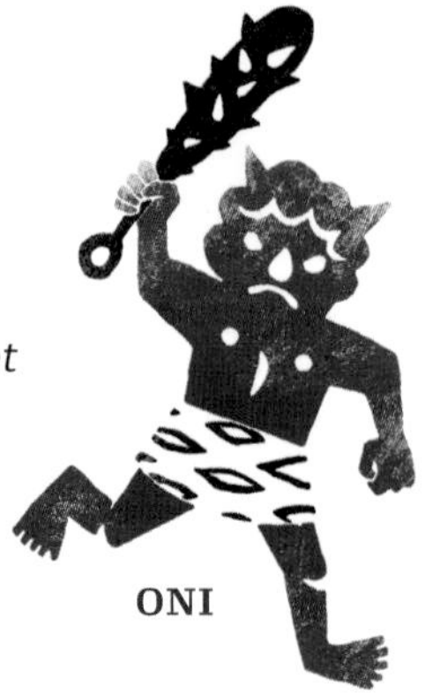
ONI

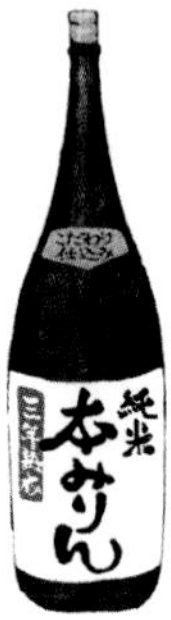
純米
本みりん
SAKE

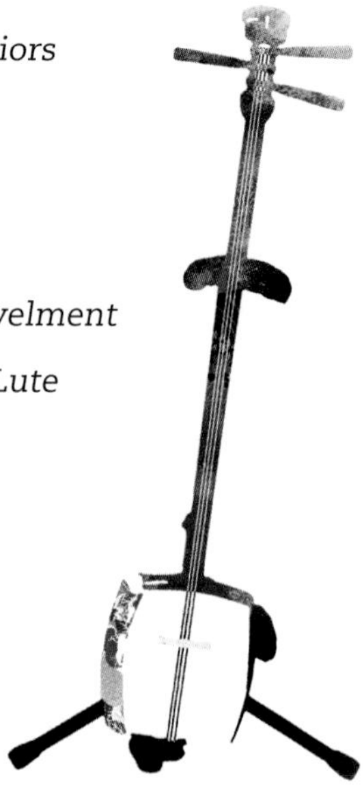
SHAMISEN

SHŌJI

UKIYO-E

WABI SABI

アイヌ
Ainu

The Native People of Hokkaido

Though less well-known than many others, the story of Japan's Ainu people is sadly reminiscent of indigenous populations around the globe: subjugation, stolen lands and the destruction of culture and language. One legend says, "Ainu lived in this place a hundred thousand years before the Children of the Sun came." In reality, it was likely thousands of years before the Japanese arrived. They once occupied the northern part of the main Honshu island, Hokkaido, and the Kuril Islands, now controlled by Russia. During the middle ages, the Japanese pushed them northward and brought diseases that, along with conflicts, decimated their populations and confined them to Hokkaido.

Ainu genetics link them to the people of Tibet, the Indian Andaman Islands, northern Myanmar and Okinawa. They were generally lighter skinned, more hirsute, had deep-set wide eyes and were bigger than the Japanese. Ainu were animistic hunter-gatherers who believed the bear to be the most important of the spirits that occupy all nature. Traditionally, the men never shaved and the women tattooed themselves around their mouths and sometimes on their forearms. They lived in villages of thatched huts and dressed in robes spun from elm tree bark, tied with a waistband, with leggings of deerskin in winter.

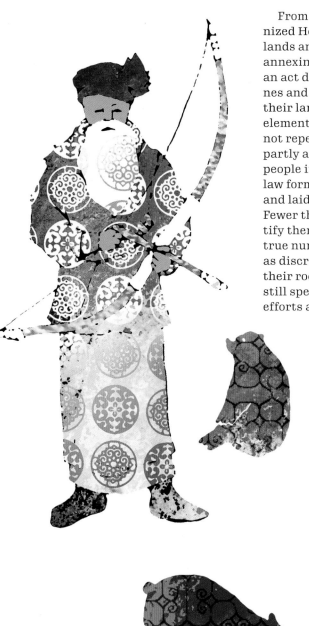

From the 16th century, Japan colonized Hokkaido, again taking Ainu lands and suppressing their culture, annexing the island in 1869. In 1899, an act declared Ainu former aborigines and forced assimilation, banning their language, tattoos and other elements of their culture. The act was not repealed until 1997 and they were partly acknowledged as indigenous people in 2008. In February 2019, a law formally recognized Ainu culture and laid out measures to preserve it. Fewer than 20,000 people now identify themselves as Ainu, though the true number may be ten times that, as discrimination led many to hide their roots. Only a handful of people still speak the Ainu language, though efforts are underway to revive it.

9

アニメ

Anime

Japanese Animated Films

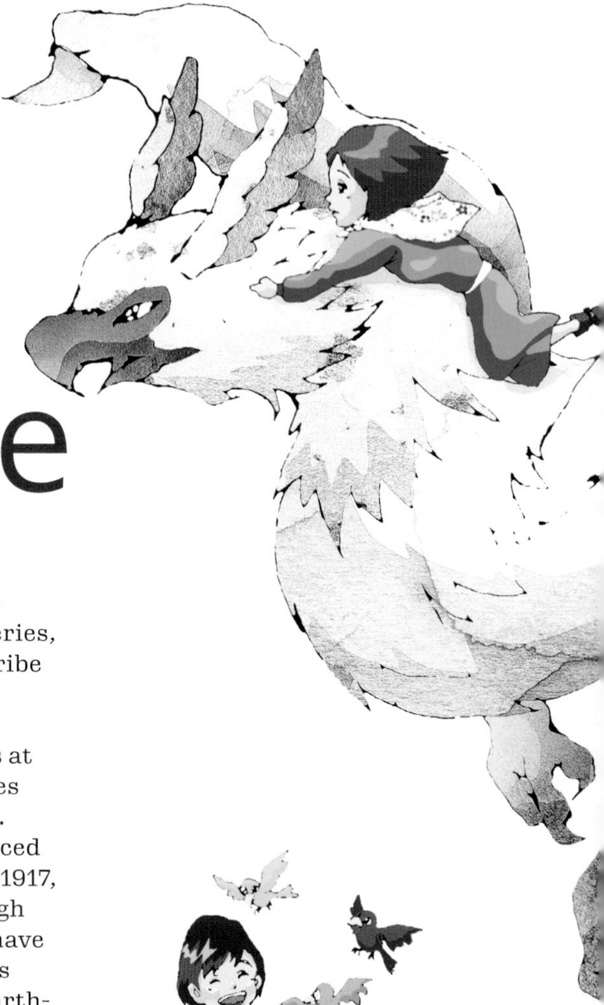

Though elsewhere *anime* refers to Japanese cartoon films and TV series, in Japan the term is used to describe all animated content.

The genres of *anime* are legion, spanning frivolous stories of kids at *ninja* school to epic dystopian tales addressing philosophical themes.

The history of *anime* can be traced back to a few short films made in 1917, including *Namakura Gatana,* though earlier productions are likely to have existed. The nascent industry was devastated by the Great Kantō Earthquake of 1923, which razed much of Tokyo. A pivotal moment came in 1948 with the founding of what is now the leading studio, Toei Animation. As well as creating some of *anime*'s seminal works, such as *Dragon Ball, Sailor Moon* and *One Piece,* Toei Animation was instrumental in the careers of directors Osamu Tezuka, Leiji Matsumoto and Studio Ghibli founders Hayao Miyazaki and Isao Takahata.

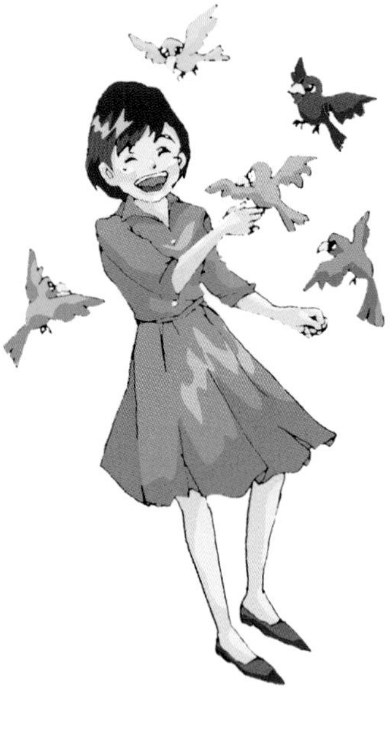

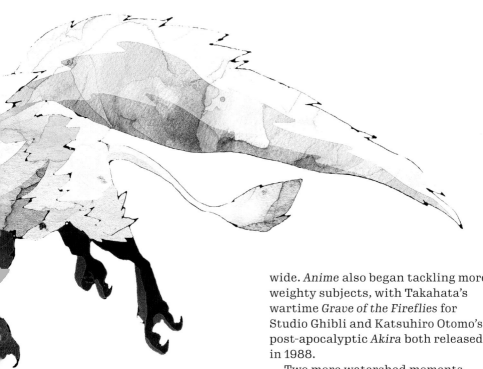

Tezuka's seminal *Tetsuwan Atomu* TV series began screening in 1963, which helped to set the pattern for *anime* adaptations of *manga* and popularize robot and space-themed productions. Other new *anime* styles born in the 1960s included sport and erotica, along with the family tale *Sazae-san,* which became a national institution with a world record of more than 7,500 weekly episodes.

The 1970s and 1980s saw the further rise of robot *anime*, with stories like *Gundam* garnering fans world-wide. *Anime* also began tackling more weighty subjects, with Takahata's wartime *Grave of the Fireflies* for Studio Ghibli and Katsuhiro Otomo's post-apocalyptic *Akira* both released in 1988.

Two more watershed moments came in 1995, with Hideaki Anno's ambitious *Neon Genesis Evangelion* series redefining the robot genre, and Mamoru Oshii's cyberpunk classic *Ghost in the Shell* asking existential questions.

Studio Ghibli was all-conquering in the late 1990s and 2000s, with Miyazaki's *Princess Mononoke* (1997) only topped by his own *Spirited Away,* which won the best animated film Oscar and set an unbeaten Japanese box office record. Today, it is a 2 trillion yen industry.

弁当
Bentō

Iconic Box Lunches

At one level, the *bentō* is simply a lunch box containing ready-to-eat food in separate compartments. But it carries a deeper meaning in Japanese culture than its function might suggest and is often referred to honorifically as *o-bentō*.

The precise origins of *bentō* are unclear, but the word has been in use since the 13th century to refer to the box itself, traditionally made from lacquer since the 16th century. *Bentō* have certainly been eaten for centuries at *hanami* cherry blossom viewing parties, as well between acts at traditional *Nō* and *Kabuki* theatrical performances.

In more recent times, the most common consumers of *bentō* have

EKIBEN

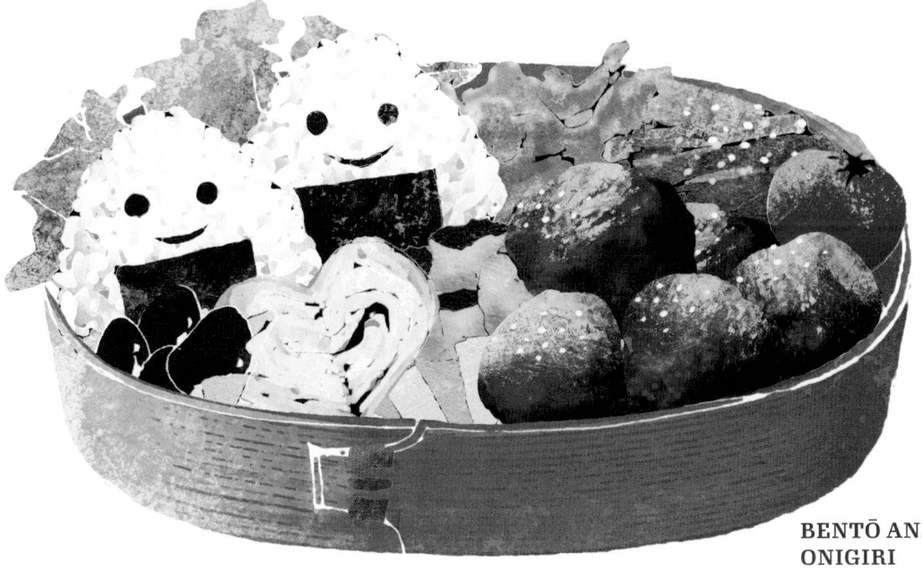

BENTŌ AND ONIGIRI

been schoolchildren and *salariiman* office workers. Homemade *o-bentō* is seen not only as a means of providing a balanced, nutritious and aesthetically pleasing meal, but also an expression of the maker's love for the recipient. That task has fallen almost entirely on women, who often feel considerable social pressure to create these mini masterpieces on a daily basis, even though *konbini-bentō* are readily available at convenience stores. As the number of working women has increased sharply in recent years, many mothers have felt obliged to get up even earlier to prepare *bentō* for their husbands and children.

These days, *bentō* boxes come in many shapes and sizes, with designs featuring characters from *anime* or *manga* popular with children. Even the food inside can be intricately prepared to form *kyaraben* (character *bentō*), which look like characters from popular culture.

Onigiri

The *onigiri* rice ball is a staple of *o-bentō* and usually consists of a filling of vegetable, fish or meat encased in white rice, often wrapped in *nori* seaweed. It is perhaps the closest Japanese equivalent to a sandwich, which are themselves sometimes found in *bentō* nowadays.

Ekiben

Ekiben, literally station *bentō,* are found at train stations, usually for consumption onboard. Now an integral part of train travel, they were first sold in 1885 on trains from Utsonomiya to Tokyo's Ueno.

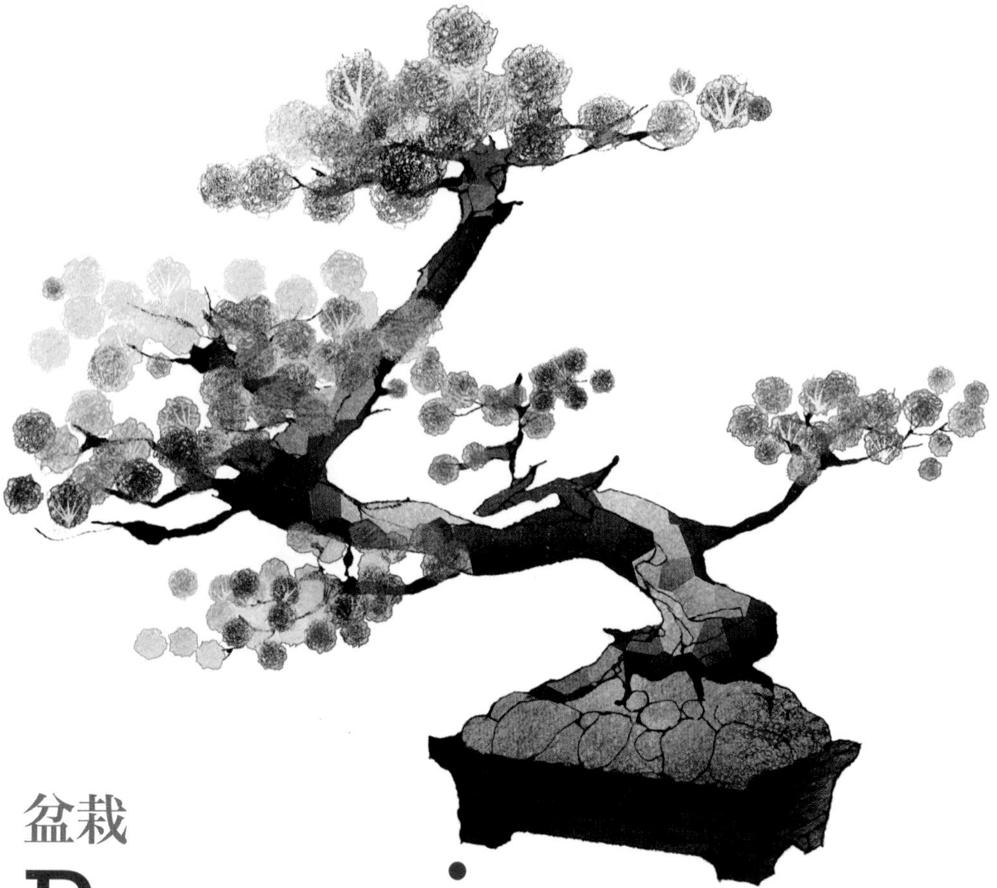

盆栽

Bonsai

Sculptural Potted Plants

The cultivation of dwarf trees in containers was developed in China and came to Japan possibly more than 1,000 years ago, likely brought by the monks whose teachings would form the basis of Zen Buddhism. Though the term *bonsai*, literally "tray plant," would not come into use until many centuries later, the art was gradually refined in Japan, adding local aesthetics and characteristics.

Many of the early practitioners were Zen monks, who brought to bear principles from the emerging philosophy on the new art form. Asymmetry, embracing the imperfections of nature and an acceptance that the cultivation of a *bonsai* tree is an ongoing process requiring prolonged attention, are all influenced by Zen thought.

Bonsai are grown from standard trees, though the practice is thought to have begun in China with dwarf varieties, which are manipulated through cutting, repotting and wiring in order to achieve the desired shape.

The art began as the preserve of the upper echelons of society, but spread to become widely practiced among ordinary folk. However, one of the best known bonsai has been in the imperial family for centuries, cared for by successive emperors. It has been granted the status of a National Treasure.

Bonseki

Bonseki is a relative of bonsai, sharing their first character. Seki means "stone," referring to the materials used along with sand to create miniaturized landscapes in shallow trays of lacquer.

Kokedama

Kokedama sprung from bonsai and consists of a plant growing from a suspended clump of soil surrounded by a moss ball—the direct translation of the term.

Both bonseki and kokedama are centuries old, and like bonsai reflect the Zen concept of wabi sabi, accepting and respectful of aging, flaws and simplicity.

武道
Budō

The Japanese Martial Arts

Although fighting systems are to be found in nearly every country, no one has codified and imbued them with intricate etiquette, rituals and spiritual elements to the extent the Japanese have. The range of Japan's martial arts is also remarkable. The Japanese Association of Budō consists of federations representing nine separate disciplines: *aikidō, jūdō, jūkendō, karatedō, kendō, kyūdō, naginata, shōrinji kenpō* and sumo. That by no means covers all the martial arts in the country.

Budō means "martial way" and it is the *dō* aspect that contributes to the distinctive nature of Japan's fighting arts. Beyond the skills to be gained by practicing such disciplines, it is the peace of mind, character development and respectfulness that traditional exponents regard as even more important than the physical attributes. The journey on the path of self-improvement towards an unattainable perfection is seen as an end in itself, and one that brings greater

rewards than a technically accomplished kick, throw or sword cut.

The mother of Japanese martial arts is often said to be *jūjitsu*, also written as *jūjutsu*, from which both *jūdō* and *aikidō* sprung, while it also influenced some schools of *karate*. There were at one time more than 2,000 different schools of *jūjitsu*, most practicing both unarmed and armed combat. Mirroring the decline of the samurai, the emphasis on *jutsu* or practical technique elements shifted to a focus on the *dō* aspects. *Jūdō* went on to become an Olympic sport and discarded much of its traditional syllabus in favor of the pursuit of medals. Meanwhile, disciplines such as *naginata*—the art of using a traditional Japanese spear—still eschew competition and remain entirely dedicated to perfecting technique for its own sake. Other martial arts, like *karate*, straddle both worlds, with some practitioners and *dōjō* focusing on competition and some on the traditional methods and goals.

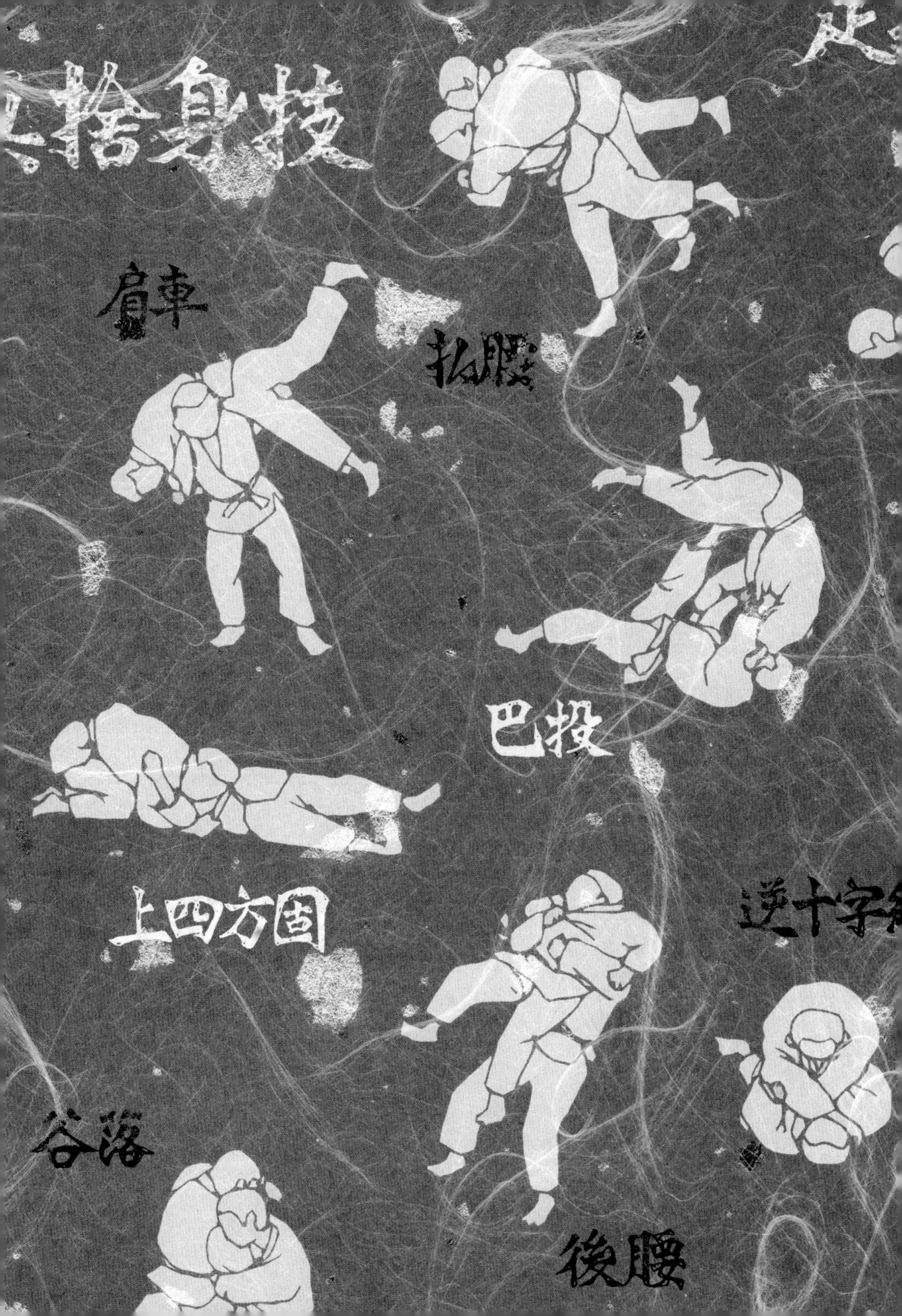
捨身技
肩車
払腰
巴投
上四方固
逆十字
谷落
後腰

Dōjō

Martial arts' training is properly referred to as *keiko* and takes place in a *dōjō,* the "place of the way." A traditional *dōjō* is a relatively sparse building, usually with a sprung wooden floor, a *shōmen* main wall that serves as its center and towards which the bows that begin and end *keiko* are directed, and training equipment. The *shōmen* will usually house a *kamidana* (shelf of the gods), a small altar that has Shintō roots and often contains a picture of the founder of the *ryūha* (style) and scrolls depicting the lineage of the *sensei* (honorable teacher).

Kyūdō

The traditional archery of *kyūdō* is one of the purest forms of *budō* in the sense that its *keiko* and rituals are focused on goals beyond technical improvement. Nevertheless, skillfully wielding a 2 m (6.5 ft) *yumi* long bow takes considerable strength and body control. Competitions are held, and *kyūdō* has a higher proportion of female practitioners than other *budō* in Japan.

Iaidō

Iaidō, the way of drawing and cutting with a *katana* samurai sword, is another discipline with lofty goals steeped in ancient traditions. Competition or sparring with live blades is disallowed, so the perfection of technique and elevation of the spirit is pursued without distraction.

Kendō

Kendō was developed to enable the way of the sword to be practiced safely without a metal sword. The *shinai* bamboo sword and armor allow *kendōka* to attack each other with full-blooded intent, but without blood being spilled. Although

AIKIDŌ

regional, national and world championships are major events, the emphasis in *kendō* remains on traditional values.

Aikidō

One of Japan's newer martial arts, *aikidō* was founded by Ueshiba Morihei in the early 20th century. The term can be translated as "the way of combining forces," and it is a system of joint locks and throws based on using an attacker's force against them. Ueshiba taught his art as a way of promoting peace, both within and between people. *Aikidō* is criticized for a lack of realism in some quarters and *ryūha* which place more emphasis on practicality now exist.

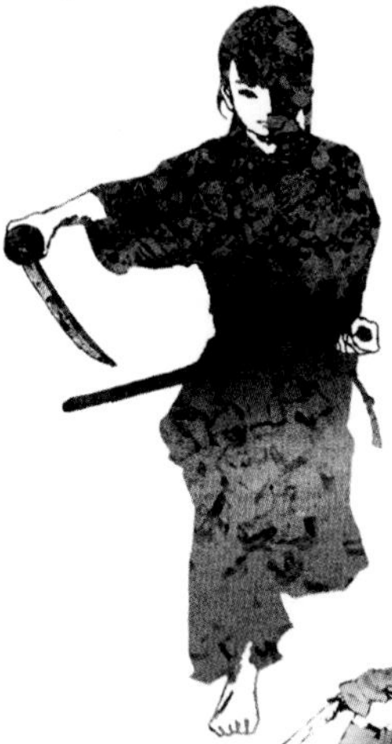

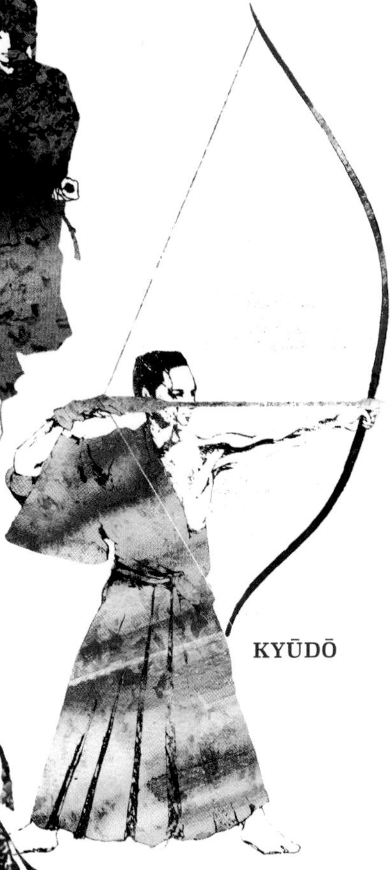
KYŪDŌ

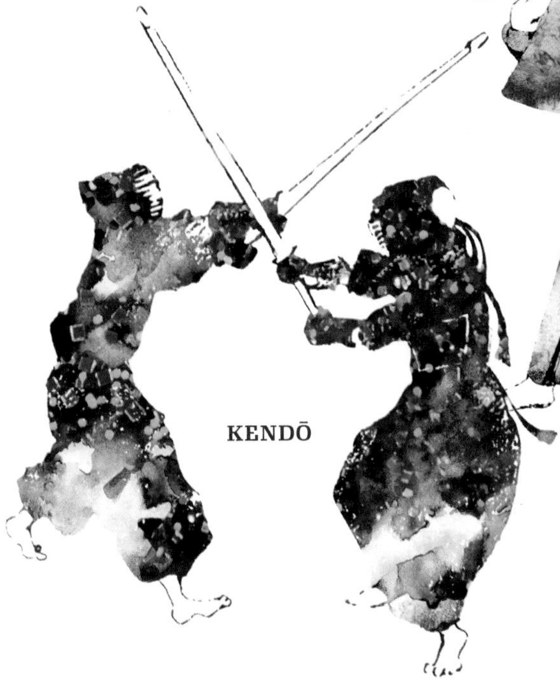
KENDŌ

文楽

Bunraku

Japanese Puppet Theater

The Japanese puppet theater is unusual in that the puppeteers are entirely visible behind the large figures they maneuver throughout the performance. Once the action begins, however, the audience ceases to notice them. They disappear like magic into the captivating flow of the narrative, into the rhythmic music, and behind the carefully controlled movements of the puppets' tiniest features. *Bunraku* or *Jōruri*, as it was initially called, is the product of the interaction of the following three arts: the narrator's recitation, which grants the characters a voice that varies in tone from time to time; the sweet and melancholic music of the *shamisen*, which underscores the dramatic moments; and the virtuosity of the puppeteer, who gives the puppet an amazingly expressive quality. Only when these three components are perfectly coordinated does the marionette acquire a soul and truly captivate the viewer.

Giri-ninjō

The person who created what we know today as *Bunraku* in the late 17th century was the brilliant screenwriter Chikamatsu Monzaemon. His dramas often revolve around a painful inner conflict between personal sentiments (*ninjō*) and duty (*giri*), which for the samurai meant obligatory loyalty to a lord, while for lovers, it meant an unbridgeable difference in caste. Suicide is nearly always the sole possible conclusion.

Shinjū

This can be translated as "union of hearts" but it actually means death. When love becomes impossible due to social prohibitions or destiny, it can only triumph through the couple's suicide. *Bunraku* and *Kabuki* plays, which are full of such tales, are inspired by a chronicle of the Edo period, when, for the first time, suicide came to be seen as an act of rebellion against authority.

Ningyō

These puppets (*ningyō* means "dolls"), which are nearly the size of humans, weigh up to 20 kg (44 lb) and are garbed in sumptuous costumes. In addition to gesturing, they can move their eyes, knit their brows, and open their mouths. Each requires three men to operate: the chief puppeteer, who moves the right arm, head and eyes—the features that convey the expressiveness of the character—and two helpers, often covered by hoods that render them symbolically invisible, who are in charge of the left arm and legs.

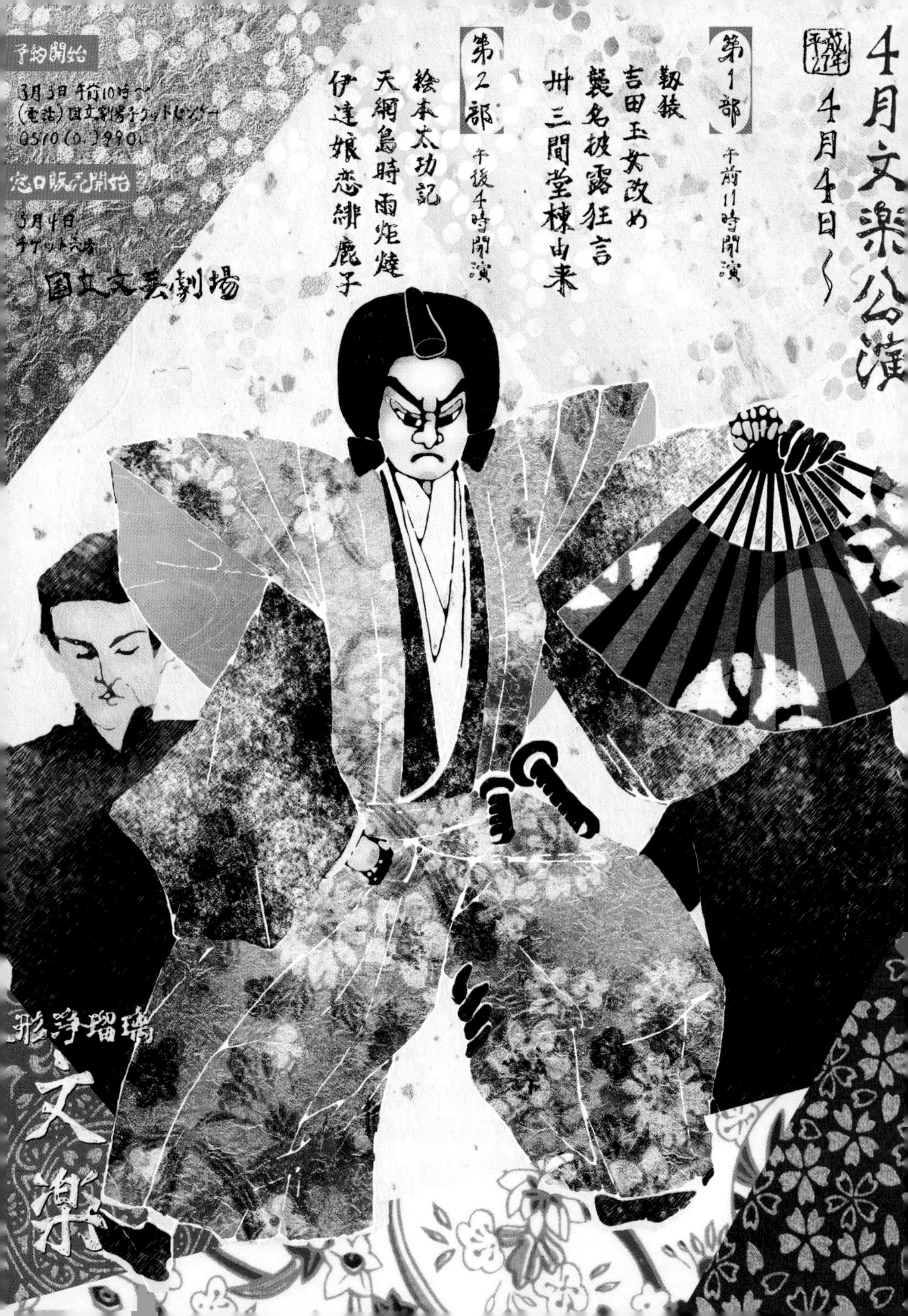
平成27年
4月文楽公演
4月4日〜
第1部
午前11時開演
靭猿
吉田玉女改め
襲名披露狂言
卅三間堂棟由来
第2部
午後4時開演
絵本太功記
天網島時雨炬燵
伊達娘恋緋鹿子
予約開始
3月3日 午前10時〜
(電話)国立文楽劇場チケットセンター
窓口販売開始
3月4日
チケット売場
国立文楽劇場
人形浄瑠璃
文楽

部落民
Burakumin

Social Outcasts of Japan

Though Japan is widely seen, and largely views itself, as homogeneous and egalitarian, that is not the whole picture. One group faced centuries of discrimination, and its descendants are yet to be freed from the vestiges of prejudice: the *burakumin*. Akin to India's untouchables, their forebears were designated outside and below the four Edo-period social castes. *Burakumin* is a euphemistic term meaning "village people" and refers to the separate neighborhoods in which they were forced to live. The origins of the *burakumin* were two separate outcast peoples. The *eta,* which means "full of filth/defilement," were those whose work brought them into contact with death, such as butchers, executioners, hide tanners and morticians, all considered unclean in Buddhism and Shintoism. *Hinin*, literally "non-humans," were comprised of beggars, ex-convicts, prostitutes, sanitation workers and certain types of entertainers. Although people were born into both groups, it was also possible to drop into them by committing unclean deeds. *Hinin* could be adopted into a family of a higher status, but for *eta*, their fate was sealed.

The 1868 Meiji Restoration dissolved the caste system, but the new commoners still faced fierce discrimination. Two rounds of legislation in the 20th century failed to end the problem, which was far more ingrained in the west of Japan than elsewhere. With employment discrimination rampant in the postwar era, some *burakumin* became *yakuza* and, along with Korean-Japanese, made up a majority of members in some major gangs.

In the 1970s, *burakumin* activists discovered a handwritten book that was being sold to companies listing the names of *buraku* areas so they could avoid employing people from them. The book was also used by families to ensure prospective in-laws had no such roots. Today, things have fortunately changed.

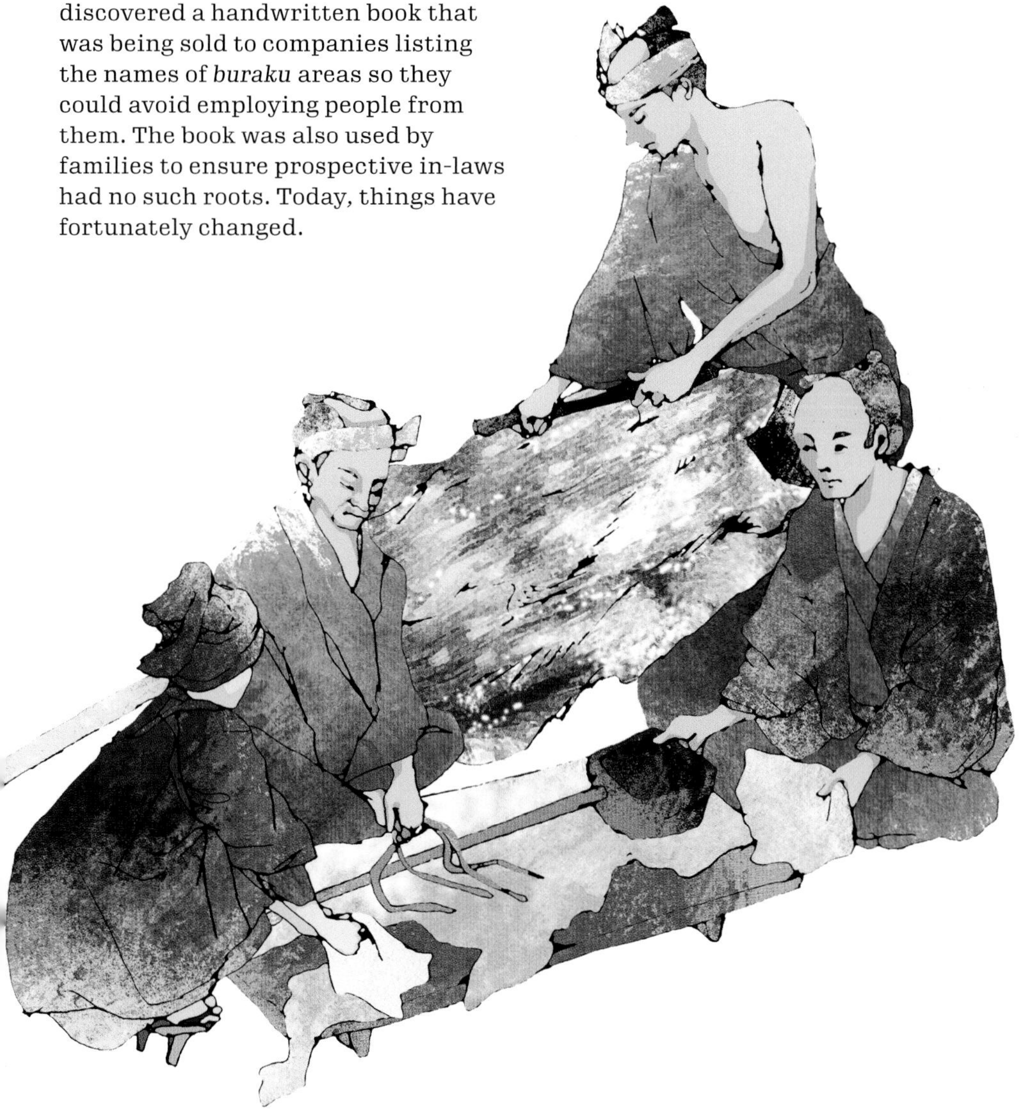

武士道
Bushidō

The Way of the Warrior

If the samurai are some of the most revered, studied and mythologized warriors in the history of warfare, then the code of *bushidō* has played a significant role in that. At the core of a set of principles for samurai to live by, is unwavering loyalty to their lord and an unflinching acceptance of death. This meant not just bravery in battle, but an acknowledgment of mortality that leads to walking a righteous path in life. A samurai in violation of the code was expected to commit the excruciatingly painful ritual of *seppuku* disembowelment with his short sword.

Bushidō, "the way of the warrior," was shaped by Confucianism and Zen Buddhism. The earliest concepts of *bushidō* are believed to have emerged more than a millennium ago, before the word samurai came into use. With the samurai's rise during the *Sengoku Jidai* (Age of Warring States) in the 15th and 16th ccenturies, which ended with them becoming the unifiers and rulers of Japan, the scope of *bushidō* broadened to take account of their elevated status.

The *Hagakure*, the text that summarizes *bushidō* better than any other, was paradoxically written during the long period of peace that began in 1600 with the Tokugawa shogunate, when many samurai effectively became noble bureaucrats and their ideal qualities shifted again.

A relaunch of the ideals in the *Hagakure* came in 1899 with the publication of Nitobe Inazō's *Bushidō: The Soul of Japan*, first written in English. Nitobe identified eight virtues in *bushidō*: rectitude (*gi*), courage (*yū*), compassion (*jin*), respect (*rei*), honesty (*makoto*), honor (*meiyo*), loyalty (*chūgi*) and self-control (*jisei*), and believed that these qualities profoundly shaped modern Japanese culture and society.

Hagakure

"The way of the samurai is found in death." So opens the *Hagakure*, a collection of thoughts on the path of the warrior with which Yamamoto Tsunetomo summarizes the samurai's code of honor. Yamamoto composed it when his lord died, in 1700, after becoming a monk, in order to pass on the ideals that founded the ethics of the warrior and the Japanese people.

武士の流儀

The Code of the Samurai

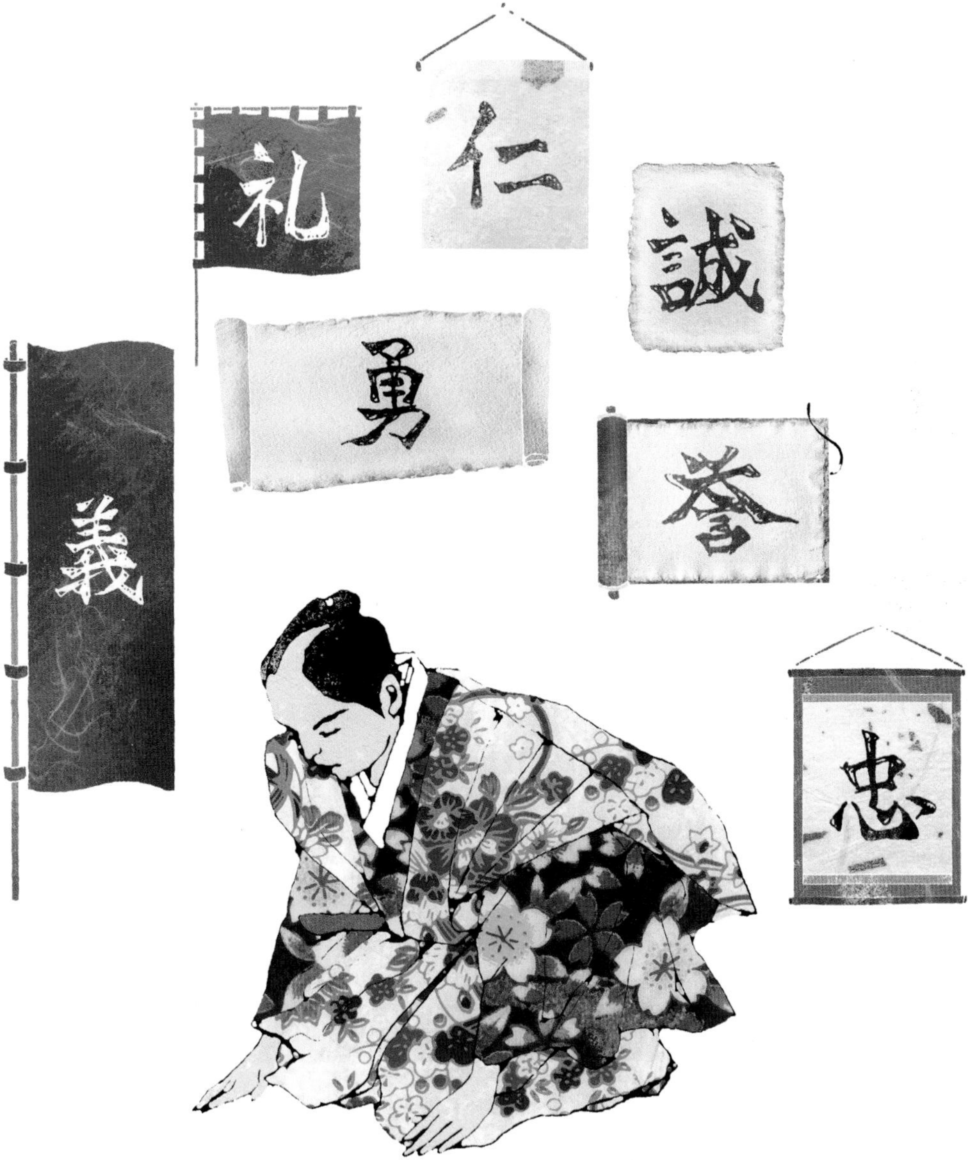

礼
仁
誠
勇
義
誉
忠

屏風
Byōbu

Painted Folding Screens

Among the very few household accessories that tradition assigns to the Japanese home, a place of honor belongs to the folding screen. In the vast halls of the ancient imperial court, *byōbu* were indispensable for creating screened areas and intimate corners within which to weave amorous intrigues or engage in political wheeling and dealing. They were equally useful later for erecting sumptuous movable backdrops in castles of the warrior aristocracy that revealed the power and wealth of their owners. While the conventional type tended to be fairly scenographic, with six or eight folds, a simpler double-paneled model was used around the bed to shelter it from drafts, or as a backdrop for an *ikebana* arrangement during tea ceremonies.

Japanese painters of all eras have had a particular predilection for these broad surfaces articulated by

panels. The panels lent themselves magnificently to serial bands of flowers or animals, while the breadth of the panels allowed for landscapes on a vast scale. The six-panel *byōbu*, in particular, was often produced in pairs that were united by a single theme but distinguishable by some variants, or with plays on two related subjects, such as the same landscape in different seasons or successive episodes of the same narrative.

Between the mid-14th and late 16th centuries, the golden age of the *byōbu*, the privileged suppliers of the court, commissioned by shogun and the most powerful *daimyō*, were the artists of the Kanō school. Their

elegant, stylized figures of birds, animals and plants were extensively adorned with gold leaf, and thus ideal for the ostentatious demands of the rampant warlords. In the shady areas where the screens were often placed, the gold of the background caught the light and reflected it back into the room, setting the contours of the image in magical relief.

The powerful general Toyotomi Hideyoshi (1536–98) wanted over 100 screens by the greatest artists of his time for his castle at Momoyama. It is said that when he went to visit the emperor at court, the 30 km (19 mi) he had to travel were lined with all these *byōbu*.

茶の湯
Cha no yu

The Zen Tea Ceremony

Also known as *chadō* or *sadō*, that is, "the way of tea," the tea ceremony is not an exercise in etiquette but rather a spiritual path, a road to inner perfection. Since the 15th century, the tea ceremony has been evolving symbiotically with Zen, from which discipline it has derived a manner, an intent and so many aesthetic preferences that it has become a true and proper form of meditation.

Like all the traditional arts of Japan, it entails a series of fixed, codified gestures, which to the eyes of the uninitiated retain an aura of mystery. Seated before the owner of the home, the guest picks up the porcelain items that are about to be used, one by one, and admires their craftsmanship in a few carefully measured phrases, excluding any emphasis that may disturb the serene tranquility of the environment. Reciprocating with the same grace and the same sequence of gestures, the officiant prepares the tea and hands it to the guest. The latter bows, accepts the bowl in the palm of his left hand, and raises it to his lips with the help of his right hand.

Throughout the ceremony, those present exchange only a few brief words, which glide over the silence yet never truly interrupt it. The result is a quiet consonance of souls, as reflected in the harmony of the gestures and the warm atmosphere in which they are enveloped.

Wagashi

These are small, traditional sweets that prepare the palate for the aroma of the tea. They can be made out of soft rice flour or be thin and dry like crackers. What is most important is that their shape and color allude to the fragrance and tones of the current season.

Matcha

The tea used for the ceremony is a bright green powdered one (*matcha*) with a strong grassy fragrance, which is whipped to a foam with a bamboo whisk, then ladled over some warm water.

Sukiya

The tea room (*sukiya* or *chashitsu*), as conceived in the 16th century by Sen no Rikyū, the greatest master of the ceremony, is deliberately small and sparse, furnished with an eye for absolute rigor: some unusual decorations, a sample of calligraphy, and an *ikebana* of utmost simplicity, often a single, still budding flower.

提灯
Chōchin

Paper Lanterns and Lamps

At sunset, when they light up over the entrances to restaurants and taverns, spreading their warm, soft illumination on the streets, they have the magical power to transform any cold iron and concrete neighborhood into a corner of old Edo.

These are the traditional balloon lanterns, white or red, with the name of the eatery or its culinary specialty imprinted in large characters. They are the antecedents of modern neon signs. One still sees them hanging from the eaves as they do in *ukiyo-e* era prints or period photographs—light, bamboo structures wrapped in *washi* paper and fixed at the ends by two wooden rings to which an electric bulb, that today often replaces the candle, is anchored.

There is a precise reason for the lightness of the frame: the *chōchin* originated as a travel lantern. The traveler used to hang such a paper lamp from the top of a stick, which he extended before him to illuminate his path at night through the treacherous alleys of 17th-century Japanese cities or along trails that scaled the mountains and led to the oldest, most highly revered temples. Like an accordion, the *chōchin*

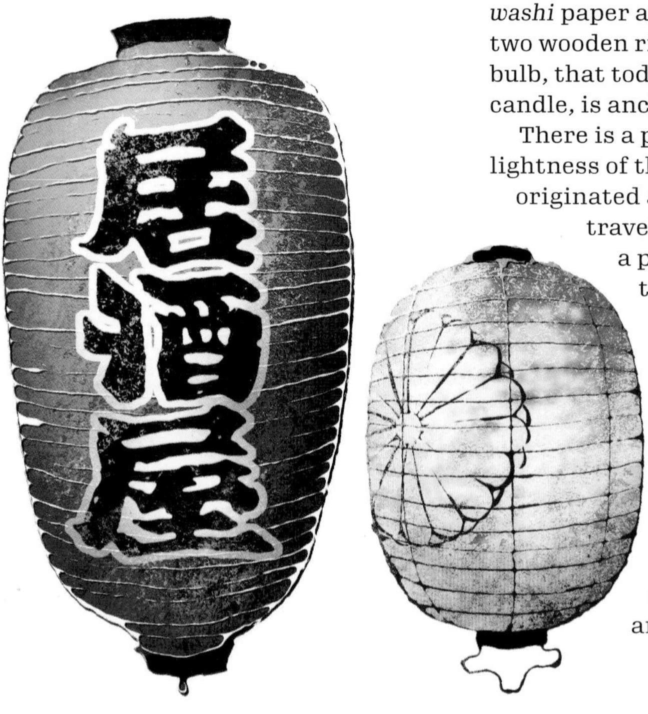
居酒屋

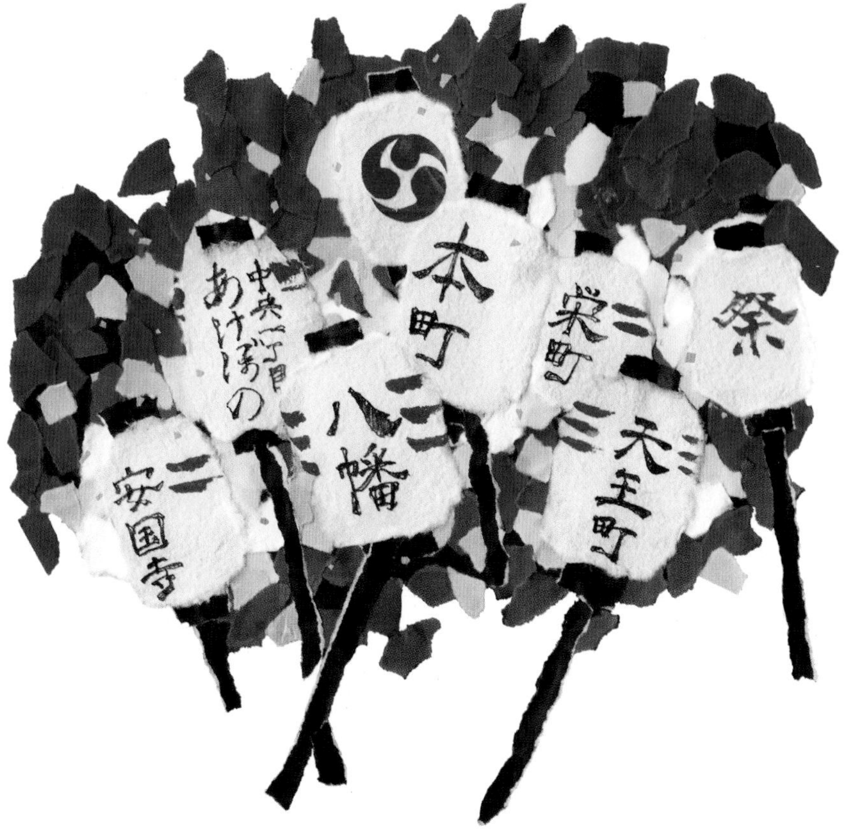
本町
祭
栄町
八幡
あけぼの
天王町
安国寺

was generally foldable, so that upon reaching his destination, the traveler could flatten it out and place it in his kimono before crossing the threshold into the warm, illuminated and safe inn awaiting him.

According to a popular belief, the *chōchin* had the power to protect one against evil spirits. For this reason, it was regarded as indispensable both at weddings and in funeral corteges. For funeral corteges taking place during the day, a white *chōchin* was used, so as to illuminate the deceased spirit's path to the world of the dead.

Takahari chōchin

Hanging from the eaves in long rows, *takahari chōchin* often illuminate the exterior of temples and shrines on the occasion of popular festivals known as *matsuri*.

Andon

The *andon*, on the other hand, is a floor lamp with a square base used for interior lighting. Perhaps the most highly sought-after lamp by antique dealers and interior decorators, it diffuses a short ray of soft light that creates an atmospheric effect.

大名
Daimyō

Feudal Lords in Traditional Times

The feudal lords of ancient Japan were known as *daimyō*, formed by the characters *dai* (big) and *myō* (name), from *myōden*, a privately owned rice field, rice being the basis of wealth at the time. By the 11th century, powerful *daimyō,* employing samurai armies, controlled many large, semi-autonomous estates. As *daimyō* took power from the increasingly enfeebled imperial government, the most powerful became the shogun, de facto ruler of the nation, beginning with Minamoto no Yoritomo in 1192.

Many *daimyō* began to collect taxes, wielding unchecked power locally, and some even issued their own cur-

rencies. During peacetime, *daimyō* enjoyed luxurious lives and indulged in cultural pursuits like *shodō*, *ikebana* and *chadō*.

There were more than 250 *daimyō* at their peak, but conflict was never far away as they vied for money, land and influence, plotting over shogunal succession. These rivalries led Japan to the bloodiest period of its ancient history, as the *sengoku* (Warring States) *daimyō* fought for supremacy from the second half of the 15th century. In the 1560s, a *daimyō* named Oda Nobunaga began a series of victories in a process later carried on by Toyotomi

Hideyoshi and then Tokugawa Ieyasu that led to a unified Japan. By the 17th century, the Tokugawa shogunate had brought most *daimyō* to heel. During the Edo period, their power was further weakened, in part by the *sankin kōtai* system. The Meiji Restoration of 1868 returned the lands of the *daimyō* to the emperor, leaving them a class of pensioned aristocrats in Tokyo.

Sankin-kōtai

Having *daimyō* stay every other year at the capital Edo (Tokyo), *sankin-kōtai* (alternate attendance) was a calculated method of control. The practice of leaving their wives and heirs as virtual hostages when they returned to Edo, keeping two residences and traveling with large retinues, strained the *daimyō* financially and prevented them from having powerful armies. However, the constant processions of *daimyō* to and from Edo led to improved roads and infrastructure.

河豚

Fugu

The Poisonous Pufferfish

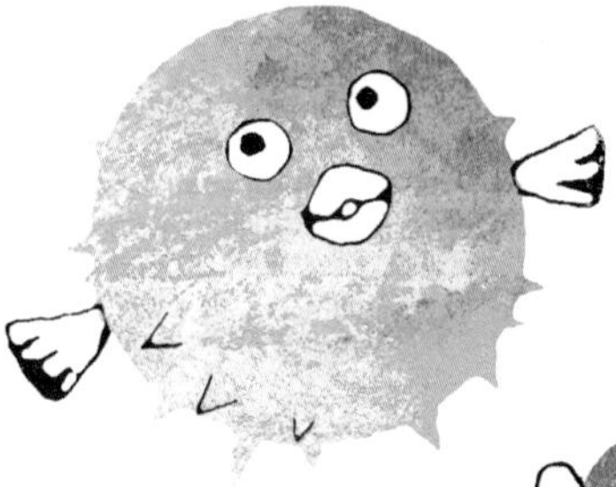

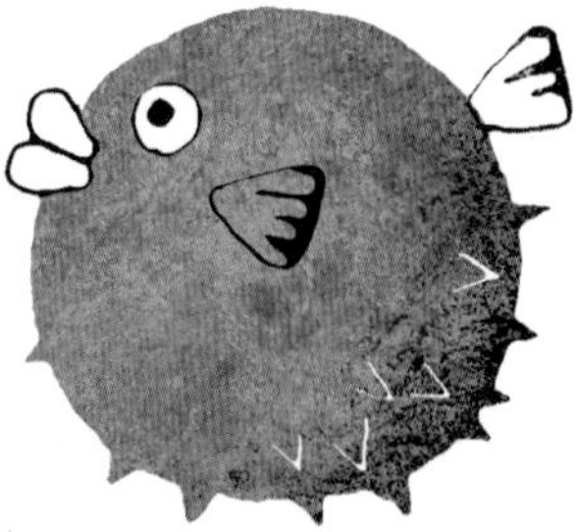

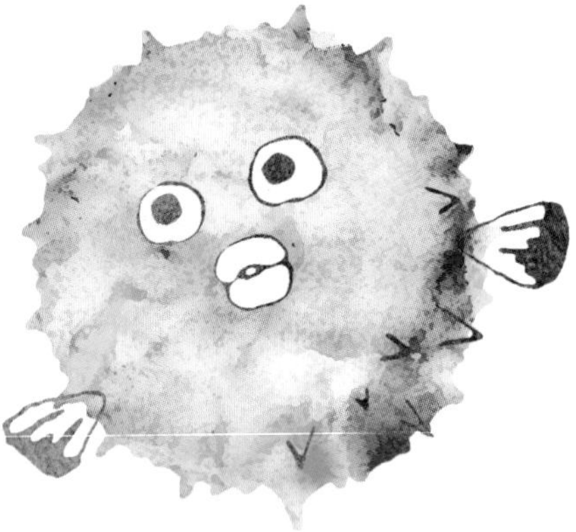

A prized delicacy, the potentially fatal properties of improperly prepared *fugu* pufferfish only add to its mystique and desirability to those brave enough to indulge. It has a long history in Japan, with the discovery of *fugu* bones suggesting it has been consumed for as long as 10,000 years. During the late 16th century, numerous samurai reportedly died after eating the fish, leading the shogun Toyotomi Hideyoshi to issue an edict prohibiting its consumption. The fish, of which there are a myriad of varieties, acquire the poison by eating other creatures carrying tetrodotoxin bacteria, which builds up in the liver, ovaries, eyes and skin. Tetrodotoxin is exponentially more poisonous than cyanide and kills by paralysis, leaving victims conscious but unable to breathe. No antidote exists and treatment consists of stomach pumping, administering activated charcoal to reduce absorption and placing the patient on life support in the hope the body can metabolize the poison. Deaths in modern Japan peaked in 1958, with 176 fatal *fugu* poisonings, after which a strict licensing system for chefs, requiring two to three years of study and practice, was introduced. The licensing has greatly reduced hospitalizations and deaths, but inevitably pushed up prices, though around 10,000 tonnes (9,800 tons) of *fugu* are still served annually. Poisonings do still occur, most frequently caused by ordinary people cooking *fugu* they have caught, but also by unqualified cooks in rural restaurants preparing the fish incorrectly, as well as the occasional mistake by an expert chef. In 1975, Bandō Mitsugorō, one of Japan's most celebrated *Kabuki* actors, died after eating four servings of *fugu kimo,* the liver and one of the most dangerous parts, at a restaurant in Kyoto. The dish was banned locally, but Bandō, who was a designated Living National Treasure, apparently believed he was immune to the poison.

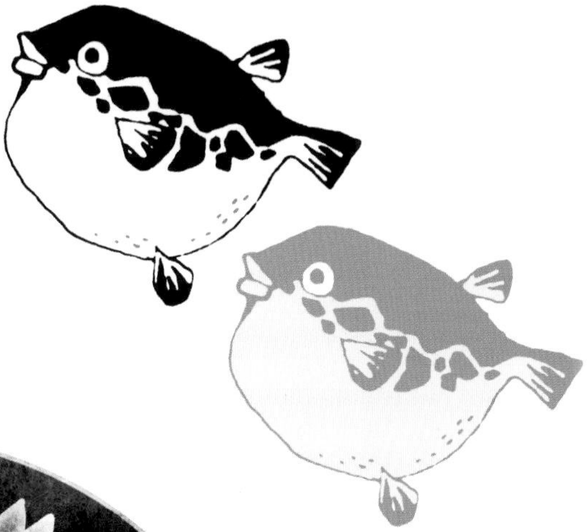

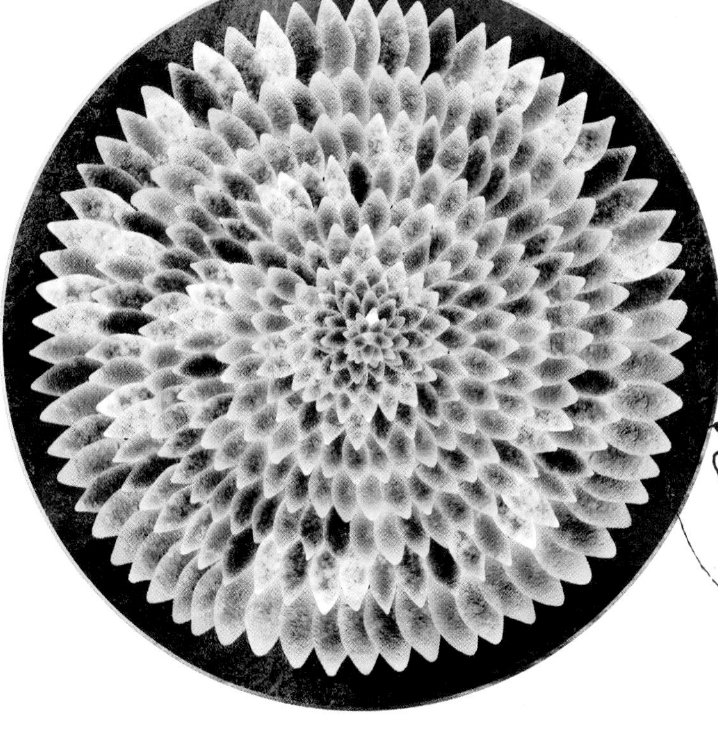

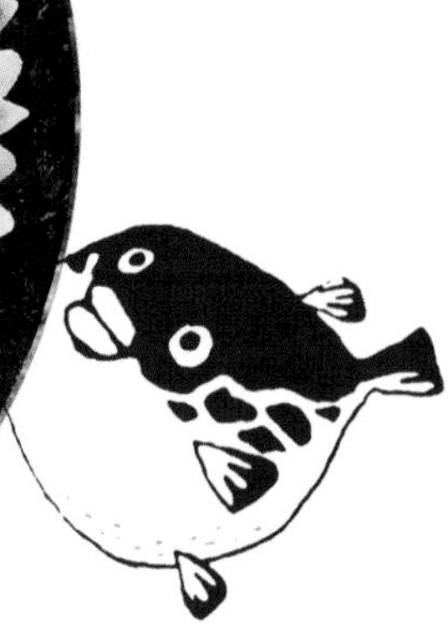

富士山
Fuji-san

Sacred Mount Fuji, the Symbol of Japan

Mt. Fuji, Japan's tallest peak at 3,776 m (12,390 ft), has long been a symbol of the nation. The perfect conical shape, often ringed with snow that enhances its beauty, as well as its religious and spiritual significance and potentially destructive volcanic power combine to give it a place in Japanese culture that exceeds even its gargantuan proportions. It is actually composed of three volcanoes, with Fuji, the youngest, resting atop the others. The diameter of the crater at its summit is 500 m (1,640 ft), while the circumference of its base is around 125 km (77 mi). The origin of the name is unclear, though it may have derived from the word for "fire" in the language of the aboriginal Ainu people. It is referred to as *Fuji no Yama* in a government document dating to 713 and still called *Fuji-yama* (Fuji mountain) today. However, most Japanese affectionately call it *Fuji-san*, though the *san* is another reading of the character for mountain, not the honorific term used for people. The mountain is 95 km (60 mi) from Tokyo and can be seen from tall buildings on a clear day. Indeed, there are numerous places, hotels, companies and other entities called *Fujimi*, meaning places where Fuji can be seen.

There are poems describing Mt. Fuji in the 8th-century *Manyōshū*, the oldest surviving collection of Japanese poetry. But it was most famously immortalized in the *Thirty-six Views of Mount Fuji* series of *ukiyo-e* woodblock prints by Hokusai, beginning in 1830. The artist later added 10 more to the series.

More than 250,000 people ascend Mt. Fuji every July–August climbing season, and though it is not a grueling trek it claims lives each year, mostly due to the huge numbers involved, as well as a few out-of-season hikers, skiers and snowboarders.

The mountain has been owned by a Shinto shrine since 1609 and some climb its slopes as a kind of pilgrimage. The last eruption was in 1707, but it remains classified as an active volcano. In 2013, Mt. Fuji was added to the UNESCO World Heritage List.

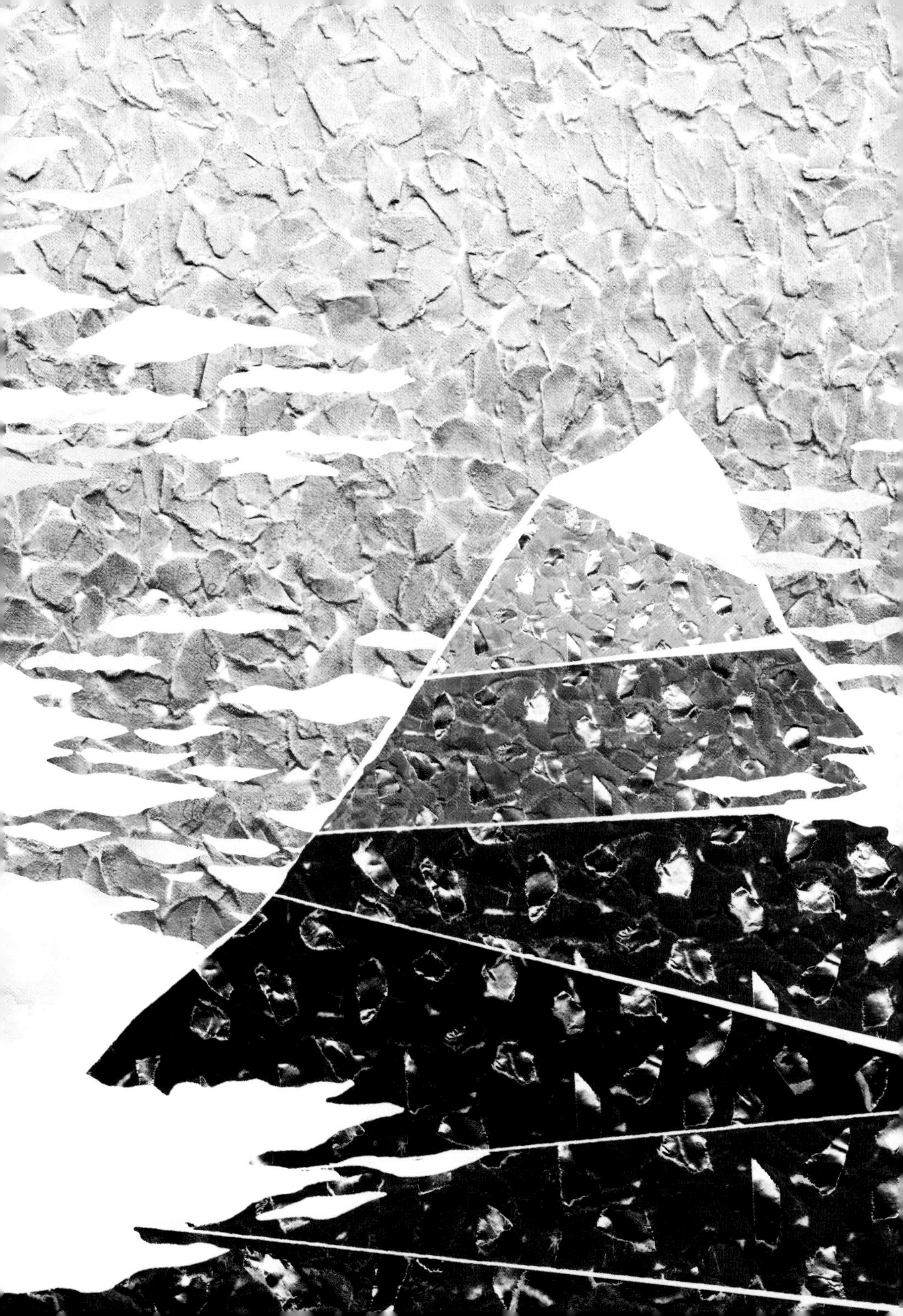

風呂敷

Furoshiki

Traditional Cloth Wrappers and Carriers

Imagine a large square handkerchief of silk or cotton, decorated perhaps with a beautiful pattern. Next, imagine knotting the corners in pairs along the diagonal to form a bundle that can be comfortably carried over the arm or shoulder. You will now have a *furoshiki-zutsumi*, a traditional and incredibly elegant way of presenting a gift.

Devised several centuries ago in the Edo period as a way of wrapping clothes and personal items, this simple square of fabric can dress an object with marvelous versatility, following its contours and protecting its fragility. With its complex folds, however, the *furoshiki* speaks above all of the giver's consideration for and attention to the gift's recipient, an attention that is reflected in a supremely refined manner in the time and care that the giver takes to wrap it.

Ochūgen and Oseibo

Ochūgen, in mid-July, and *Oseibo*, around New Year, are the two annual holidays when the Japanese customarily exchange gifts. On these occasions, those who feel they owe a debt of gratitude or wish to emphasize a bond, present a gift, usually fruit, sweets or a clothing item. The packages, always very elegant, are sealed with a special auspicious symbol, the *noshi*.

Noshi

Noshi is one of the oldest forms of *origami*. It consists of a strip of paper—yellow or sometimes with a flower or pine needle pattern—wrapped in a white and red sheet, then folded into a characteristic cone. It accompanies a gift presented on the occasion of a wedding, birth, graduation or other happy event as a token of good luck.

Omiyage

Omiyage can be translated as "souvenir," but its importance as a ritual in Japanese culture is unparalleled elsewhere. Woe to anyone who returns from a journey without a small gift for relatives, friends and colleagues, even if that means spending more time shopping for these than on seeing the sights.

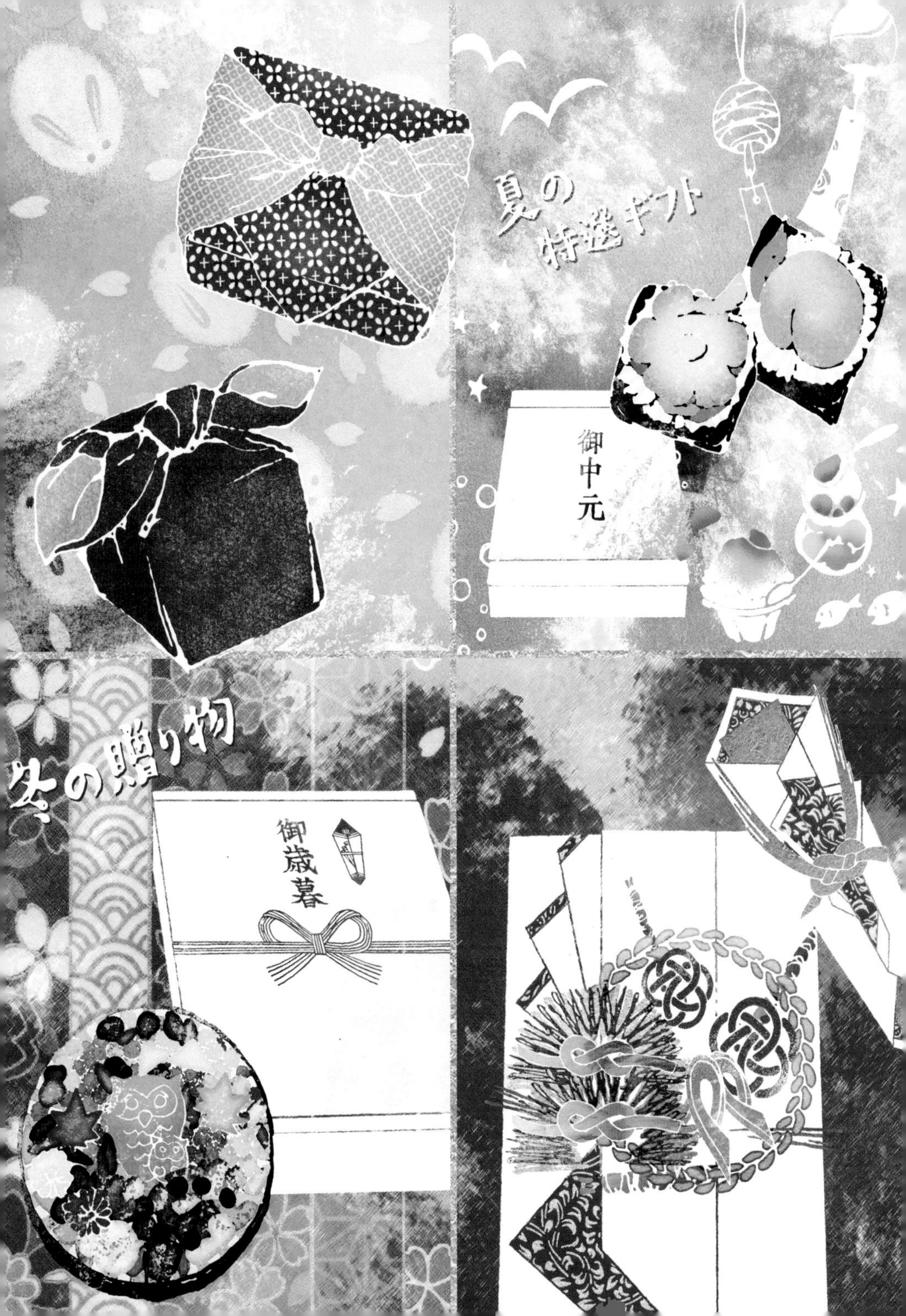
夏の特選ギフト
御中元
冬の贈り物
御歳暮

我慢
Gaman

The Japanese Concept of Stoicism and Strength

Visitors from Western countries, in particular, though from other parts of the world as well, often experience a mixture of wonder, admiration and bewilderment at many of the ways in which Japanese society operates. There is, of course, no single cause or explanation for this, but one significant factor is the concept of *gaman*. It is difficult to pin the term down with a single explanation, but it refers to the capacity for and practice of endurance, tolerance, self-control, self-denial and strength in the face of hardship. Its origin lies in Zen Buddhism, where it more specifically refers to enduring the unendurable with grace and patience. The two characters that make up the word don't provide particularly clear

clues to its meaning. The first part, *ga*, means "I," "the self" or "selfish," while the second part, *man*, means "ridicule" or "laziness." To be *gaman-zuyoi* is to be particularly virtuous and patient in this respect, even by Japanese standards; the latter part coming from *tsuyoi*, meaning "strong." The notion is not peculiar to Japan as parallels can be drawn with the stoicism of the ancient Greeks and the British "stiff upper lip." What

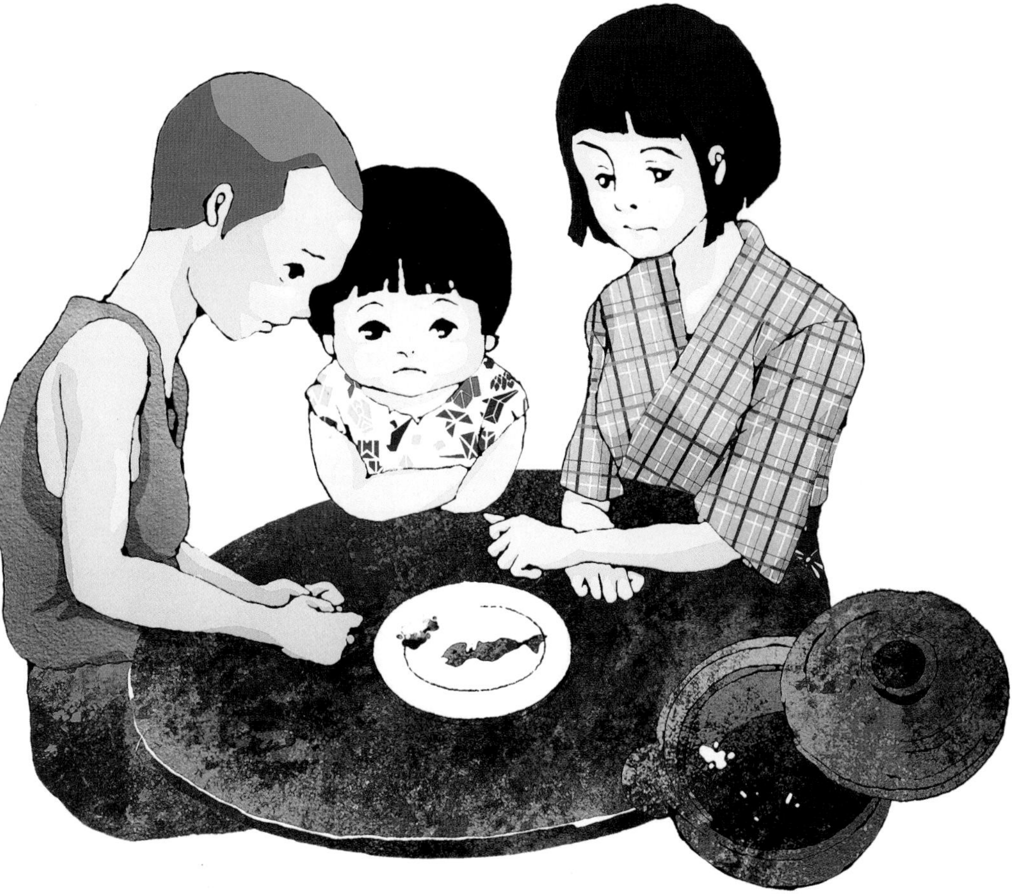

gives it a Japanese flavor is the way it is so strongly linked to being harmonious with, and considerate of, those around you. Some argue it was born out of and shaped by nature and the physical environment. The Japanese rice-based agricultural tradition required regular cooperation within communities. The disaster-prone nature of the country also demands an ability to endure, while the crowded environment of the modern country makes respect for others a necessity. *Gaman* played an important role in rebuilding Japan from postwar devastation into an economic superpower. More recently, *gaman* was seen in the way survivors of the 2011 earthquake, *tsunami* and nuclear crisis conducted themselves with dignity, patience and consideration for others in the face of seemingly unbearable challenges.

頑張って
Ganbatte

Giving One's Utmost

If someone in Japan is taking a test, competing in a sport, looking for work, putting up a shelf or undertaking any activity that requires effort, the call of encouragement from those around will almost always include some form of the word *ganbatte*. The plain form of the verb is *ganbaru,* though it is sometimes transliterated as *gambaru*. Its basic meaning is "to do one's best" or "keep at it," and it can be seen as the active counterpart to the more passive endurance of *gaman*. The *gan* character means "stubborn," "foolish" or "firm," while *haru* (which becomes *baru* when combined with *gan*) is to "stretch," "spread" or "strain." However, while

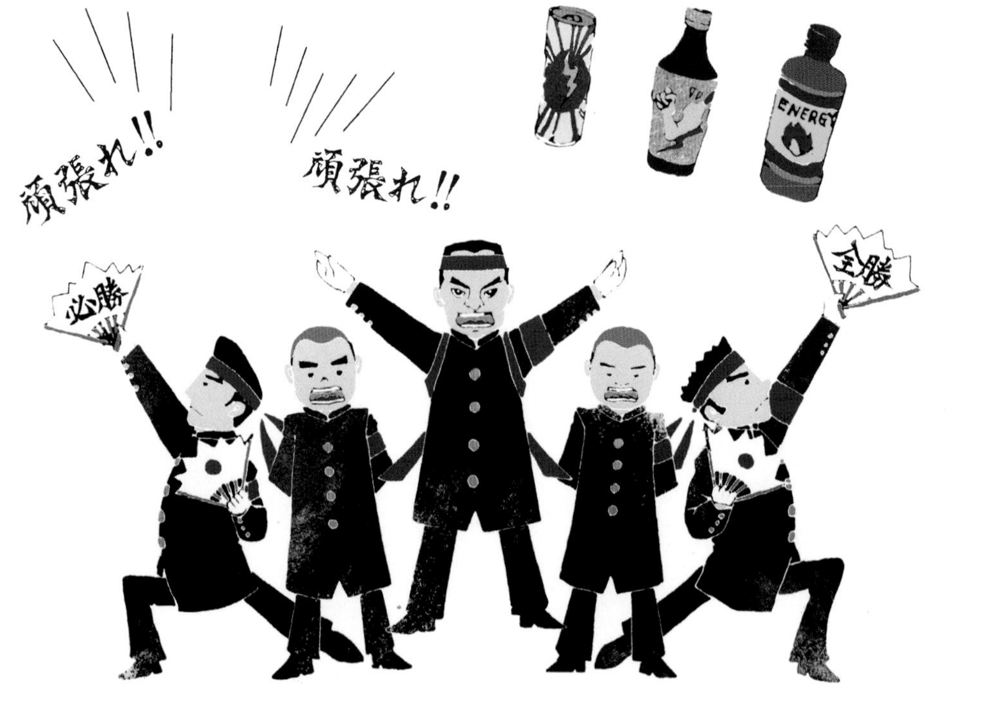
頑張れ!!
頑張れ!!
ENERGY
必勝

it may seem those components give clues as to its meaning, they are actually *ateji*: characters used because their reading is the desired sound rather than containing the correct meaning. The etymology of the term is a matter of debate among linguists, but the fact that there were once at least 40 different regional ways of expressing *ganbaru* speaks of its deep significance in Japanese culture.

Although today *ganbaru* is used everywhere in Japan, there are multiple forms and it can be written in *kanji*, *hiragana* or *katakana*. These include *ganbatte-ne*, a gentler and more feminine version. *Ganbatte kudasai* adds please, while *ganbare* and *ganbarō* are imperative forms, but often used for cheering sports or for extra emphasis. If a response is appropriate, it is usually *ganbarimasu*—"I will do my best."

And to do one's very best is regarded in Japan as one of the ultimate virtues. Like *gaman*, it is drilled into children from a young age. If there is a statistical expression of *ganbaru*, it is perhaps that the average Japanese worker only takes half their annual paid holidays. Although it is possible not to try your best—*ganbaranai*—there is no widely accepted antonym for the word.

芸者

Geisha

Highly Refined Female Entertainers

The word *geisha* or *geiko* means "artist." The fact that among the entertainments she offered until the 19th century were those of the bedroom does not detract from her mastery of numerous refined arts. The *geisha* had to know how to dance and sing, play the ancient three-stringed instrument known as the *shamisen,* wear elaborate kimonos, serve *sake* with impeccable grace, and entertain with intelligent conversation. She placed this talent at the complete service of her customer, a wealthy businessman or powerful politician, who for a few hours could grant himself the rare privilege of a highly refined companion, an immensely cultured interlocutor, who would dance and sing for him alone, cuddle him, banish his worries, while using the correct words to reinforce his ego. To embody the ideal woman as conceived by every man's fantasy, the *geisha* had to undergo a long, rigorous apprenticeship. And if the most beautiful and talented of them came to be viewed as goddesses, envied by other women and enveloped in an aura of luxury and fame, the price they paid was often very high. Their brilliant, worldly existence did not, in fact, differ much from the seclusion of a nun.

In the 17th and 18th centuries, becoming a *geisha* in Japan was less a matter of choice than an extreme measure dictated by poverty. Starving families gave female offspring between the ages of eight and ten to the *okiya* where they would embark on this lifetime career. Like a slave, the *geisha* was destined to remain forever bound to her *okiya*, where she would live a lonely existence without hope of love or marriage.

Today, being a *geisha* is practically like any other profession, chosen consciously by young women who, upon graduating from high school, decide to undertake the long and demanding study of the traditional arts of Japan. There are not many of them, of course, and nearly all are concentrated in Kyoto, where there are as many as five neighborhoods with teahouses in which around 200 of these extraordinary "women of art" still reside.

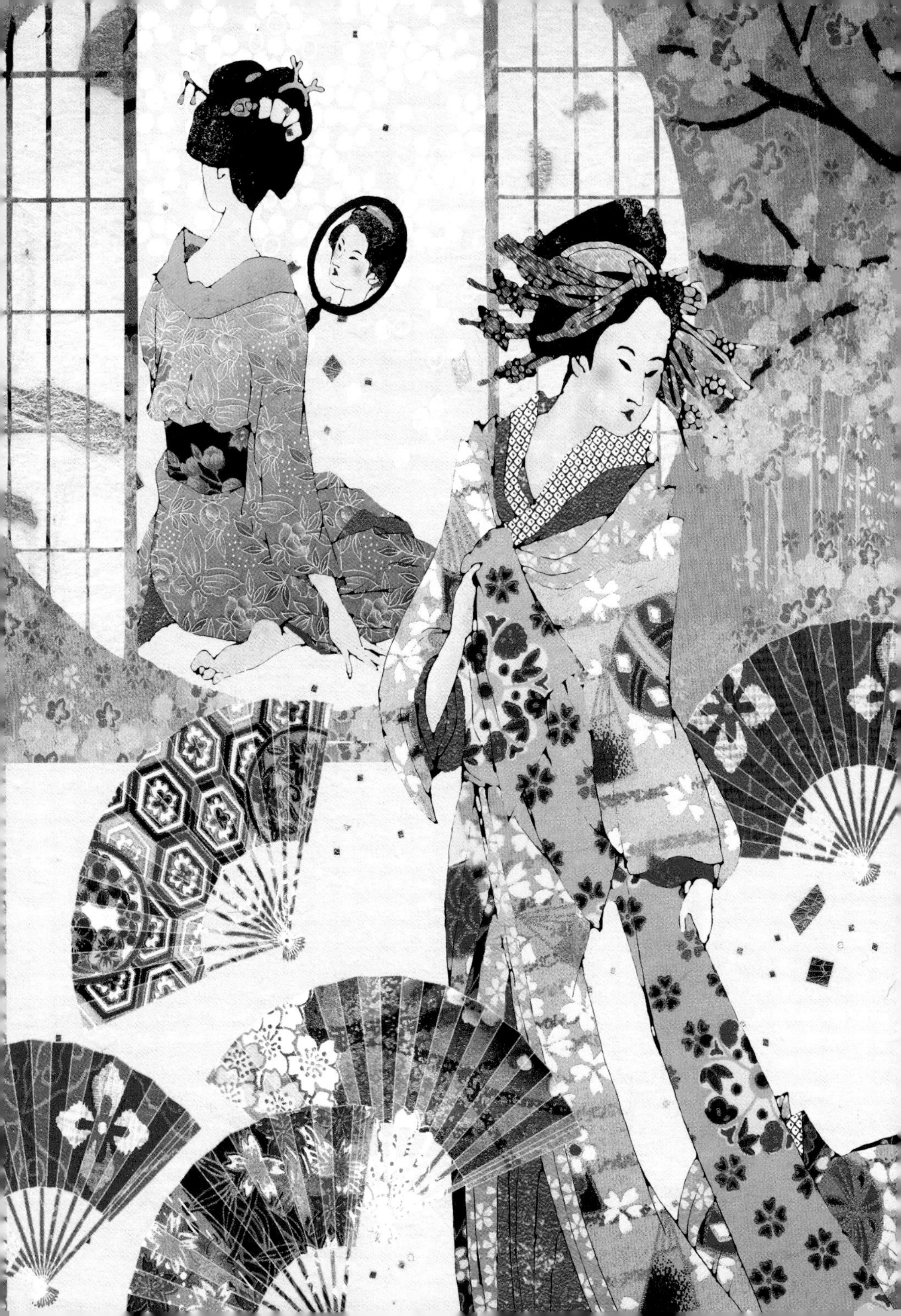

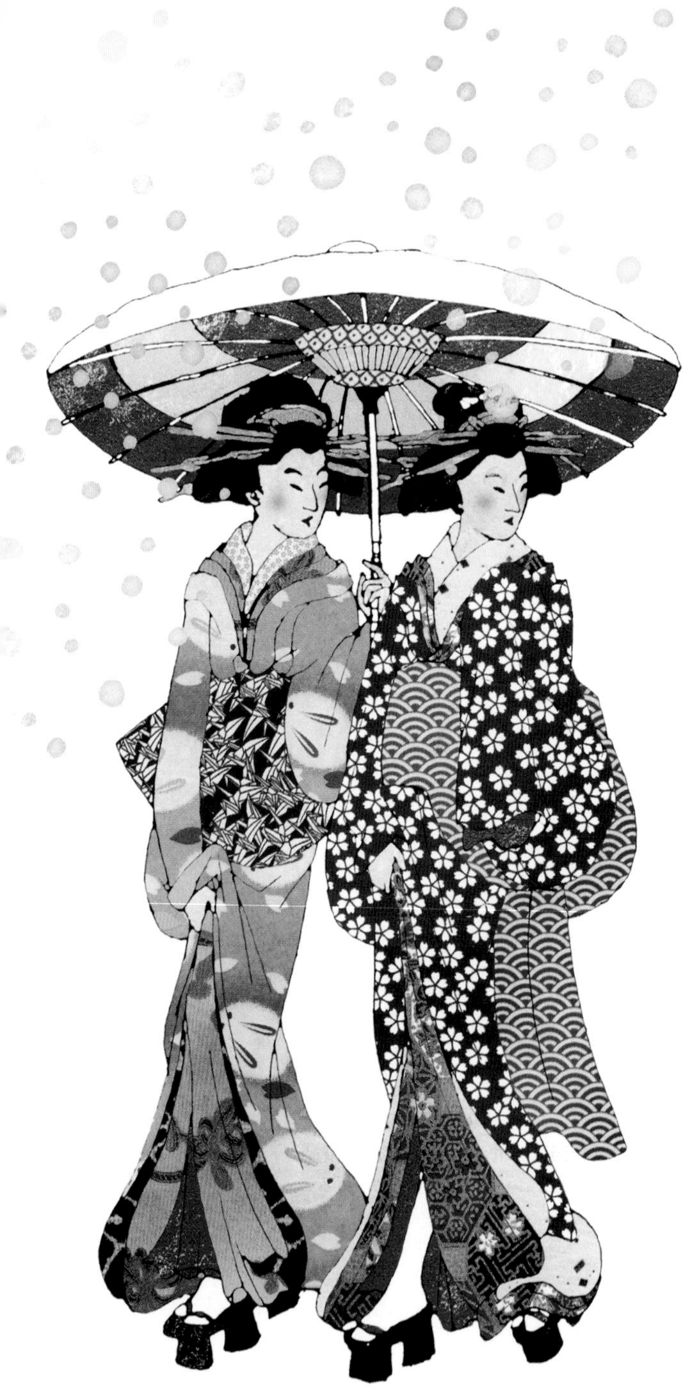

Maiko

The *geisha* apprentice is known as a *maiko* (dancer) and is recognizable by a number of distinctive signs. First is a kimono with lively patterns in which the color red predominates. Her lips, lined to appear narrower, are equally scarlet. Unlike the *geisha*, the *maiko* does not wear a wig, and leaves a thin strip of bare skin untouched by white grease paint around her hairline.

Okiya

The *okiya* is the residential institution that instructs the *geisha* in the various arts of entertainment, and endows her with the deportment of a queen and the taste of an artist. It was here that she entered as a little girl and remained until her death, in the vain hope of one day being able to redeem her freedom and repay the enormous debt contracted by her apprenticeship and luxurious kimonos. Life for women in these communal residences was often harsh, plagued by ferocious intrigue and rivalry over the favor of the most prestigious clients.

Cha no ya

With its sliding screens and *tatami*, the so-called tearoom, *cha no ya*, is actually the traditional location for the refined banquets at which the *geisha* and *maiko* were in attendance. The exorbitantly high bill (hundreds of thousands of yen) was euphemistically known as *ohanadai*, or the "cost of flowers."

Oiran

The highest-ranking courtesans in Edo's "nightless cities" were not *geisha* but *oiran*,

true divas, who were admired, unattainable and reserved for the wealthiest clients. The annual spring procession in which they participated attracted huge crowds of men enchanted by their grace and women dazzled by their sumptuous hairstyles and kimonos.

Danna

The *geisha*'s success is also measured by the number and prestige of customers willing to become her *danna*, or sugar daddy. The *danna* took charge of the huge sums needed to redeem the *geisha*'s freedom from the *okiya* and support her high standard of living while indulging her with gifts. He would not marry her, however, usually because he was already married to another woman of his own rank.

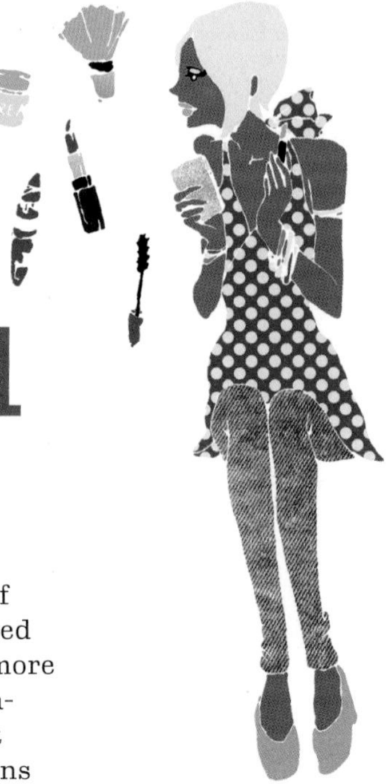

ギャル

Gyaru

Modern Fun-loving Gals

Rather than a single identifiable trend, *gyaru* comprised a series of styles and subcultures that evolved and fused into one another over more than two decades. *Gyaru* is a Japanized version of "gal," which first came into focus via a brand of jeans in the 1970s. Fun-loving young urban women had been labeled *modan-garu* (modern girls) back in the 1920s, and the moral panic it induced was not unlike that caused by their successors. The first signs of *gyaru* culture appeared in the 1980s, and the term was used for young office girls who spent their time partying in Tokyo's discos and furiously shopping for fashion.

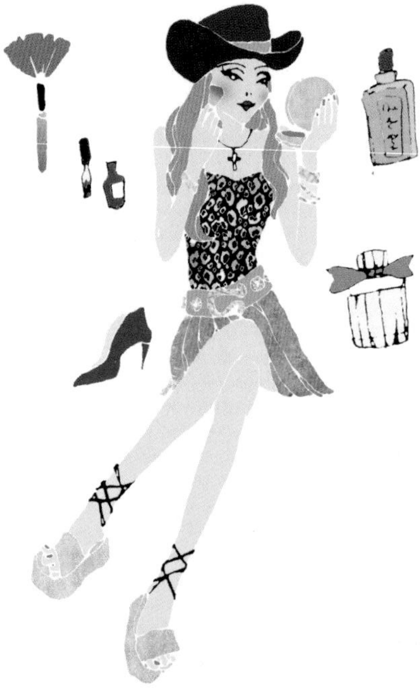

At the dawn of the 1990s, what became known as *kogyaru*—the *ko* coming from *kōkōsei*, meaning "high school students"—first appeared in Shibuya. The earliest *kogyaru* were private school students in Tokyo who sported tans, dyed brown hair, shortened school skirts, Burberry scarves, loafers and knee-high white socks. Their take on the school uniform was

eventually adopted by girls across Japan, but also fetishized in the tabloids and pornography. Meanwhile, the mainstream media was full of tales of moral decline and *kogyaru* engaging in *enjo kōsai* ("compensated dating," a euphemism for paid sex) with older men to buy designer gear. In many ways, the *gyaru* inverted ideals of Japanese femininity with their rough slang, aggressive attitude and dark skin. As the ranks of *gyaru* broadened to include working-class girls, by the end of the decade their style would become extreme, morphing into *ganguro* and *yamamba*.

Ganguro

Perhaps partly in reaction to their portrayal as sex objects, *ganguro* ("black face") took the tanned look to extremes so that only very light make-up could be seen against it. With platform heels, wild accessories and hair bleached or brightly dyed, the look shocked the mainstream.

Yamamba

The *yamamba* ("mountain witches") *gyaru* went even further. With pitch black faces, even brighter make-up and multicolored stringy hair, they were the antithesis of *kawaii* cuteness.

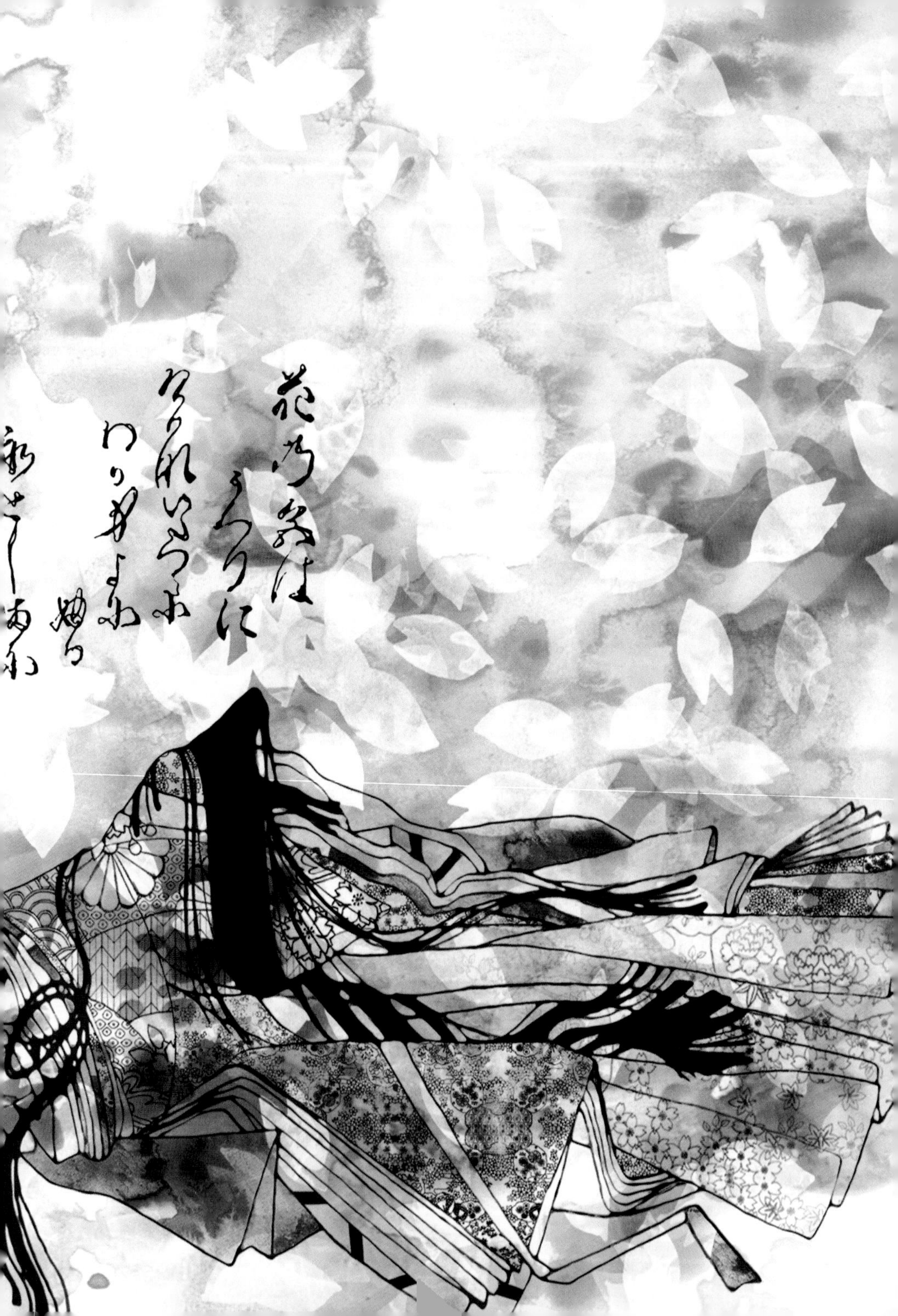
花乃色は
うつりに
けりないたつらに
わか身よにふる
なかめせしまに

俳句

Haiku

Japanese Poetry

When one speaks of Japanese poetry, one immediately thinks of *haiku*, a short composition of three verses of 5, 7 and 5 syllables, respectively. Sharp as the blow of the *katana* and brilliant as a flash of light, it isolates a fragment of reality, capturing its atmosphere.

Haiku is a "democratic" form of poetry that does not require much talent to generate results. In fact, nearly everyone in Japan practices *haiku* from childhood. This does not mean that it has not attracted great poets, above all Matsuo Bashō, who, in the 17th century reinvented what was a comic and popular genre by infusing it with a Zen sensibility. With unpolished and concise words that banish all sentimentality, his *haiku* captures the poignant beauty of minute things—a frog's plunge into a pond, the emergence of a clump of violets on a path—and of *kigo*, a reference to the season that speaks of the passage of time and our transformations in sync with nature.

The bell is silent,
like a chime, the fragrance of flowers
vibrates in the evening
—Matsuo Bashō (1644–94)

The double corollas emit their fragrance and wither into cherries under my eaves, but no one but the wind has come to visit me.
—Princess Shikishi

Waka

Historically, feelings in Japan have been expressed in 31 syllables, the number of those in *waka*, the country's oldest poetic form, one so ingrained in the psyche of the archipelago that its very name means "Japanese poetry." It is *waka* that created nature in the land of the Rising Sun: the full moon in the mountains, the ephemeral magic of the cherry tree, the flaming nuances of autumn leaves—in short, nature as it was interpreted over the centuries.

Waka was fashionable at court where nobles recited verses of past poets from memory and, in turn, challenged each other to composition contests. Thus, in the 13th century was born the most famous of anthologies, the *Hyakunin isshu* (A Hundred Poems for a Hundred Poets), which was turned into a game of cards, each of which bears a composition and is illustrated with a portrait of the poet.

花見

Hanami

The Art of Cherry Blossom Viewing

"To admire flowers," which is what *hanami* means, has always been an exquisite pleasure for the Japanese. However, the term does not pertain to all flowers: there is only one flower par excellence in the Japanese archipelago, namely the cherry blossom. With its poignant and ephemeral beauty, the cherry blossom has for centuries embodied the Japanese sense of life, elicited the melancholy of poets and lovers and recalled the courage and death inherent in the samurai's destiny. As it did ten centuries ago, today its buds are anticipated and watched with trepidation, and when the first signs of blossom appear, people, as if under a spell, swarm outdoors and go en masse to see the show. *Hanami* entails going to a place renowned for the beauty of its cherry trees, preferably a place where their branches frame some ancient sanctuary, a mountain range or a romantic lake, and to lie there idle or to stroll, embark on a leisurely boat trip or, more often, spread out blankets and mats and enjoy a picnic with friends.

Whether the destination is quiet, such as Yoshino on the hills of Kyoto, a favorite for generations of viewers, or the park of Ueno in Tokyo, where the blossoms turn into a boisterous *matsuri*, what matters is that everyone in Japan stops running, calculating and planning for an instant each spring and looks up at the pink clouds above their heads while savoring a moment of pure poetry. This, too, is as fleeting as the cherry blossom.

Sakura

In Japan, the cherry blossom or *sakura* comes in over 400 varieties. The most classic is *Somei-yoshino* (*Prunus yedoensis*), which has five petals of an almost imperceptible pink, but can also come in pure white, pearl gray, pale yellow and a deep pink. The blossoms of some of its species change color, from white to pink, for example, during the same flowering. The most lyrical is undoubtedly the *Shidare-zakura*, with its long hanging branches that turn into vaporous cascades of silk.

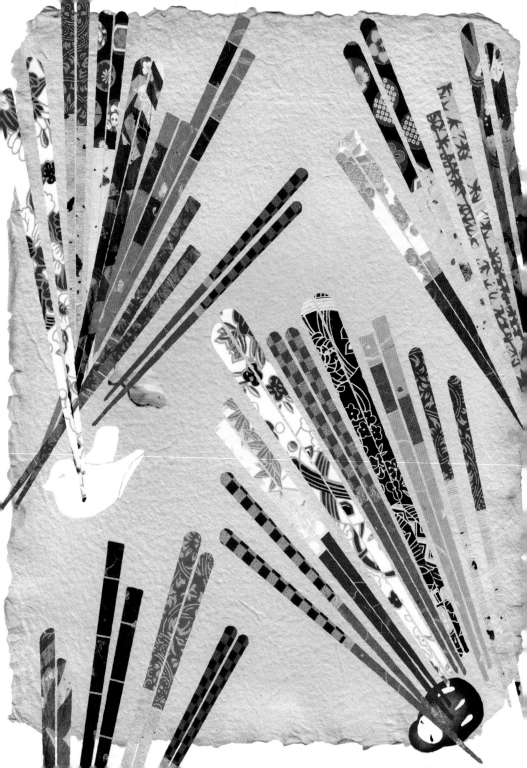

箸
Hashi

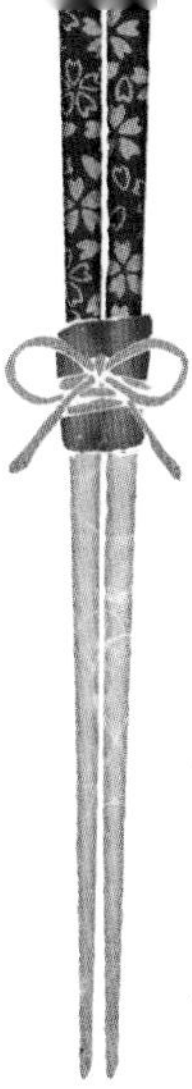

Chopsticks

Pairs of chopsticks are the only cutlery provided at the Japanese table. Historically, they have exerted a tremendous influence on Japanese cuisine, orienting it towards a preference for foods that are already broken down into chopstick-sized morsels. In truth, however, *hashi* are more versatile than they appear: they can gather, separate, break off and extract. When inactive, they can rest with their tips pointing leftward and aligned with the table's edge, beneath the bowl on a small three-dimensional ceramic holder, a *hashioki*.

If one does not wish to risk upsetting one's fellow diners, one must take into account a series of etiquette rules. Three gestures are strictly forbidden because they threaten to bring about bad luck: *saigoshi*, crossing chopsticks with one's neighbor; *utsuribashi*, taking food from various dishes without alternating it with rice; and *hashiwatashi*, passing food from chopsticks to chopsticks. Even planting chopsticks vertically in a rice bowl brings misfortune as it recalls an offer to the dead. Moreover, it is simply in poor taste to point chopsticks at someone, use them to push or pull a plate and, above all, pierce food like a skewer even when, in the case of certain difficult morsels, it would seem the best option.

Using *hashi* is not all that difficult. They must first be held between the thumb and forefinger, while resting (like a pencil) on the middle finger. Second, they must be held in the hollow of the thumb and over the first phalanx of the ring finger. The second remains fixed, while the first is maneuvered by movements in the index and middle fingers.

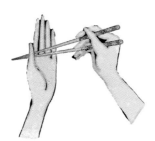

平和ボケ

Heiwa-boke

Complacency in Peaceful Times

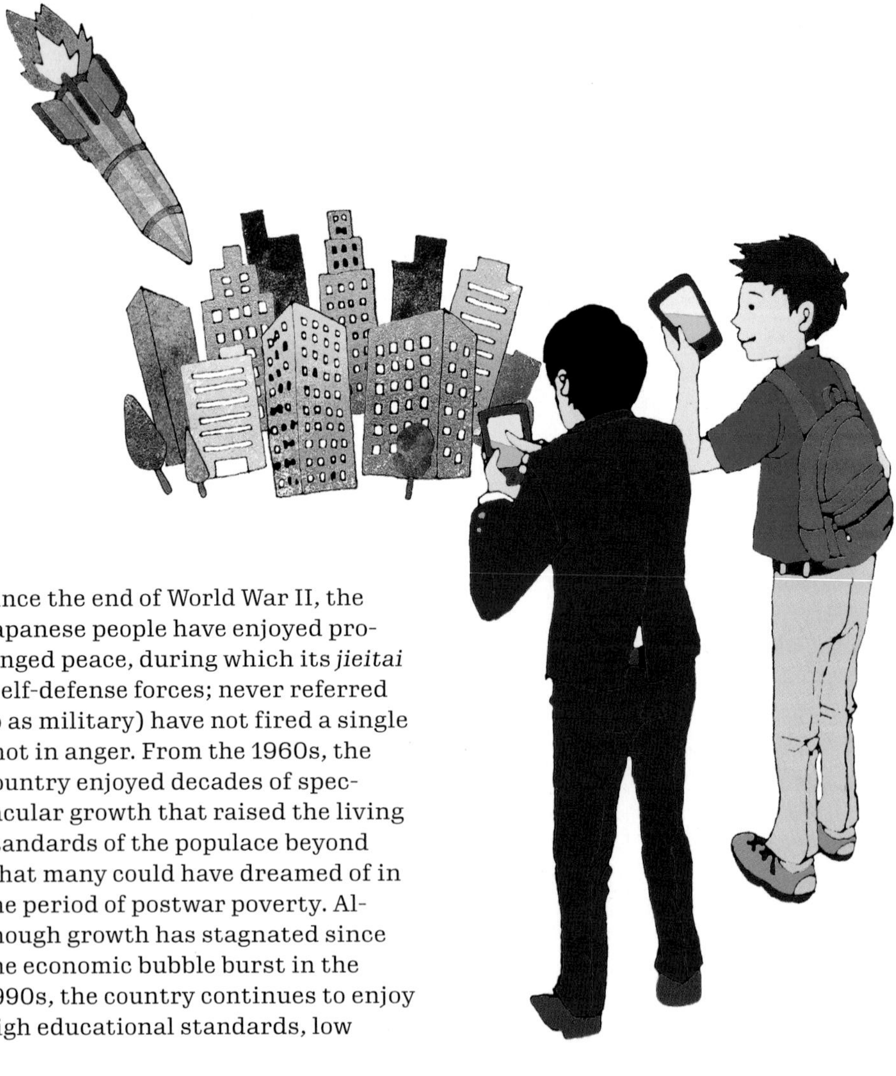

Since the end of World War II, the Japanese people have enjoyed prolonged peace, during which its *jieitai* (self-defense forces; never referred to as military) have not fired a single shot in anger. From the 1960s, the country enjoyed decades of spectacular growth that raised the living standards of the populace beyond what many could have dreamed of in the period of postwar poverty. Although growth has stagnated since the economic bubble burst in the 1990s, the country continues to enjoy high educational standards, low unemployment, superb healthcare and one of the world's longest average lifespans. And while Japan is not utopia, to these may be added extremely low crime rates, particularly violence, superlative levels of service and a society noted worldwide for its etiquette and respectfulness. If every rose has its thorn, then the downside to all this peace, prosperity and politeness is what the Japanese call *heiwa-boke*. *Heiwa* means "peace" and *boke* has a range of meanings: "stupid," "unaware," "out of focus," "senile," "vacant" or "the fall guy" in a comedy duo. Although separately some of these terms have different *kanji*, when combined with another character they are written in *katakana*, bringing their meanings together. For example, *jisa-boke* is literally "time-difference-stupid," used for jetlag.

Heiwa-boke itself is also used in different contexts. It can describe gullibility toward criminals and tricksters that Japanese often display when abroad. Some point to a cultural infantilization and an obsession with *kawaii* as a form of *heiwa-boke* because of an overly safe and stable existence. It is even used in a geopolitical context to criticize a complacent belief that the pacifist Clause 9 of the Constitution will spare Japan from conflict even in the face of a belligerent North Korea and an increasingly assertive and expansionist China. Even though Japan can be shaken out of *heiwa-boke*, as it was in the years after the 2011 mega-quake, *tsunami* and nuclear disaster, when the term *heiwa-boke* was rarely heard.

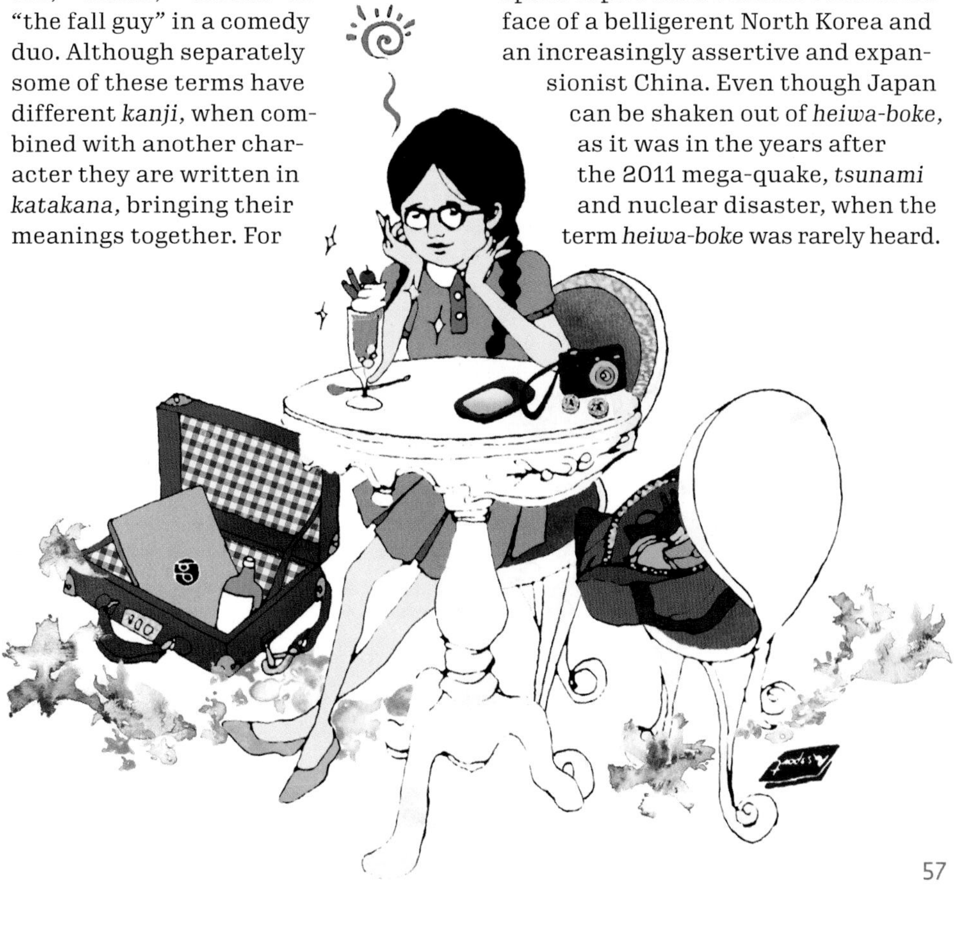

雛祭り
Hina matsuri

The Japanese Doll Festival or Girls' Day

On March 3, all Japanese households with daughters celebrate Girls' Day with a spectacular array of dolls. These are not just any dolls, but ancient *ohina*, who atop their red velvet-covered pedestal, stage a royal wedding at the court of Heian and therefore don the sumptuous attire of the 10th-century aristocracy. At the apex of the pyramid sit the emperor and empress, followed by ministers and court ladies, musicians, armed guards and possibly servants on the levels below. The entire ensemble is surrounded by enchanting miniature carts, trunks and dishes on which girls pretend to serve food.

In ancient times, it was customary to exorcise bad luck by making paper dolls, then entrusting them to the current of a river on the third day of the third month. The belief was that they would absorb human misfortunes and carry them far away. Later, when more durable clay dolls appeared on the scene, they were surrounded by offerings of food meant to convince them to absorb the family's misfortunes.

The splendid *ohina* of today, often handed down from mother to daughter, are simply the heirs of those shamanic puppets. For this reason, parents are willing to make any sacrifice to present them to their daughter and thus avoid the risk of an unhappy or, worse, unmarried life.

Gosekku

Hinamatsuri, which falls on the third day of the third month, is one of the five festivals, or *gosekku,* that mark the Japanese year. It is followed by *Tango no sekku*, Boys' Day, on the fifth day of the fifth month; *Tanabata*, the festival of the stars, on the seventh day of the seventh month; *Kiku no sekku*, the chrysanthemum festival, on the ninth day of the ninth month; and *Nanakusa*, the feast of the seven herbs, on the seventh day of the first month.

Hishimochi

Hishimochi is the typical rice sweet eaten during *Hinamatsuri*. It is packaged in three different colors: green to symbolize sprouting grass; white to commemorate the winter snow that has begun to melt; and peach blossom pink to herald spring. The latter festival is also called *Momo no sekku,* or the peach blossom feast.

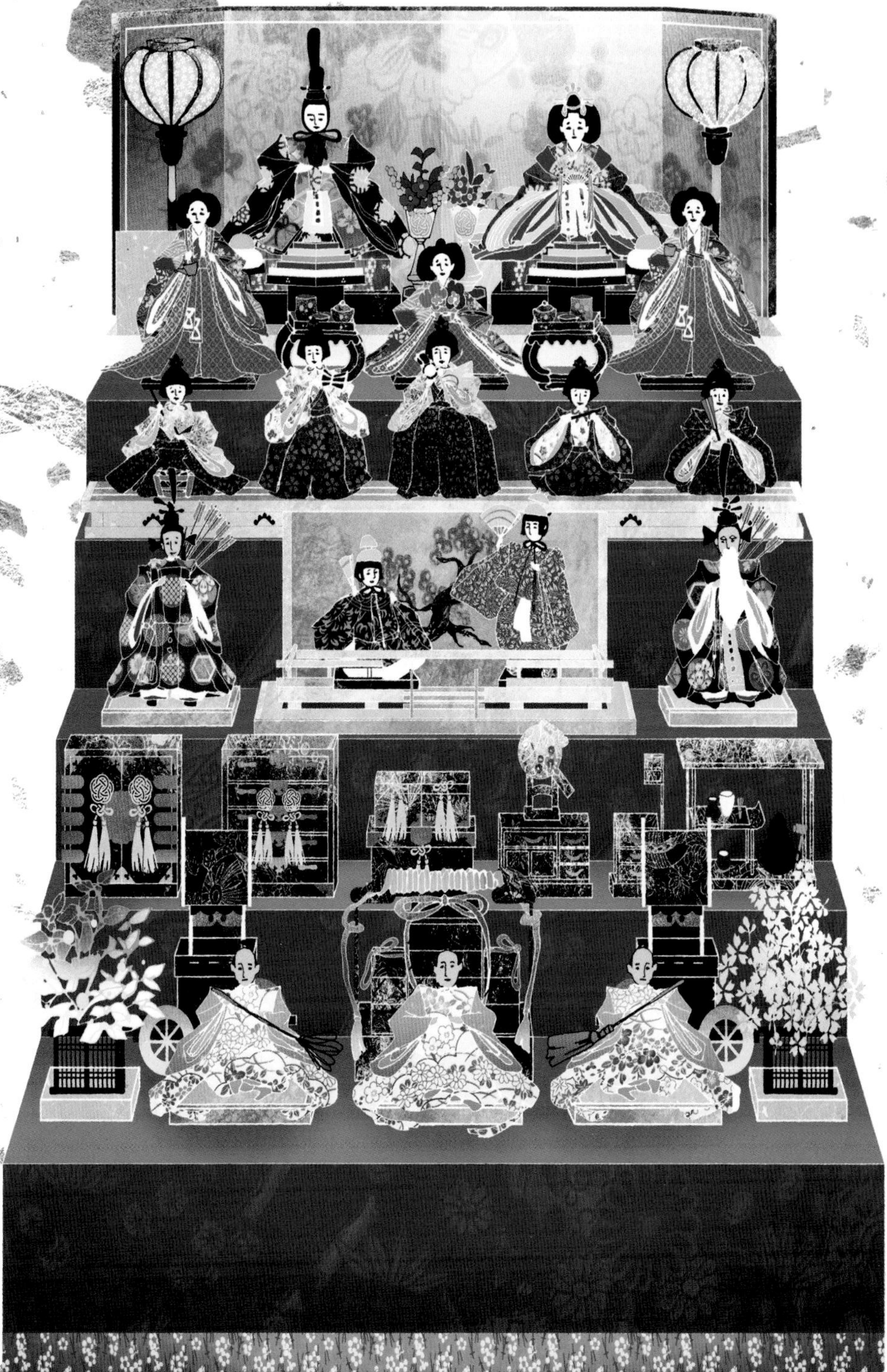

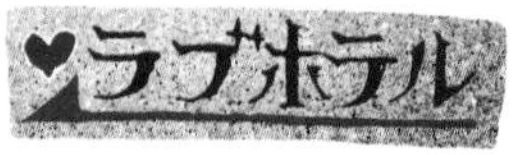
ラブホテル
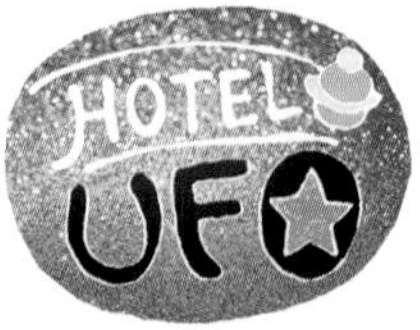
HOTEL
UFO
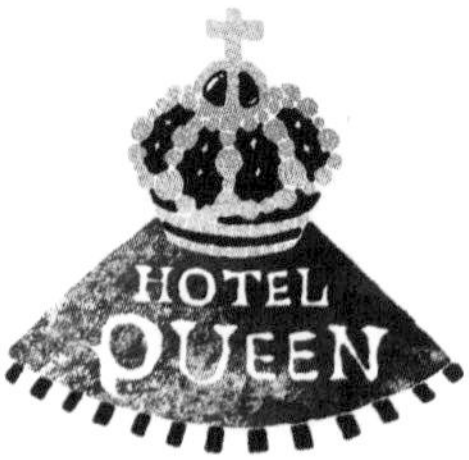
HOTEL
QUEEN

ホテル

Hoteru

Hotels and Other Tourist Accommodation

From traditional *ryokan* inns to luxury hotels, Japan has a huge range of temporary accommodation, all referred to casually as *yado*. There are also numerous themed places to stay: bookshop hotels, places with rooms decked out *anime* style, and robot hotels where automatons check guests in and carry their luggage. But two categories are probably the most symbolic of Japan: love hotels and capsule hotels.

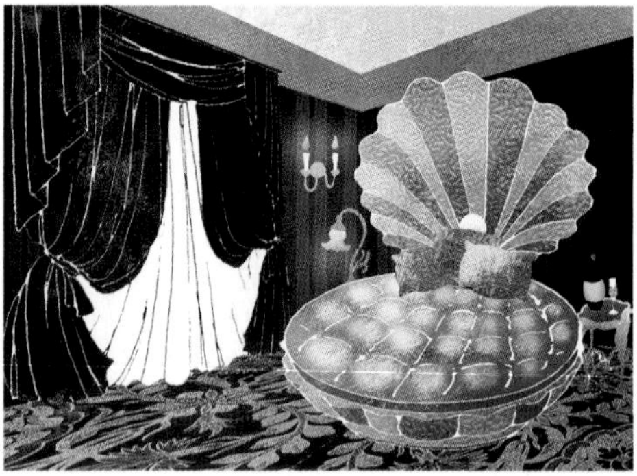

Rabu Hoteru

Known as *rabu hoteru*, often shortened to *rabuho*, love hotels provide a space for intimacy that can be leased for two or three hours, referred to euphemistically as *kyūkei* (rest), or for the night. Space is a key word. Their forerunner, *tsurekomi yado*, were born out of a need for privacy, even for married couples, who often lived in cramped multi-generational family homes. Love hotels first appeared in the late 1960s, with the Meguro Emperor in Tokyo becoming a landmark for its striking European castle design when it opened in 1973. Although they are used for prostitution and affairs, *rabuho* are still frequented by couples looking for privacy. The entrances are discreet, minimizing contact with other guests and staff, with room designs to suit every taste, from train carriage replicas to S&M dungeons. More than a million people are estimated to use love hotels each day, making it a huge industry. Recent years have seen many broaden their appeal and offer services such as food, saunas, rooftop baths and large screen TVs. Some of these hotels now market themselves as resort hotels.

Kapuseru Hoteru

Capsule hotels, pronounced *ka-puseru hoteru*, became synonymous with hard-working salarymen of the bubble era who either worked late or drank with colleagues into the night. Enclosed pods with just enough room to sleep and shared washing areas, they provide a reasonable alternative to expensive taxis home. Like their romantic cousins, capsule hotels have moved upmarket lately, with incarnations like designer versions, hybrids with bigger individual spaces and those catering solely to women.

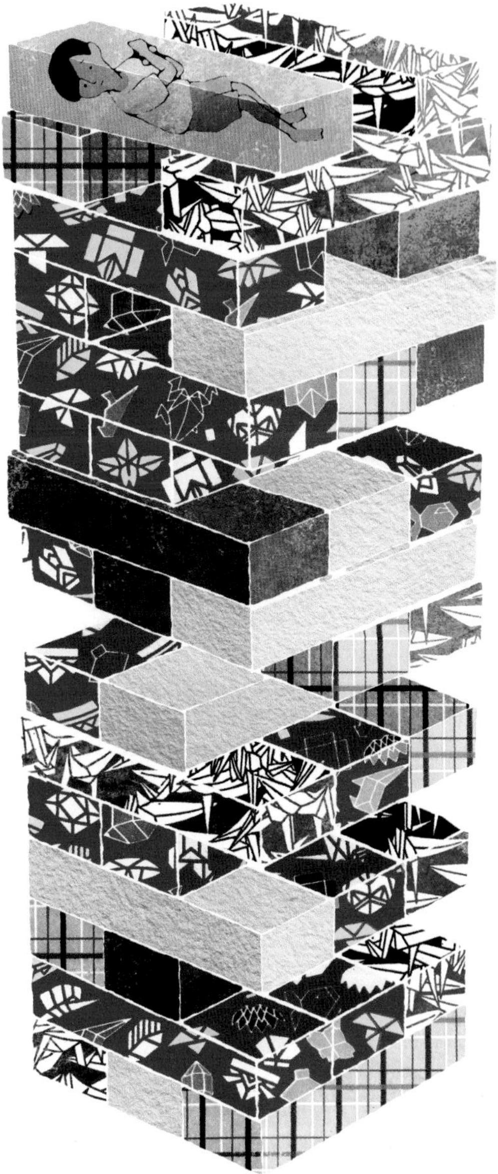

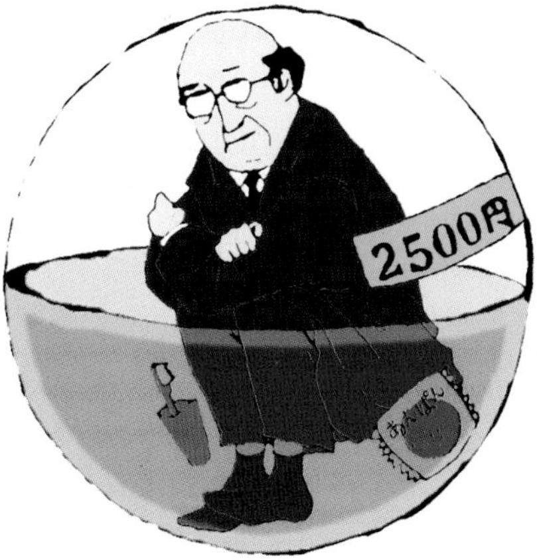
2500円

生け花

Ikebana

The Art of Flower Arrangement

If you believe that a floral composition is something akin to an ornament, a beautiful object with which to adorn the home, then you are at odds with the spirit of *ikebana*. The "live flowers" (the literal meaning of the term) that go into the vibrant plant sculpture know as *ikebana* are a great deal more than that. Their aim is to suggest the natural universe in its totality within an enclosed room, to create a bond between inside and outside, to make the viewer feel part of the vast harmony of the cosmos.

The ability to express the very essence of nature with a few flowers or twigs obviously requires sophisticated artistry, one through which clever artifice can convey natural spontaneity. Once various items are placed in a container, shears are used to adjust the lengths of stems and shapes of leaves. Lines are curved by hand to emphasize gentleness, arranged in diagonals to express dynamism or set along vertical and horizontal axes to transmit tranquility. Playing with negative and positive space, criss-crossing lines of force, reveals a state of mind and generates an ambience.

Along with the other arts of Zen, *ikebana* aims at simplicity and harmony and favors asymmetrical lines, but it is also open to variations on these aesthetic principles as evidenced by a myriad of schools and styles. The oldest is *Rikka*, which derives from the tradition of placing floral offerings on Buddhist altars, a sumptuous and scenographic style that is ideal for feasts and ceremonies and was widely used between the 14th and 17th centuries to decorate the temples and castles of the warrior aristocracy.

The first style taught to beginners is *Moribana*, in which vertical or slightly oblique stems rise from trays and short vases. The *Nageire* vessel, on the other hand, is tall with a narrow mouth, which allows for picturesque, cascading compositions.

But regardless of the school one chooses to follow, while creating an *ikebana* an artist always searches for external forms in the depths of his or her soul. Only in this way can "the way of flowers" (*kadō*) become an instrument of spiritual growth and refinement.

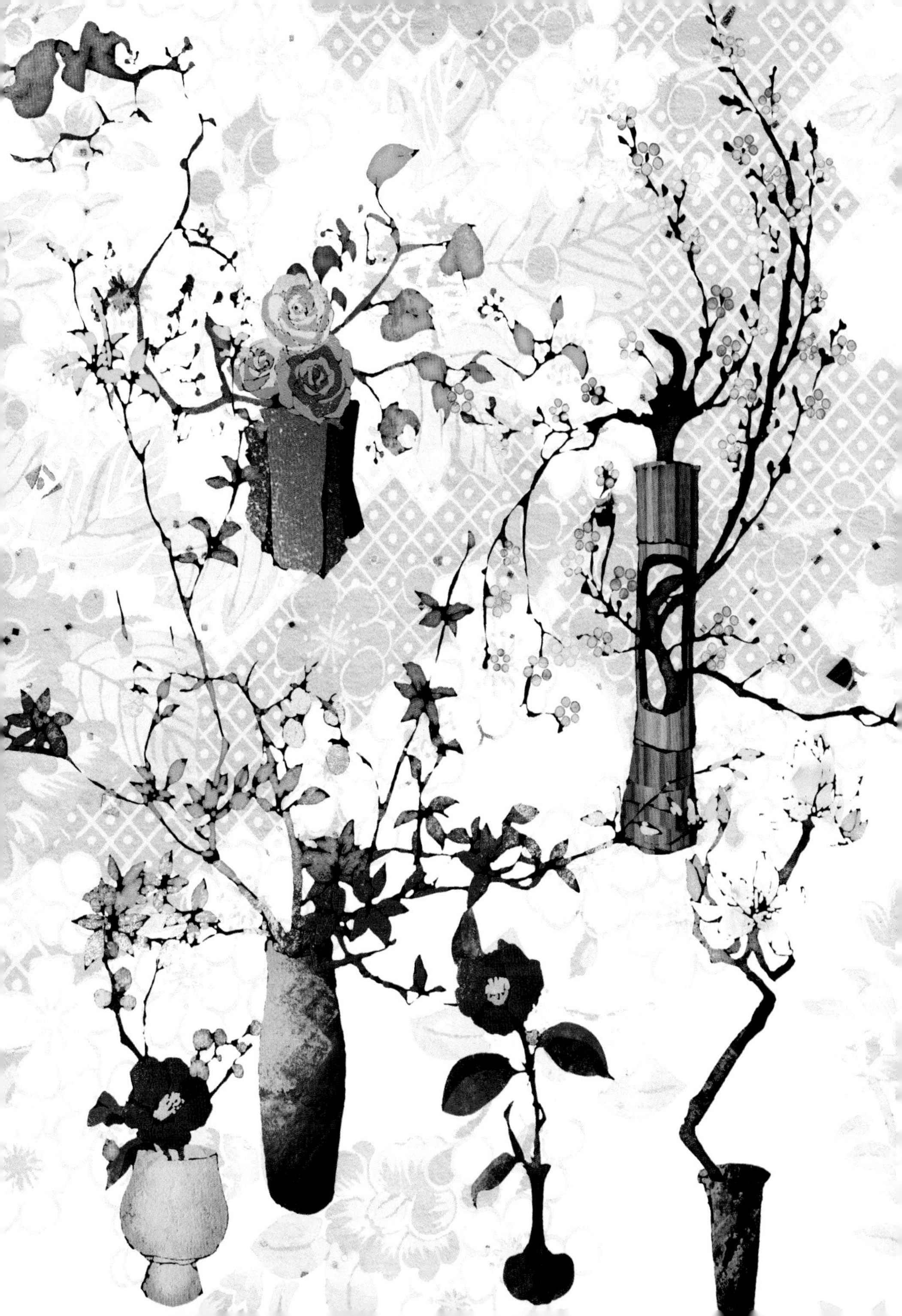

粋
Iki

Elusive, Fleeting Beauty

Indistinct, ambiguous and full of inner resonance, this aesthetic concept, which emerged at the dawn of the 19th century, accounts for many choices made by *ukiyo-e* artists and is often still evident in the taste trends of the Rising Sun. The only person who has attempted to pinpoint it is the philosopher, poet and inimitable dandy Kuki Shūzō (1888–1941), a friend of Heidegger and Claudel, who was as much in love with aesthetics as with the cosmopolitanism of Paris, and who dedicated his entire life to studying this elusive definition of beauty.

We can attempt to get an idea of the meaning of *iki* from his 1930 essay, "The structure of *iki*," which, using imagery rather than definitions, conveys the notion in a relatively comprehensible manner to us laymen. *Iki*, for example, lies in the allusiveness of transparent silk that comes in contact with flesh, a collar of a kimono that dips slightly to reveal the nape of the neck, or the slightly messy hair with several tousled locks typical of a person who has just woken up.

Iki is also about raising a corner of the kimono with the hand, making the red of the undergarments and the whiteness of the bare foot in a high wooden sandal flicker with every step. Above all, *iki* is a woman after emerging from a bath with a light garment carelessly cast over her body but one shoulder inadvertently bared, from which the

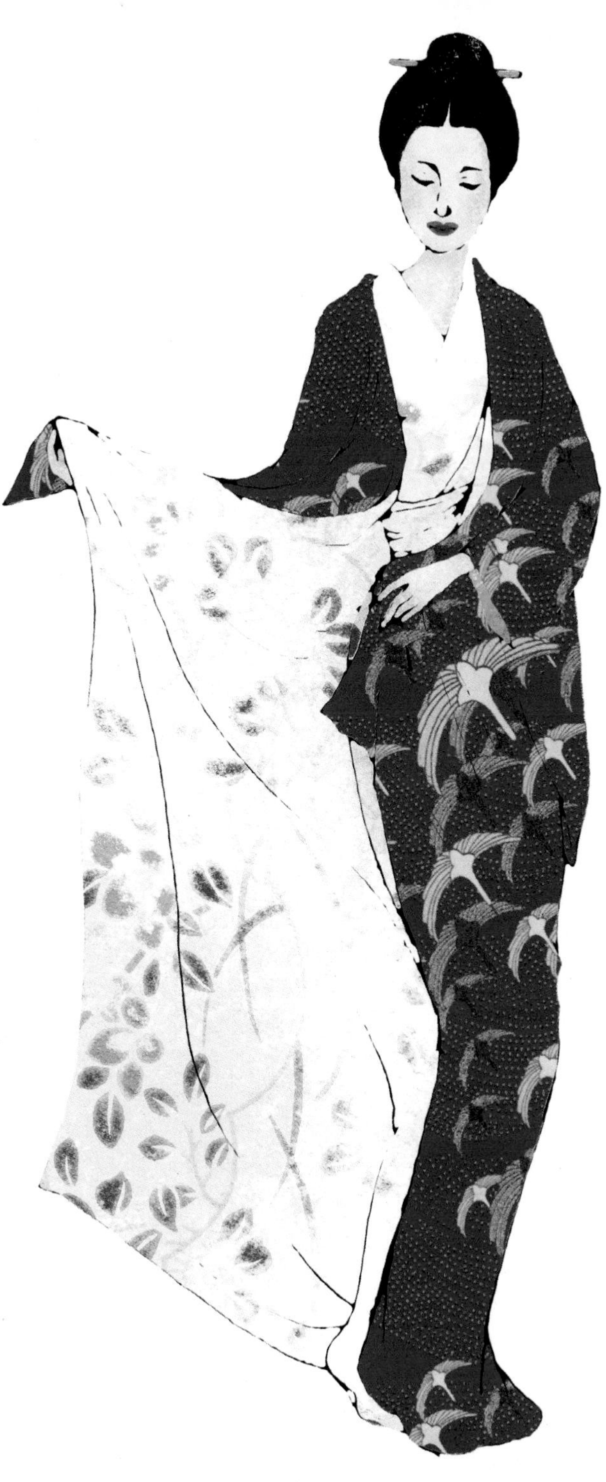

scent of still-warm skin wafts. Without question, the bottom line of *iki* is seductiveness.

The beauty in which *iki* is embodied is not objective elegance but a subtle charm, erotic tension, something akin to coquetry. A beauty allowed to scintillate but never fully reveal itself, always in some casual, unselfconscious manner, a carelessness that arises equally from a contempt for material things and earthly attachments, such as that of certain *geisha* from Edo who would reject a supremely wealthy client simply for being overly clumsy.

入れ墨
Irezumi

Traditional Japanese Tattoos

The origins of the Japanese art of tattooing, known as *irezumi*, may go back thousands of years. Ainu women of Hokkaido and the Ryukyu (Okinawan) islands certainly had a tradition of tattoos for many centuries, although mainland *irezumi* appears to have developed separately.

Tattooing criminals as a way of branding them may have started as early as the Kofun period (300–538), but was definitely widespread in later centuries, usually in the form of a straight line on offenders' arms or foreheads for each conviction.

It was during the Edo period that extravagant full-body *irezumi* was born. Many who sported tattoos were engaged in risky professions, as firefighters, messengers, steeplejacks and gamblers, as well as *kyōkaku*, folklore street heroes who protected the weak and were seen by some as predecessors of the *yakuza gangs*.

Ukiyo-e artists began to depict characters with elaborate tattoos, boosting their popularity, and some are said to have gone on to also work as *horimono*, or *irezumi* practitioners. The images of dragons, demons, birds, *koi* carp, samurai, *geisha* and mythical creatures that became favored *irezumi* at that time continue to be so today, particularly among *yakuza*.

Traditional *irezumi* use Nara ink and are hand-poked in a lengthy, painful and expensive process.

After Japan opened up to the West in the Meiji period, the government thought *irezumi* would appear primitive and in 1872 outlawed it. In fact, many visitors were enamored with the intricate designs and a number of foreign dignitaries got inked. In the 1880s, King Edward VII sent his sons, the Dukes of Clarence and York, to Yokohama *irezumi* master Horichiyo, where the Duke of York, later King George V, had a dragon tattooed on his arm.

Legalized by the US occupation authorities in 1948, inked GIs introduced many Americans to the style. It was after this that *irezumi* became synonymous with *yakuza* gangsters, with some of them now spending millions of yen and hours under the needle, often over years, as a mark of endurance and status.

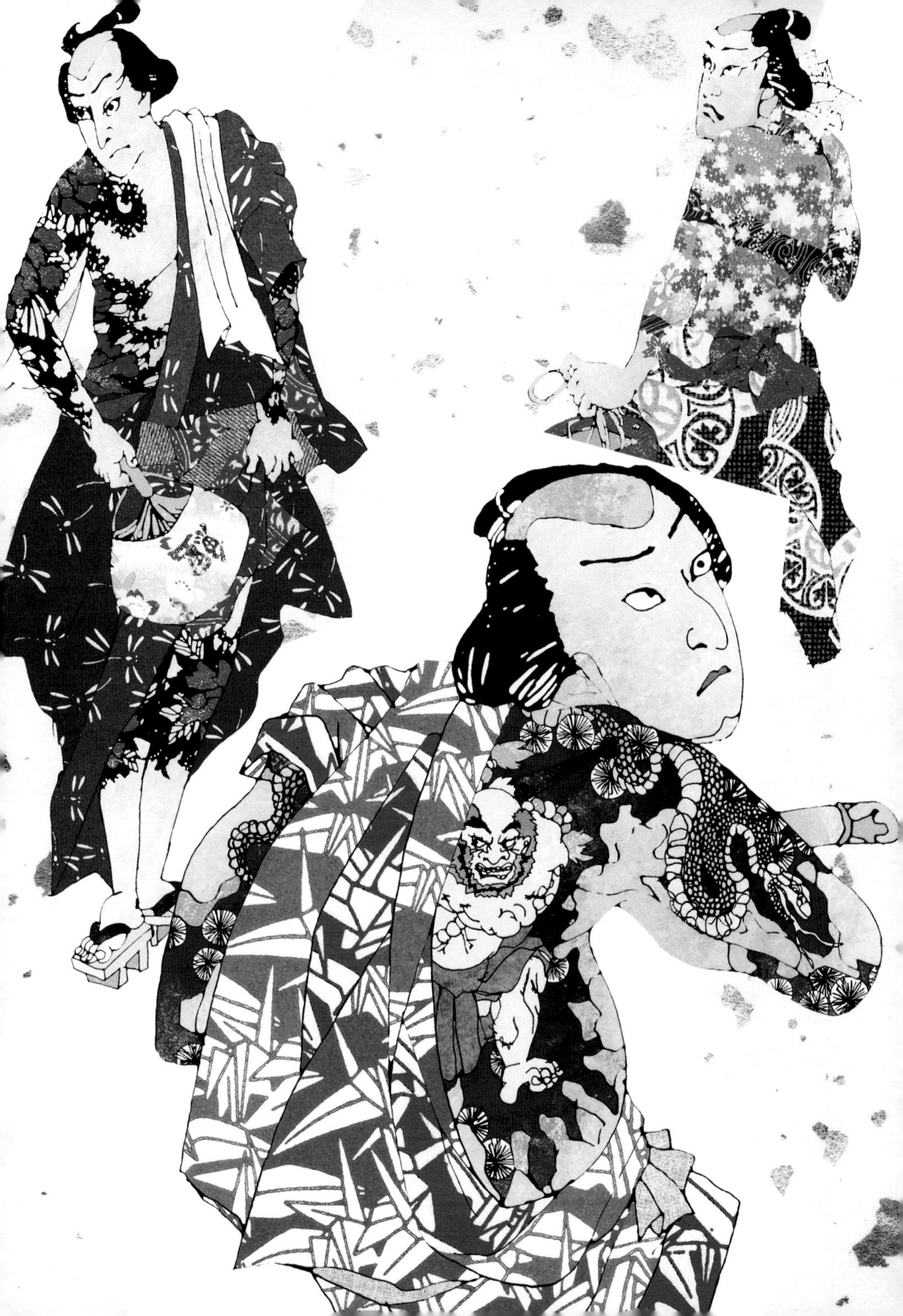

囲炉裏

Irori

The Japanese Hearth or Kitchen

This is the common method of heating a traditional Japanese house, and the equivalent to our concept of the hearth as the home's ideal center, where families seek warmth and cook food. The *irori* is a kind of metal-lined square tank built into the floor and used for burning wood or coal. Above it hangs a bamboo rod ending with a hook from which a cast-iron teapot or pot is suspended over the fire. The height of the rod is adjusted with a particular type of counterweight, usually in the shape of a fish. There is not a single Japanese person for whom the sight of an old soot-covered

irori does not evoke the simple life of a rural family huddling around the fire, waiting for dinner on a winter evening and discussing the day as skewered fish slowly broil on the embers.

Hibachi

The *hibachi*, more convenient than the *irori* because it was transportable, came to be used more widely to warm hands and teapots in the 19th century. The term means "vase of fire," and it often does, in fact, assume the shape of a large bronze or porcelain vase, especially in the version intended for the tea ceremony. Sometimes,

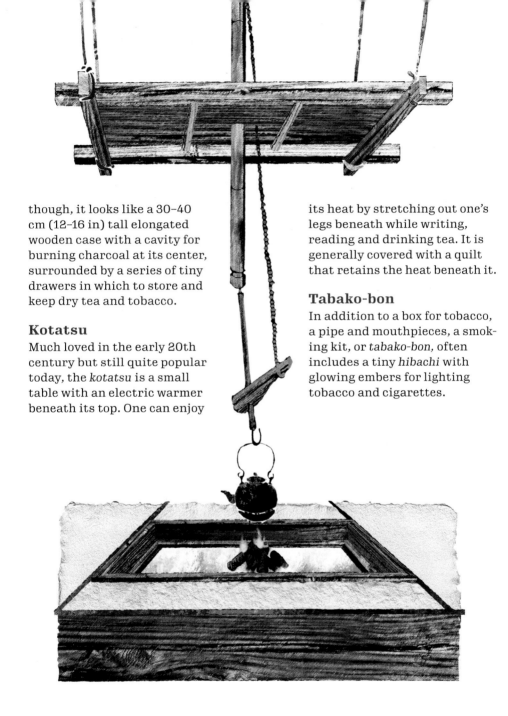

though, it looks like a 30–40 cm (12–16 in) tall elongated wooden case with a cavity for burning charcoal at its center, surrounded by a series of tiny drawers in which to store and keep dry tea and tobacco.

Kotatsu

Much loved in the early 20th century but still quite popular today, the *kotatsu* is a small table with an electric warmer beneath its top. One can enjoy its heat by stretching out one's legs beneath while writing, reading and drinking tea. It is generally covered with a quilt that retains the heat beneath it.

Tabako-bon

In addition to a box for tobacco, a pipe and mouthpieces, a smoking kit, or *tabako-bon,* often includes a tiny *hibachi* with glowing embers for lighting tobacco and cigarettes.

Jポップ

J-pop

Japanese Pop Music

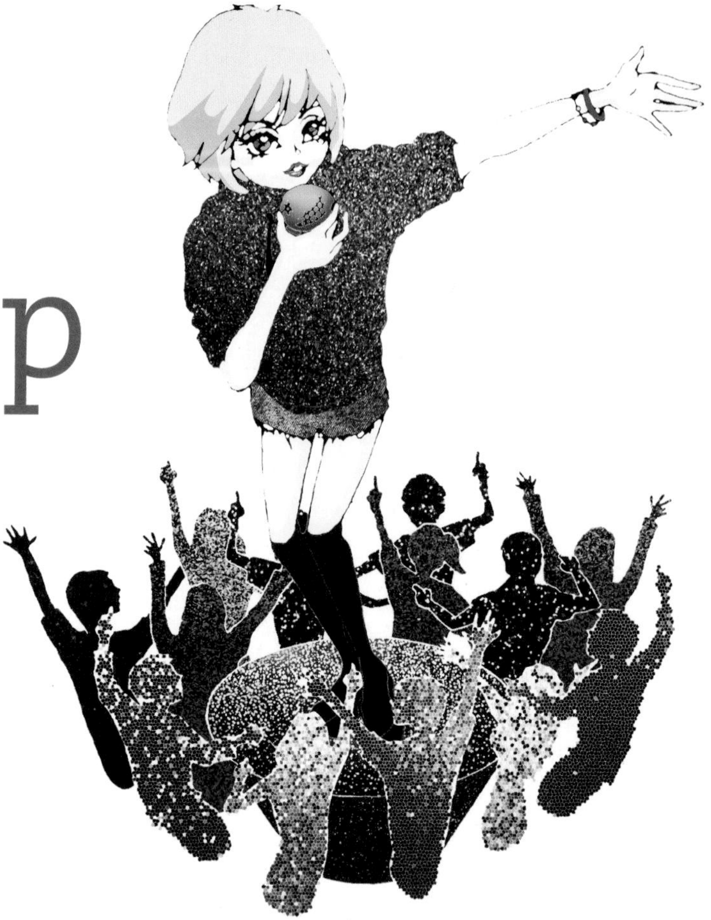

The origins of J-pop, pronounced *jē-poppu*, can be traced back to the 1960s when local musicians began incorporating elements of Western pop into their compositions, as well as producing localized covers. The sound became known as *kayōkyoku*, literally "lyric-sing-music," and bore the influence of Japan's *enka* folk music. In the 1970s, artists like the multi-million selling duo Pink Lady, with choreographed dance routines, sexy outfits and English song titles, helped lay down the blueprint for the J-pop and idol groups that would appear later. With Japan's music industry then the world's second largest, the 1990s were dominated by J-pop acts, including Amuro Namie, produced by Komuro Tetsuya, with combined sales of more than 170 million. The end of the decade saw Utada Hikaru's R&B-tinged debut sell 10 million copies, a J-pop record that still stands, and a renaissance of the all-girl idol group.

Aidoru

Parents down the years have dismissed their children's musical heroes as bereft of talent, and for many of Japan's *aidoru* (idol) groups, that rings true. Members of boy and girl bands put together by Japan's all-powerful talent agencies are often deliberately chosen for their lack of musical ability. Even some members of SMAP, born out of dominant agency Johnny's & Associates, and who between 1988 and 2016 became the bestselling Asian band in history, are known for being unable to hold a tune. Top idol groups like SMAP and label-mates Arashi, who are truly omnipresent, also work as actors and have hosted their own prime-time TV variety shows. The young members of female groups, especially, such as Morning Musume and AKB48, are chosen for their girl-next-door looks, and their lack of ability or rhythm is presented as *kawaii*. This is said to appeal to their fans, who are, somewhat disturbingly, often older men. Tales of exploitation and abuse are rife, while most wannabe idols are poorly paid and often bound by restrictive contracts that control even their love lives.

受験地獄
Juken jigoku

Exam Hell

Japan's postwar national mission to raise educational standards lifted it to near the top of international rankings despite allocating a relatively low proportion of GDP to public education. As more people began to complete high school and go on to tertiary education, competition to get into the best schools and universities intensified, leading to what is known as *juken jigoku,* or exam hell. The synonymous *shiken jigoku* is more commonly used for exams other than those for high school and university entrance, such as exams for some kindergartens and preparatory schools to ready children for them.

The importance of entrance exams in Japanese society is illustrated by the more than 100 compound words formed with *juken* recognized by the National Institute of Japanese Language and Linguistics. Students who are in full preparation mode to become a *juken-sha* (candidate) are transformed into a *juken-sei* (exam student). And when *juken-kyōsō* exam competition reaches its peak, it is called *juken-sensō,* or exam war.

The country's skewed demographics—decades of low birth rate mean just 12 percent of the population is under 14 compared to 36 percent immediately after the war—might have been expected to ease the competitiveness. But a rise in single-child households has also meant that *kyoiku mamas* (education-driven mothers) now often focus all their energy on just one offspring.

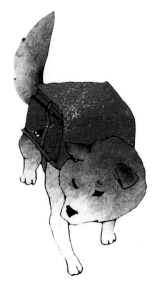

A multi-billion dollar education industry has been fueled by these pressures, with cram schools at its heart. Although *katei-kyōshi* (home tutors) and correspondence courses play a part, it is the tens of thousands of private, after-hours *gakushū juku* schools, usually known simply as *juku*, that are attended by a majority of elementary schoolers and a significant proportion of older students. Despite mirroring the often criticized rote learning style of Japanese public education, the *juku* Kumon has found favor overseas with thousands of schools in more than 50 countries.

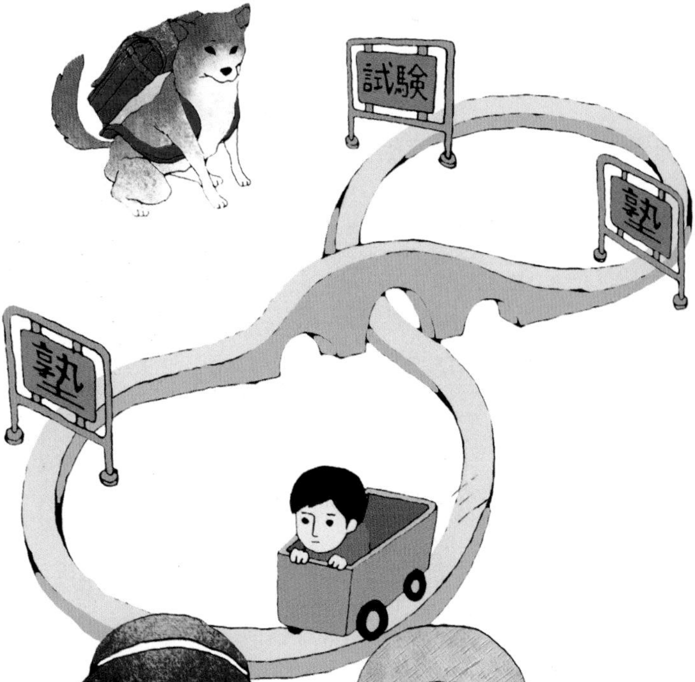
試験
塾
塾

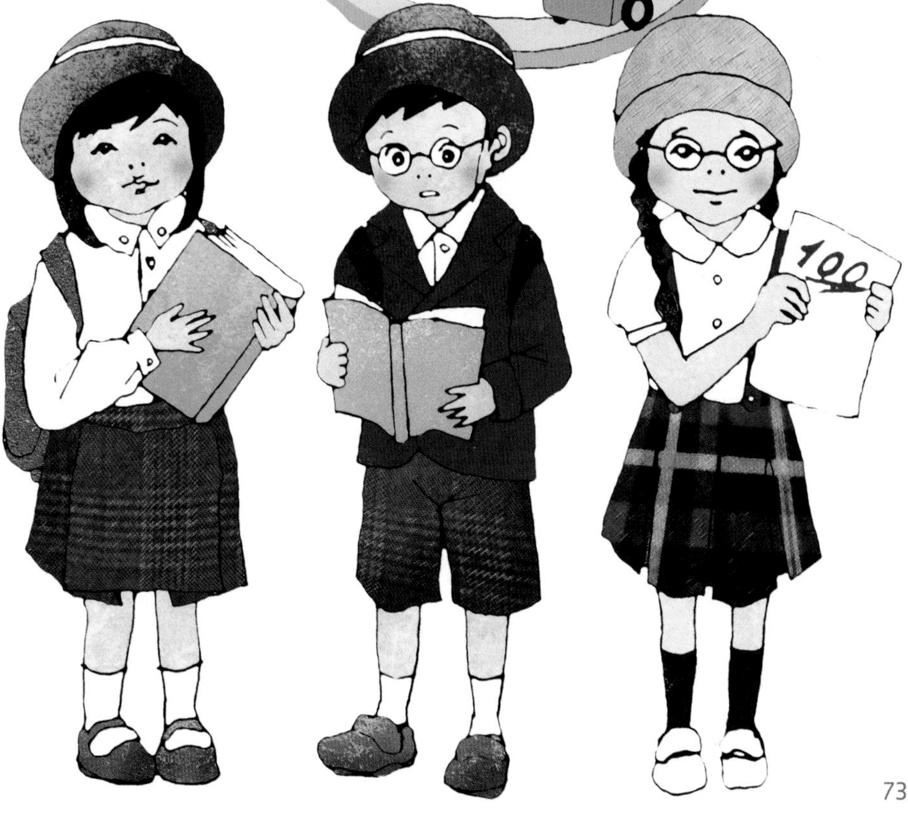
100

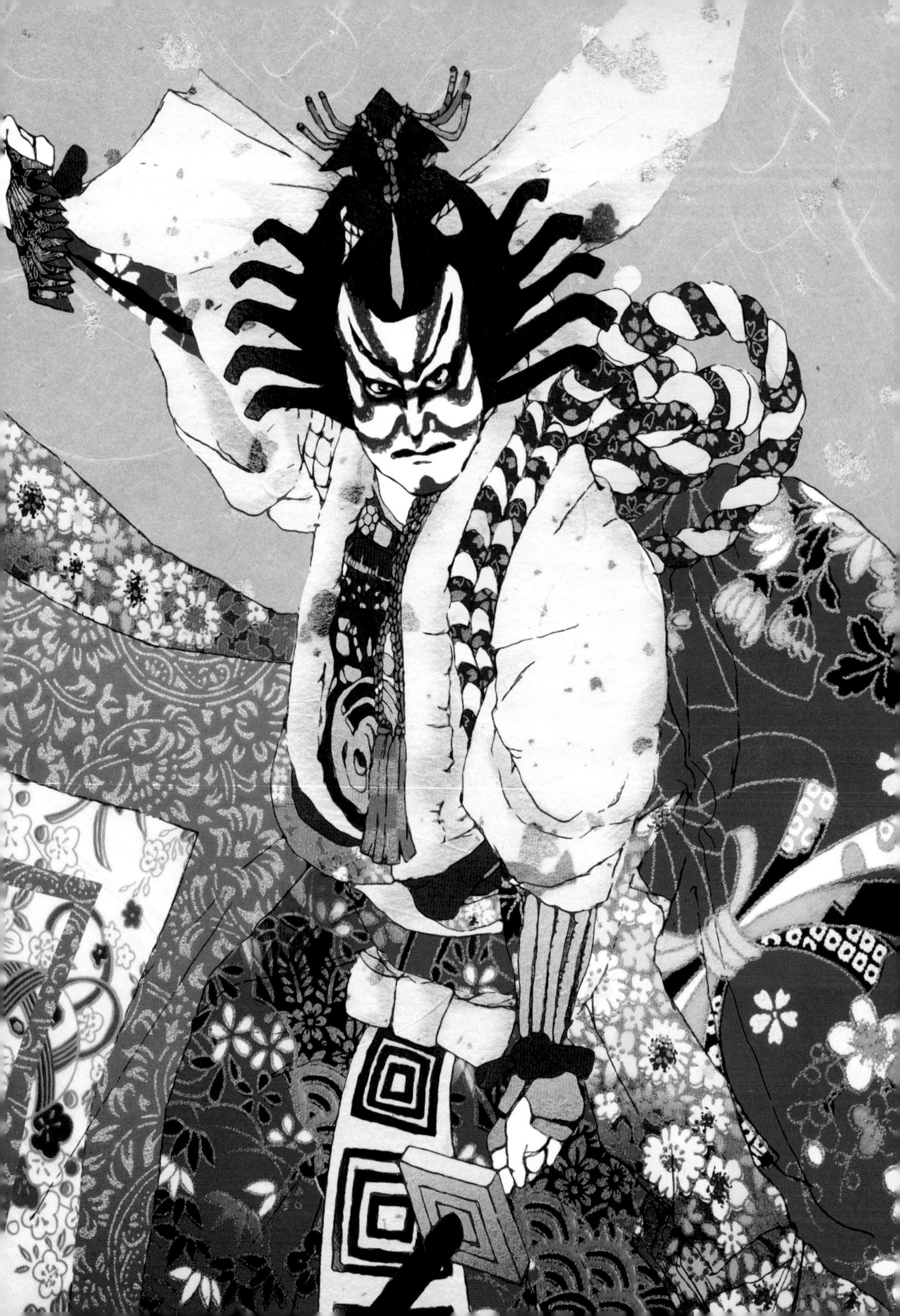

歌舞伎
Kabuki

Spectacular Theatrical Performances

Kabuki, the word derived from *ka* (song), *bu* (dance) and *ki* (technique), merges all the components of this popular form of theatrical entertainment: intricate textures, sumptuous costumes and scenes, spectacular dance, virtuoso acting. Whether presenting gruesome historical episodes or passionate melodramas inspired by ancient chronicles, the combat between good and evil, virtue and vice, heart-driven aspirations and social convention is always displayed in bold colors on the stage. *Kabuki* also chooses themes involving the merchant and artisan class that began emerging at the turn of the 17th century. The stories, composed largely for this new middle class, reflect the contradictions of a developing society that no longer accepts the rigid ideals of the old feudal system but does not yet have the power to impose its own values. Thus, though the historical works of the genre generally focus on the courage and loyalty of the hero, the romantic ones often end with the suicide of lovers tragically trapped in the dead end of class distinctions or a feeling unrecognized by the status quo.

The success of a work was often attributable to the actor's charisma, his ability to arouse collective excitement and also influence fashion.

Onnagata

This is the male actor who plays female characters, the most difficult ones, which require the great effort of transforming his body to appear as fragile as a woman's. For the sake of public morality, the shogunate decreed in 1652 that all parts be entrusted to men, and so it has remained to this day.

Hanamichi

The "road of flowers" is a walkway which extends into the audience from the main stage, where the actors make their triumphant entry or exit. It is also often the site of the *michiyuki*, the journey of the protagonists, the climax of the tragedy when two lovers decide to commit suicide together.

Mie

The test of a great actor, this is a sort of snapshot image in which an action appears frozen in a static pose of great visual impact. It requires more energy and a better sense of balance than do most movements of the wildest dance. The audience explodes with enthusiastic applause during such hypnotic moments of suspension.

神楽

Kagura

Ancient Ritual Music and Dances

According to legend, a deity, Uzume, invented dance for a specific purpose. Offended by her brother Susanoo, Amaterasu, the goddess of the sun, had barricaded herself in a cave, plunging the world into freezing darkness. To rouse her curiosity and convince her to reappear, Uzume mounted an upside-down skin and began to thump her feet to a rhythm. The stratagem worked. The goddess peeked out and spring returned to earth. That dance was the *Kagura*, which originated as a shamanic ritual for invoking the deity and inviting her to manifest herself so that the life cycle of man and nature would revive, the earth be fertile and the crops abundant. Over time, it was appropriated by appropriate Shinto liturgy, which heightened its ecstatic and divinatory aspects in order to turn it into a ceremony of the shrine and court. It is still performed regularly on the occasion of *matsuri* by priestesses, who, accompanied by drums and flutes, assume highly suggestive priestly gestures.

Kamigata Mai

This elegant and refined dance emerged from *Nō* theater, whose shuffling steps and particular circular movements, some performed with fans, it retains. It was developed in the region of Kyoto and Osaka in the 16th century, when it was performed by blind dancers, not in theaters but in private residences for the amusement of a *daimyō*. Later, it became a typical form of entertainment by courtesans in houses of pleasure.

Bugaku

If *Kagura* is the dance of Shintoism, then *Bugaku* is the most typical form of Buddhist dance. It came to Japan from India in the 7th century along with Buddhism, its sacred texts, sculpture and temple architecture. Slow and solemn pantomime, sometimes nearly martial, it is performed within a kind of circle of dancers in gorgeous costumes and grotesque masks, who stage symbolic battles between good and play out evil encounters with fantastical animals or other episodes drawn from legend.

神風

Kamikaze

Japanese Suicide Pilots

In the West, the two *kanji* characters that form this word are commonly read as *kamikaze*, at least when referring to the pilots who carried out suicide attacks in World War II. However, in Japanese they are more commonly known as *Shinpū*, an alternate pronunciation of the characters. *Shinpū* ("divine wind") were the 13th-century typhoons that twice saved Japan from Mongol attacks, devastating the enemy fleet. Many centuries later, towards the end of the Pacific War, when the exhausted country found itself having to face a US invasion, the "divine wind" was again called on to save the

敗北より死

"Better death than defeat"

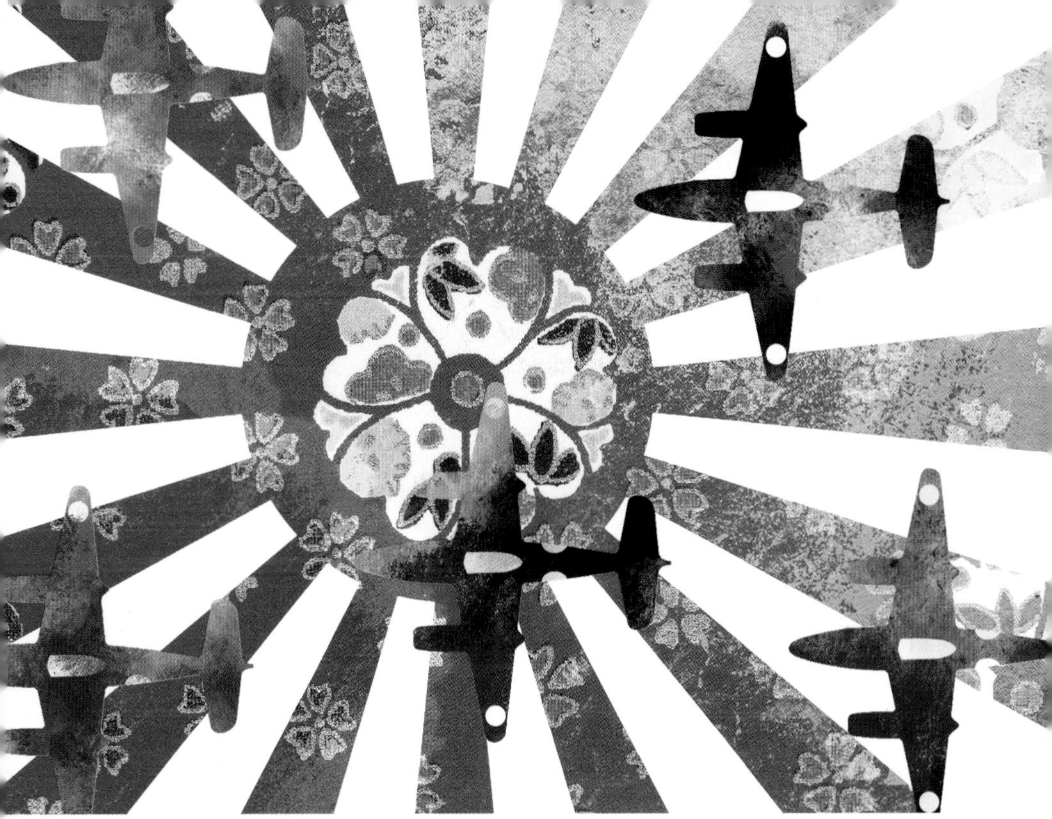

nation, this time in the form of young pilots willing to fly directly into enemy ships in small planes laden with explosives. It was Ōnishi Takijirō himself, the admiral who conceived the so-called *tokkōtai* (*tokubetsu kōgeki tai*), or special attack units, who baptized the units engaged in suicide operations with the glorious name of *shinpū*.

It was never a problem for the Japanese command to find volunteers, who were always in greater numbers than necessary. Generally, the *kamikaze* were recruited among university students between 20 and 23 years old, who were moved by patriotic feelings and aspirations to honor and glory, as well as by the principles of the ancient *bushidō* samurai code. They were trained in seven days and before the last mission they underwent purification rites and tied on the *hachimaki*, the scarf with the *hino maru*, the symbol of the rising sun.

From October 1944 to August 1945, more than 2,000 suicide attacks were carried out and 47 American and British ships were sunk with another 300 damaged, but the desperate Japanese strategy turned out to be ultimately futile.

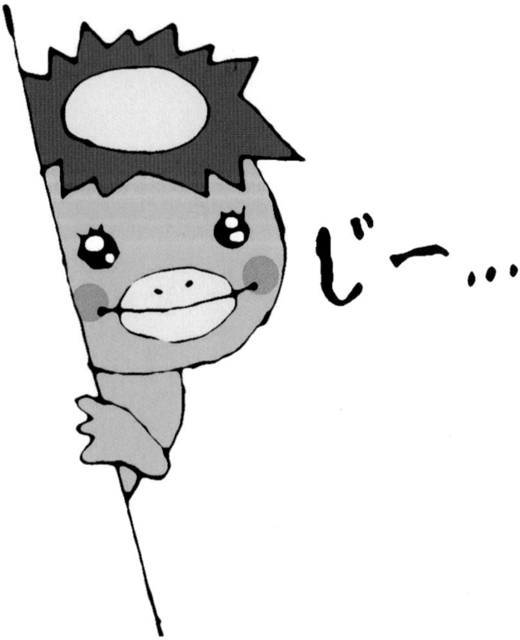
じー…
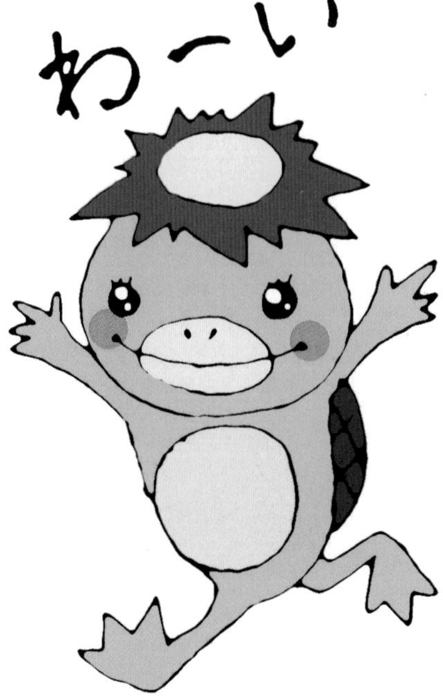
わーい

河童

Kappa

Mystical Water Sprites

Bizarre and mischievous creatures who inhabit rivers and streams, the *kappa* are recognized by their greenish skin, often slimy or covered with scales, and webbed hands and feet that allow them to swim with lightning speed. Although they resemble children between the ages of 5 and 10, they have an anthropomorphic appearance combined with turtle, frog, monkey or tiger features, as in the illustrations. The *kappa* are often represented with a beak or with a tortoise shell on their backs.

The *kappa's* most prominent feature is a concave indentation on the top of its head in which water, the source of its strength and the element vital to its well-being, is pooled. Despite its comic appearance, it is extremely dangerous. It can sneak out of a river and drag children, women, oxen or horses into it. It sucks out their organs through their anus, then leaves behind their empty carcasses.

If one runs into a *kappa*, there is only one way to render it harmless: by

おやすみ

はぐはぐ

recipes for medicines, retrieve precious objects lost in water and supply fish. This strange blend of generosity and maleficence actually reflects the dual nature of water. A vital element and essential to the cultivation of rice, water turns into a threat and a destructive force in the event of a flood. As the advance of science and technology has gradually allowed us to control its power, the sprite of the rivers has also been placated. Indeed, since the 1960s it has enjoyed a popularity boom and become the hero of various comic strips, including Mizuki Shigeru's famous *Kappa no Sanpei*. With the proliferation of gadgets accompanying its fame, the fellow has been definitively rehabilitated, from an ugly and dangerous little monster into a nice commercial *kawaii* icon.

depriving it of the water stored on its head. This is not too difficult a task; one needs simply to make a deep bow, as the *kappa*, who is very polite, cannot help but bow in return and thus spill his precious liquid.

Once captured, the *kappa* will make a pact with its human captor that will render it benevolent. At this point, it will reveal secret

ふ〜っ

過労死
Karōshi

Death from Overwork

Japanese workers have a mostly deserved reputation for dedication and loyalty to their companies, but some end up making the ultimate sacrifice. The *karōshi* (over-work-death) problem has long been around, but it was only after several high-profile deaths of young workers in recent years that this was highlighted. The cultural roots of *karōshi* lie in the traditions of loyal service, a reluctance to question or defy authority, the value placed on the group over self, the tendency to endure, or *gaman*, and the acceptance of fate encapsulated by *shōganai*. Such

tendencies helped natural resource-poor Japan produce an economic miracle derived almost exclusively from the strength of human capital. But it came at a price: long hours and few holidays meant little time with families and strained health. It was during the 1970s that the problem began to be recognized and the term *karōshi* coined. During the bubble economy of the 1980s, when *salariiman* sleeping overnight in the office was commonplace, apparently healthy high-flying executives began dying and the government started to

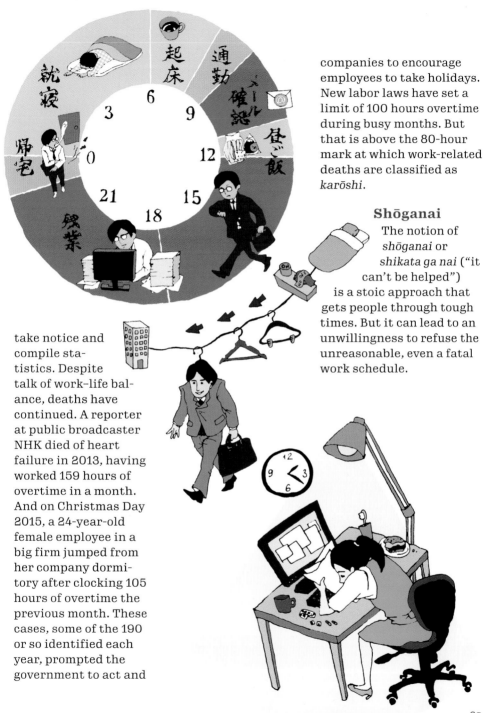

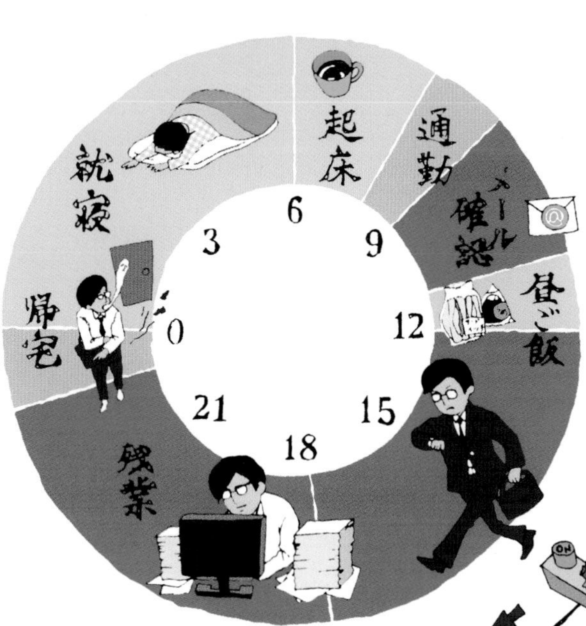
起床
通勤
メール確認
昼ご飯
残業
帰宅
就寝
6
9
12
15
18
21
0
3

take notice and compile statistics. Despite talk of work–life balance, deaths have continued. A reporter at public broadcaster NHK died of heart failure in 2013, having worked 159 hours of overtime in a month. And on Christmas Day 2015, a 24-year-old female employee in a big firm jumped from her company dormitory after clocking 105 hours of overtime the previous month. These cases, some of the 190 or so identified each year, prompted the government to act and companies to encourage employees to take holidays. New labor laws have set a limit of 100 hours overtime during busy months. But that is above the 80-hour mark at which work-related deaths are classified as *karōshi*.

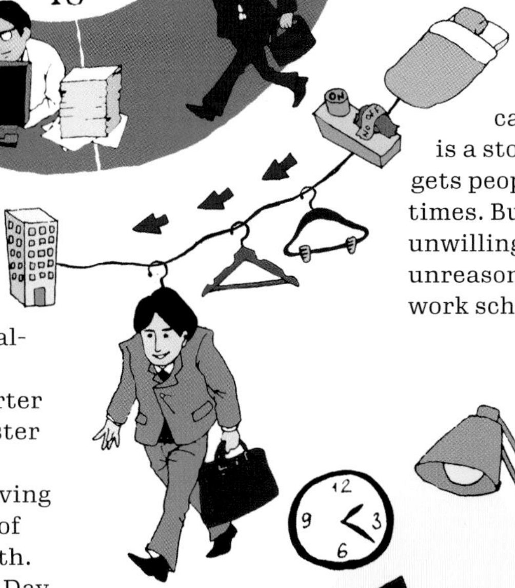

Shōganai

The notion of *shōganai* or *shikata ga nai* ("it can't be helped") is a stoic approach that gets people through tough times. But it can lead to an unwillingness to refuse the unreasonable, even a fatal work schedule.

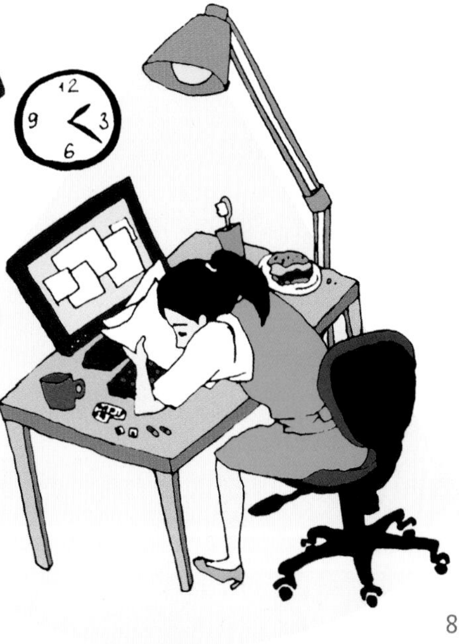
12
3
6
9

刀

Katana

The Samurai Sword

The most iconic bladed weapon in the history of warfare, the *katana* swords of the samurai are also works of outstanding craftsmanship. The early long swords used in Japan were double-edged and based on Chinese designs. The distinctive curved blade design of the *katana* is believed to be the result of the attempted Mongol invasions of the 13th century. The swords of the time often caught in the hardened leather armor of the Mongol warriors, sometimes snapping when their bearers pulled them out. To combat this, swordsmiths adopted a new forging method that created a more flexible spine and sharper blade. This was achieved by repeatedly folding the *tamahagane* steel, which is smelted and then cooled by coating the two parts of the sword with different thicknesses of a wet clay concoction. The difference in the temperatures changes the composition of the steel and causes the curvature of the blade, known as the *hamon*. The *hamon* is then accentuated during the weeks-long polishing process performed by a specialist. The *katana's bo hi* groove was introduced to make the blade lighter and more resilient, but not, as sometimes stated, to allow blood to run off. This forging method and design remained largely unchanged for centuries, though the length fluctuated between 60 and 73 cm (24 and 29 in).

During times of peace, elements such as the *tsuba* guards, *tsuka* handles and *saya* scabbards become more decorative. A *katana* was paired with either a *wakizashi* short sword or a *tantō* dagger, the two weapons being the mark of a samurai. Though the *katana* is sometimes referred to as the soul of a samurai, and it no doubt held special meaning for them, it was not their main battlefield weapon. The samurai were primarily horseback archers who would also use spears or *naginata* pole arms before resorting to swords at close quarters.

The 1876 Haitōrei Edict forbade the samurai from carrying swords and was one of the most visible signs that their era was at an end.

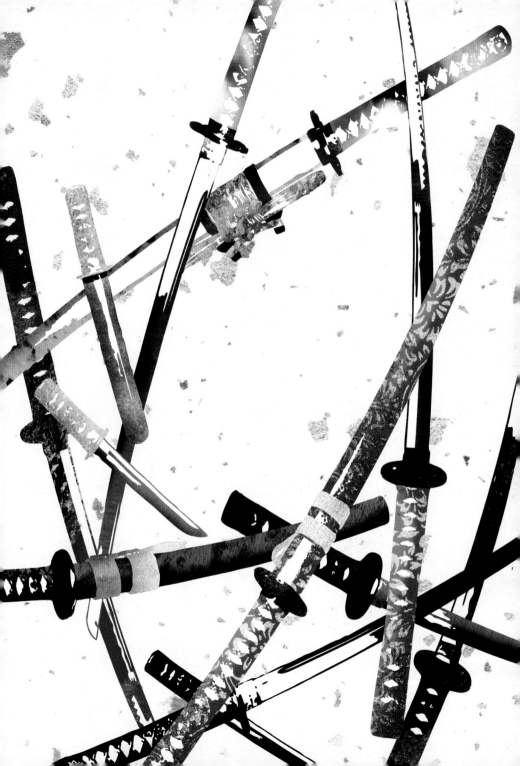

可愛い

Kawaii

The Japanese Concept of Cuteness

The word *kawaii* is truly ubiquitous in Japan, particularly among young women, and is used to describe everything from food to clothes to personality traits and much more in between. The Japanese concept of "cute," which also embraces an idea of purity and innocence, has entered the vocaulary of international pop culture. There is debate as to *kawaii*'s etymology. Some point to its use in *The Tale of Genji* (*Genji monogatari*), written by the imperial court lady-in-waiting Murasaki Shikibu in the 11th century, where it was used to mean "touching." In later centuries, it came to designate the sense of tenderness inspired by children and fragile and defenseless women.

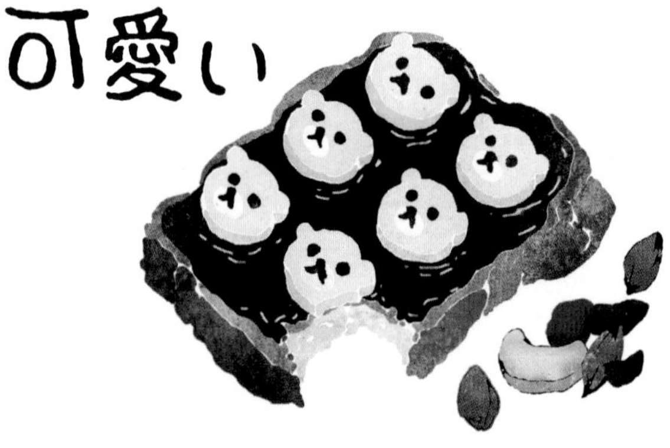
可愛い

The current *kawaii* trend is often traced back to a writing style that teenage girls developed in the 1970s. The overly curved characters were peppered with little pictures and faces (that may also have been the precursors of *emoji*—a combination of emotion and *ji*) and the occasional alphabet letter. The style enraged teachers but was adopted by magazines, *manga* and advertisers. Another 1970s-born symbol of *kawaii* is the mouthless cat Hello Kitty, which has gone on to be a multi-billion dollar merchandising franchise and even a tourist ambassador of Japan. One official embodiment of *kawaii* is *yuru-kyara* ("carefree character") mascots, which exist for nearly every area, campaign and entity in Japan, including some prisons. The government's embracing of *kawaii* has been criticized for portraying Japan as kitsch and promoting infantilization, especially of women. Japan

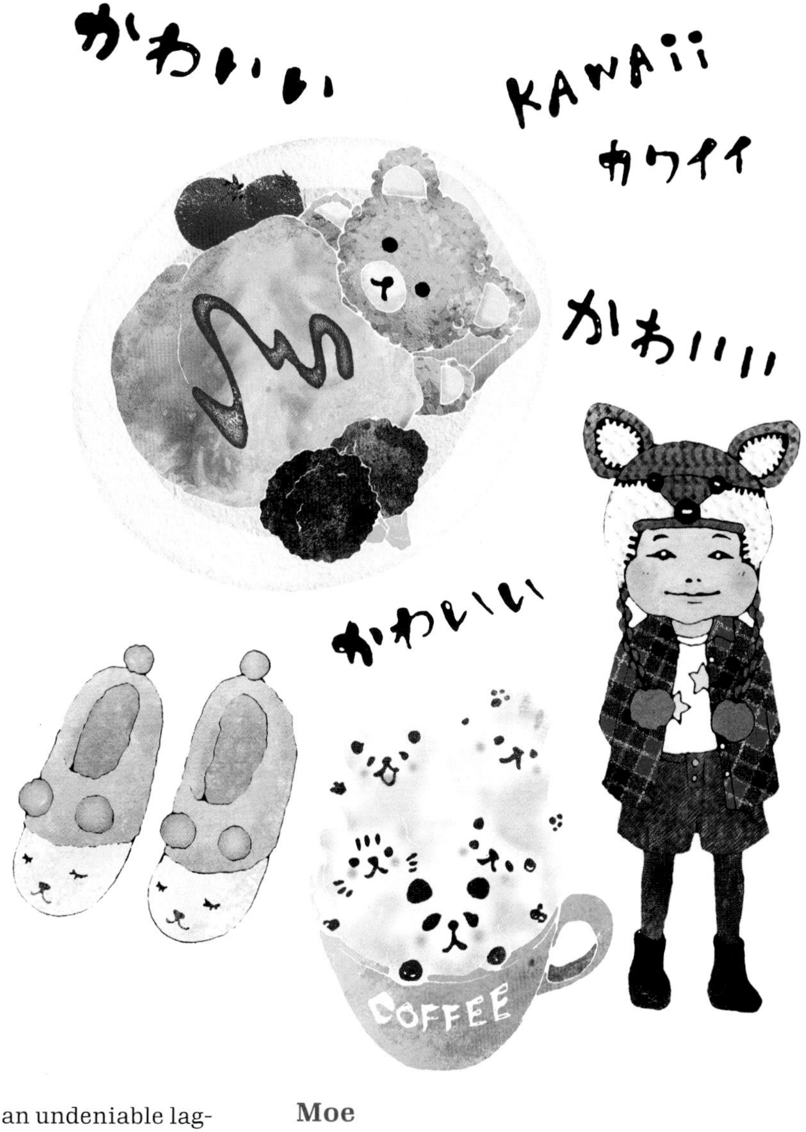
かわいい
KAWAii
カワイイ
かわいい
かわいい
COFFEE

is an undeniable laggard in gender equality, and the childlike, docile ideals of *kawaii*, which many young women feel pressured to strive for, are hardly conducive to empowerment.

Moe

In the slang of *anime* consumers this word assumes a meaning similar to that of *kawaii*. The term *moe* (with emphasis on the final "e"), which originally indicated the passion for a cartoon or video game character, is now often used to define a charmingly sweet and naive girl without any experience in relationships with the other sex (*moekko*).

着物
Kimono

The Iconic Japanese Garment

Kimono means "garment." This says a lot about the universality and exclusivity of this form of attire in Japan before the arrival of Western clothing. Even afterwards, it continued to coexist peaceably with the inevitable business suit or designer outfit worn by university students, while carving out its own impregnable niche. Putting on the kimono is still practically mandatory for New Year celebrations, weddings and funerals, graduations, and coming-of-age ceremonies. Those used on such occasions are often family heirlooms, passed down from generation to generation and stored in an equally precious cedar chest.

The kimono that we see today is actually the result of a drastic simplification process. The *jūnihitoe* worn by 10th- and 11th-century court ladies consisted of 12 superimposed kimonos of different colors and designs, reflecting the subtle combinations that had conformed to a complex aesthetic code as well as to the colors and atmosphere of the current season.

Nonetheless, there is still a precise etiquette involved in choosing the appropriate kimono for a specific occasion, age and time of year. For example, the fine silk *furisode* with brightly painted or embroidered patterns and sleeves are formally reserved for young, unmarried women and used for graduations or twentieth birthdays.

The *hōmongi* is suitable for married women and has a black or solid colored background decorated with an elegant motif running along the full hem. It used to be gifted to the bride as a symbol of a change in status. A married woman's kimono can be identified by a more compact sleeve that is convenient for taking care of household chores and for storing a handkerchief or purse. An obligatory rule, also visible in *ukiyo-e* prints, makes it compulsory that the garment reflects the season: bright colors, irises and cherry blossoms for spring and summer; red or golden leaves and chrysanthemums for autumn, while the New Year kimono is preferably decorated with bamboo, pine or plum trees, which are regarded as auspicious omens for the coming year.

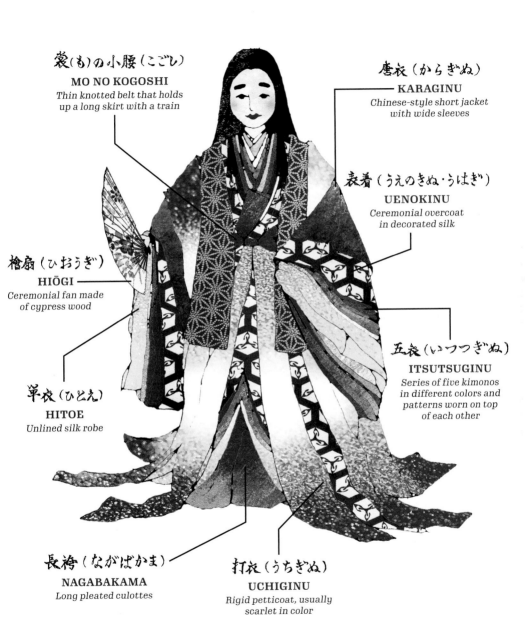

裳(も)の小腰(こごし)

MO NO KOGOSHI

*Thin knotted belt that holds
up a long skirt with a train*

唐衣(からぎぬ)

KARAGINU

*Chinese-style short jacket
with wide sleeves*

表着(うえのきぬ・うはぎ)

UENOKINU

*Ceremonial overcoat
in decorated silk*

檜扇(ひおうぎ)

HIŌGI

*Ceremonial fan made
of cypress wood*

五衣(いつつぎぬ)

ITSUTSUGINU

*Series of five kimonos
in different colors and
patterns worn on top
of each other*

単衣(ひとえ)

HITOE

Unlined silk robe

長袴(ながばかま)

NAGABAKAMA

Long pleated culottes

打衣(うちぎぬ)

UCHIGINU

*Rigid petticoat, usually
scarlet in color*

Yukata

The *yukata* is the brightly colored fresh cotton and unlined summer kimono, suitable for occasions that are not too formal. For example, it is perfect for *matsuri*, the ancient local festivals, at which tradition is emphasized.

The term derives from *yu* ("bath") and *katabira* ("linen"), as this was the garment that nobles of the court used after their bath. It is invariably found in hotel rooms, typically in a white geometrical pattern on a blue background, or vice versa.

Obi

This is the wide rigid band used to tie the kimono. Knotted in a complex fashion at the back, it is the trickiest part of the entire dressing ritual, especially if the wearer chooses a sophisticated knot. The movements of a woman bound by the kimono will naturally no longer be the same once it has been pulled tight: the posture of her shoulders, her gait, the inclination of her neck will all acquire that enchanting, indefinable charm of the prints of two centuries ago.

Geta and Zōri

The *geta* are the sandals most typically worn by *ukiyo-e*'s harrowing beauties as well as the rugged heroes of *Kabuki*. They have a flat wooden base, supported by two high "protrusions," to which the characteristic V-shaped strips of fabric of the thong are attached. Men still wear them at traditional festivals, ceremonies or sometimes when using public bathrooms. The rare *geisha* that can still be glimpsed in Kyoto can generally run without tripping on particular thick *geta*. Today, however, ordinary women wearing a kimono inevitably opt for *zōri*, straw flip-flops, nowadays conveniently manufactured in printed vinyl.

OBI

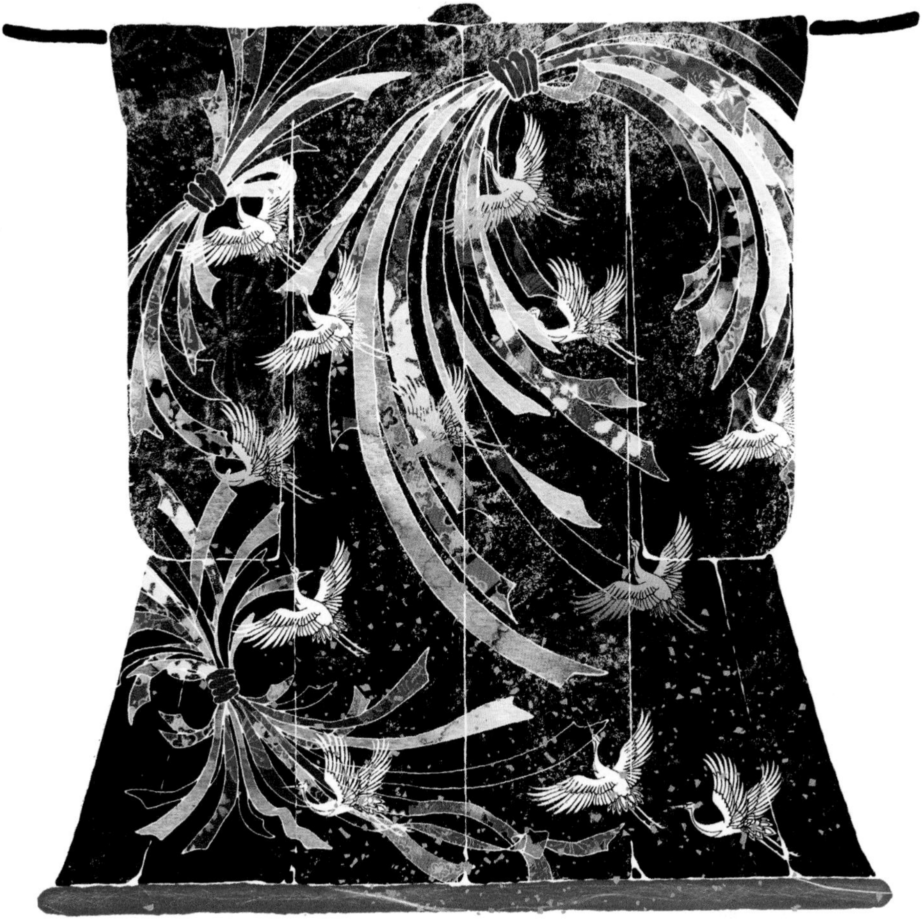

Tabi

Worn with traditional sandals, *tabi* are white cotton socks in which the big toe is separated from the second toe so that the foot can slip through the thong. The courtesans of Edo avoided wearing them even in mid-winter in order to bewitch men with a sexy bare foot.

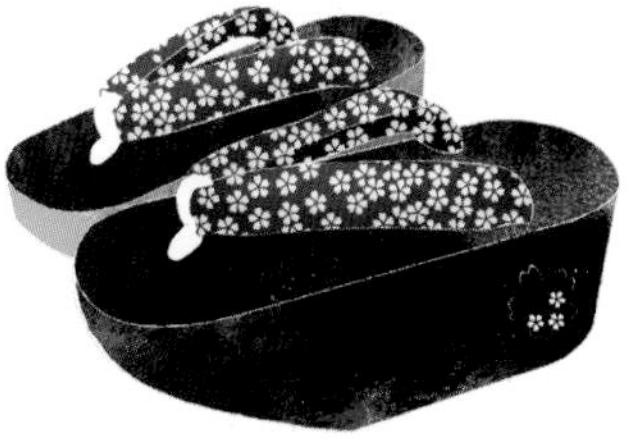

GETA

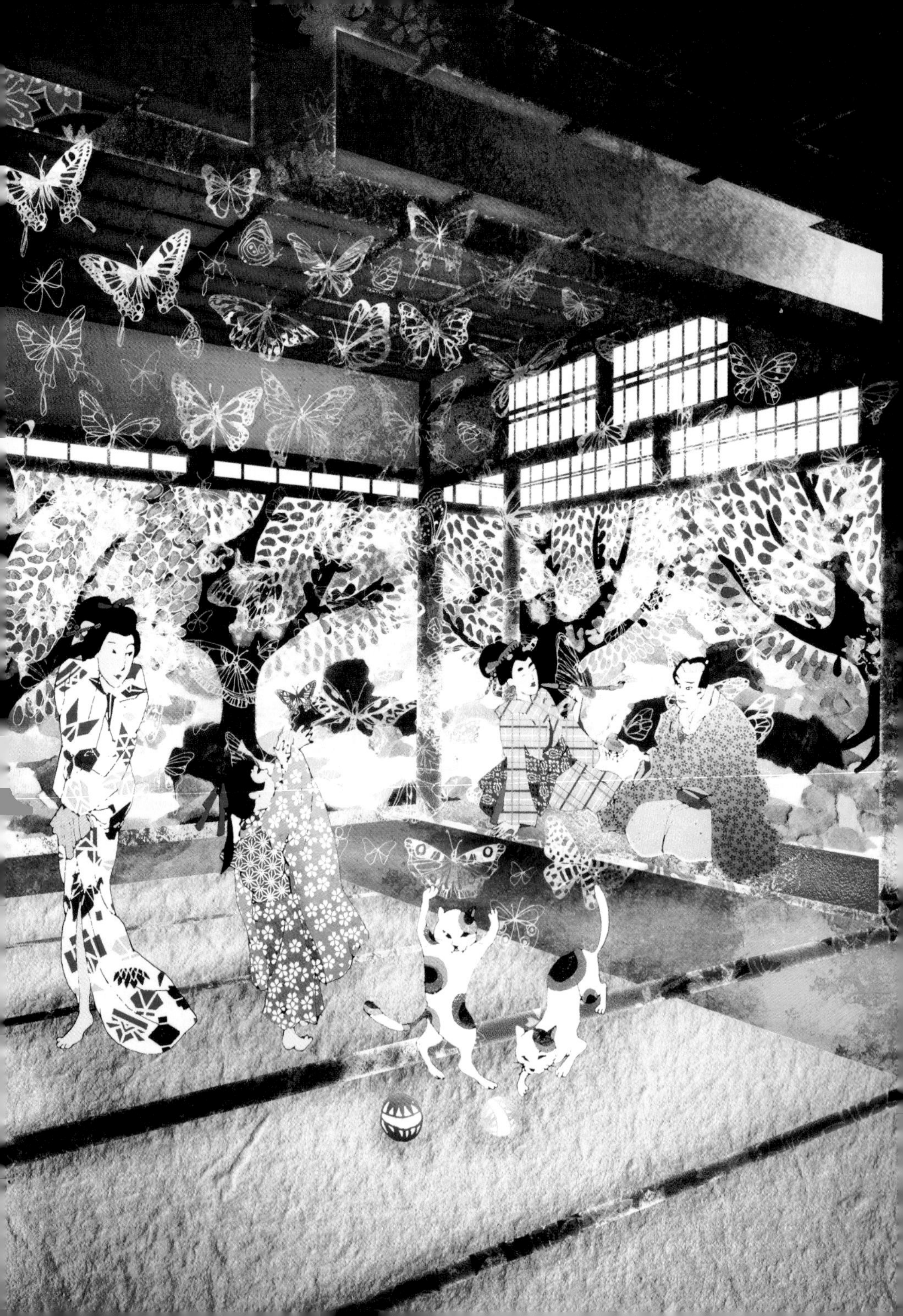

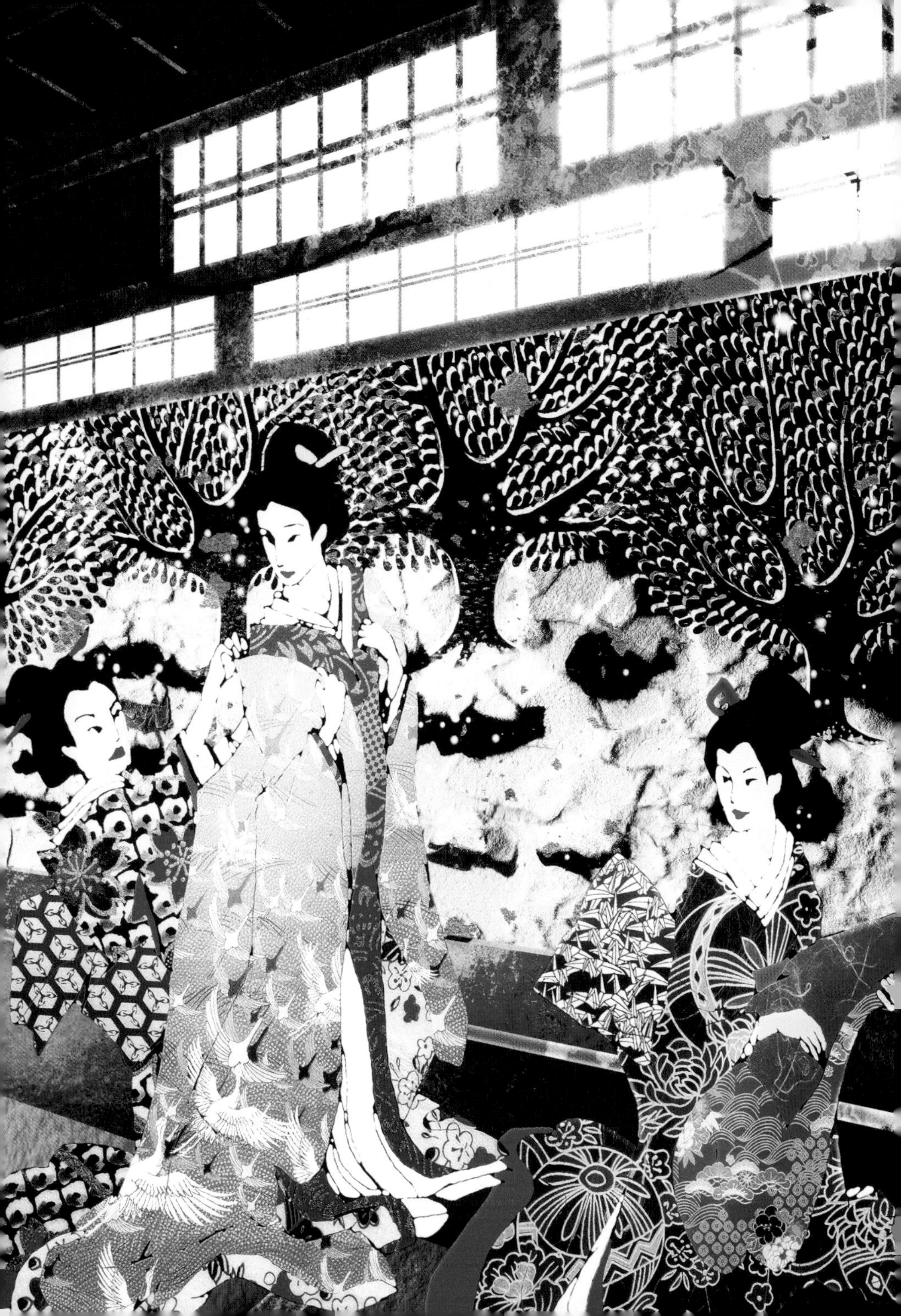

金継ぎ
Kintsugi

The Art of Exalting Imperfection

Known also as *kintsukuroi*, *kintsugi* can be defined as the art of exalting imperfection. It apparently began with a stubborn shogun who fell in love with beauty and who was taught by Zen to care for and love small things. Although he belonged to a line of warriors, Ashikaga Yoshimasa was a man of profound spirituality and a refined sense of aesthetics—two qualities that blended in beautifully in the arts of 15th-century Japan, such as ink painting, *ikebana* and the tea ceremony.

Legend has it that one of the cups used by Yoshimasa for a ritual, indeed his favorite one, broke. Not wanting to lose it at any cost, the shogun sent it to China for repair. How terrible was his disappointment when he saw it come back bound together by unsightly metal ties. Desperate, he then entrusted the item to some Japanese artisans who, moved by his concern, came up with the idea of suturing the cracks with molten gold, thus creating a delicate gleaming lattice in the ceramic material. They turned a no longer usable vessel into a masterpiece.

In Japan, the crack, which in the uncompromising idealism of the West is a lamentable sign of a distancing

from the divine perfection that we strive to pursue, the symptom of decay and corruption, is precious testimony of uniqueness. It tells the object's story, it speaks of its presence in our everyday life, of the memories that bind it to our life, and thus render it even dearer. Emphasizing its fragility, it serves as an image of the passage of time, which pulls everything with it. And in this feeling of transience, which corresponds to our own mortality, it invites us to live more fully in the short period that still awaits us.

Instead of masking the defect, *kintsugi* artistically highlights the cracked line of pottery with gold or silver, implying all this and far more.

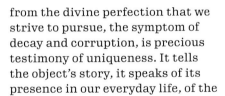

鯉のぼり
Koinobori

Carp Streamers to Celebrate Boys' Day

All over Japan from April to early May, in public housing blocks, outside houses and stretched out across rivers and fields, long windsocks brightly decorated with pictures of koi (carp) can be seen fluttering. These *koinobori*, or "carp climbing," represent strength and resilience. Indeed, a Japanese proverb, *koi no takinobori*, meaning "carp climbing the waterfall," denotes to achieve success through effort.

Koinobori are flown to celebrate *Kodomo no hi* (Children's Day) on May 5, the last day of the Golden Week holidays. Although the day is now officially dedicated to children of both genders, the focus is on boys, and girls have a separate day on March 3 known as *Hinamatsuri* (Doll's Festival), though it is not a national holiday. The carp, believed to be one of the toughest fish, represents the hope that boys will grow up to be strong, healthy and successful. The origins of *koinobori* are uncertain, with estimates of when it started ranging from 700 to 1,500 years ago. Until 1948 it was celebrated as *Tango no sekku*, one of five *sekku* celebrations once held at the imperial court, including *O-shōgatsu* on January 1, *Hinamatsuri* on March 3 and *Tanabata* on July 7.

The carp streamers may have been inspired by the banners that samurai used to identify themselves and their units on the battlefield, but now come in a set with different colors representing the various members of a family. They vary in size from mini versions hung inside houses or out of windows, to meters-long creations strung across rivers. A festival in Kazo, Saitama, north of Tokyo, boasts a 100 m (328 ft)-long *koinobori* that has to be raised by a crane. The other major component of *Kodomo no hi* celebrations are the *yoroikabuto* displays in houses of miniature samurai armor. *Yoroi* is the intricate body armor, while *kabuto* is the helmet.

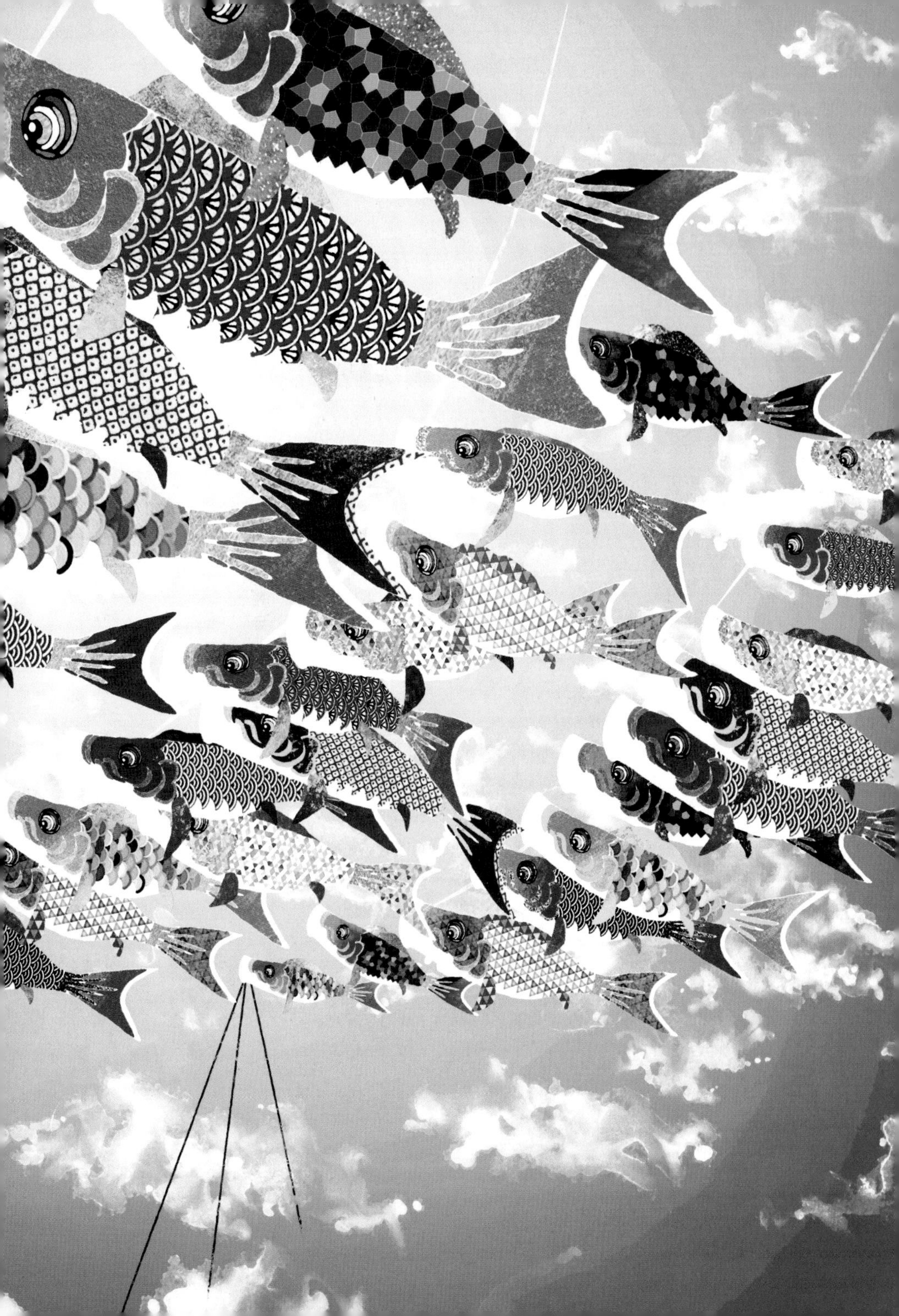

コスプレ
Kosupure

Costume Play or Cosplay

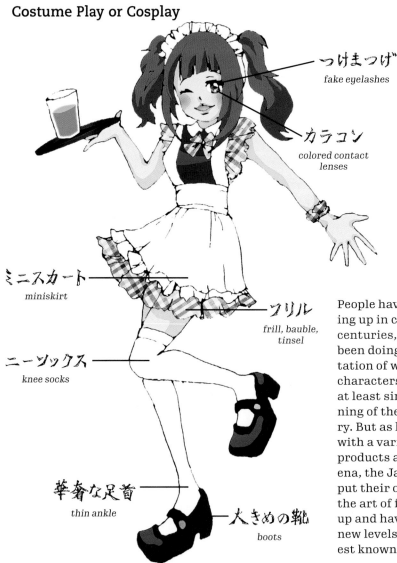

つけまつげ
fake eyelashes

カラコン
colored contact lenses

ミニスカート
miniskirt

フリル
frill, bauble, tinsel

ニーソックス
knee socks

華奢な足首
thin ankle

大きめの靴
boots

People have been dressing up in costumes for centuries, and have been doing so in imitation of well-known characters from fiction at least since the beginning of the 20th century. But as has happened with a variety of trends, products and phenomena, the Japanese have put their own twist on the art of fancy dressup and have taken it to new levels. The earliest known Japanese cosplayers actually dressed up as characters from Western science fiction novels at conventions during the mid-1970s. And the term *kosuchūmu purei* (costume play) was coined by writer Nobuyuki Takahashi in a magazine article he wrote covering the 1984 World Science Fiction Convention in Los Angeles. The word was shortened and combined, as often happens with both Japanese and imported English phrases, into *kosupure*, coming into widespread use by the 1990s as the practice itself grew in popularity.

Japanese society is in some ways still very conformist and restrictive. The popularity of *kosupure* is probably in part a reaction to this, giving people an escapist outlet to express themselves, and a mask behind which to do so. With *anime* and *manga* providing such a rich roster of visually striking characters to base *kosupure* on, they almost inevitably became the source of inspiration for most costumes.

One of the largest *kosupure* events in Japan is the biannual Comiket (comic market) in Tokyo, a non-profit convention built around fan-written *dōjinshi manga*. The event attracts more than half a million attendees to its summer and winter editions, making it the largest fan convention in the world. Japanese *kosupure* has heavily influenced fan conventions worldwide and extravagant costumes are now commonplace at events from New York to Helsinki. The latest manifestation of *kosupure* in Japan is the enthusiastic embracing of Halloween in recent years, which sees tens of thousands of wildly attired revelers hitting the streets of central Tokyo.

Kunoichi girl

漫画
Manga

Japanese Comic Books

The word *manga* consists of two characters; the first has multiple meanings, including "restless" and "unrestricted," while the second simply means "image." It is the unrestricted element of *manga* which defines and somewhat distinguishes it from comics elsewhere. There is a vast array of *manga* published every week, targeting audiences from young children to office workers. The storylines range from horror, sci-fi, human drama and erotica, through to politics, business and social commentary, told with structures and character development often unconventional by Western standards.

The word probably came into use in the late 18th century to describe the *kibyōshi* subgenre of *kusazōshi* picture books characterized by their yellow covers. They featured one illustration per page, with dialogue written in the available spaces in the pictures. Movable printing type for Japanese was a challenge because of the multiple syllabary and thousands of characters, so carving text directly onto the woodblock with the images made more sense. This meant the text and images had a synergy rarely found in other medium, a characteristic that has lived on in *manga* today.

The term became more widely known with the publication of the Hokusai *manga* books in the early 19th century, which contained more than 3,000 drawings from the legendary *ukiyo-e* artist Hokusai and were intended as instruction manuals for his devotees. Although magazines and newspapers carried comic strips from

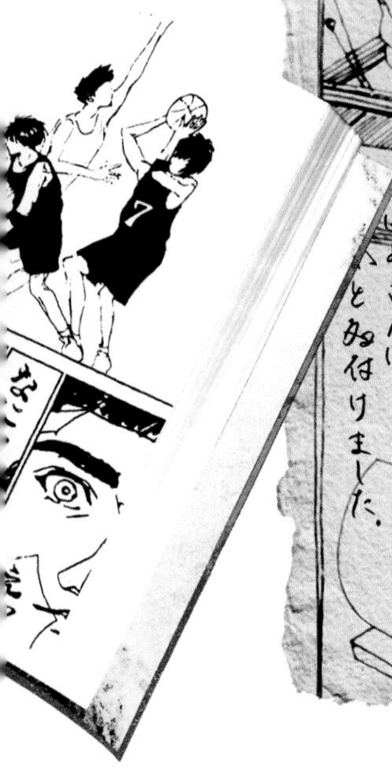

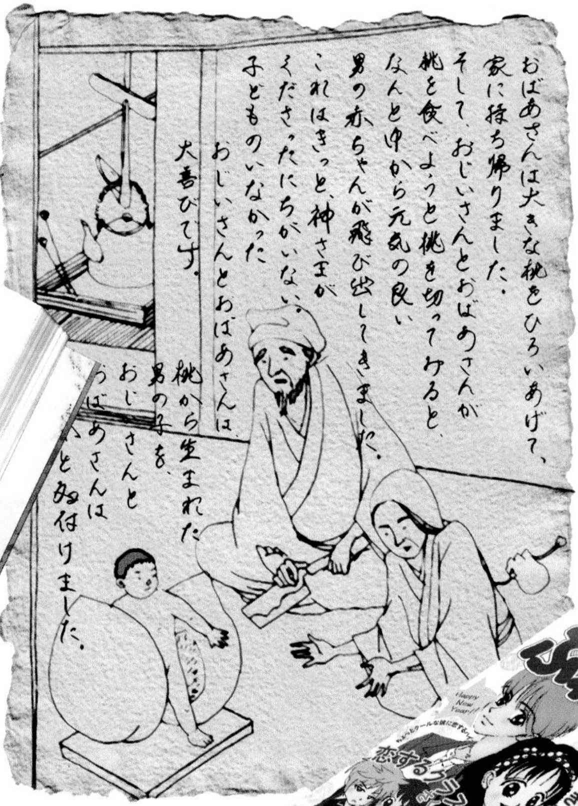

おばあさんは大きな桃をひろいあげて、
家に持ち帰りました。
そして、おじいさんとおばあさんが
桃を食べようと桃を切ってみると、
なんと中から元気の良い
男の赤ちゃんが飛び出してきました。
これはきっと、神さまが
くださったにちがいない。
子どものいなかった
おじいさんとおばあさんは
大喜びです。
桃から生まれた
男の子を、
おじいさんと
おばあさんは
と名付けました。

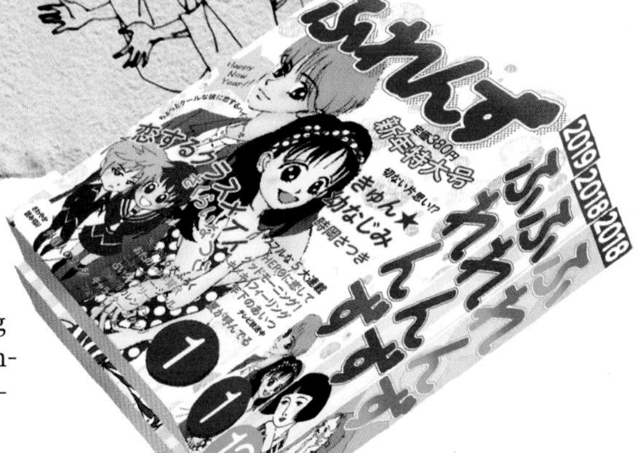

ふれんず
2019 2018 2018
定価380円
新年特大号
切ない片思い!?
きゅん★幼なじみ

the early 20th century, it was during the 1960s that the weekly and monthly *manga* magazines carrying installments of multiple series came into being. *Manga* never looked back and its bestsellers have shifted hundreds of millions of copies in total. Nearly every famous *anime,* from *Ghost in the Shell* to *Dragon Ball,* started life as *manga*. In fact, the adaptation route from *manga* to *anime* to TV drama to live action movie is so well worn that some in the film industry bemoan a lack of opportunity for original scripts.

祭

Matsuri

Japanese Folk Festivals

These can be defined as traditional commual festivals, the feasts held on specific dates at villages or sanctuaries. Each is marked by its own peculiar features and atmosphere that set it apart from others, but in all lives the peasant spirit of a population that has long articulated the year according to the agricultural cycle. Thus, the *matsuri* in spring, now often reduced to romantic contemplation of blossoming vegetation, actually refers to an older festival celebrating fertility.

Today, much like 2,000 years ago, the feast centers on the divinity's (*kami*) arrival at the sanctuary, where it is welcomed with offerings of food, music, dance, prayer and various forms of divination. The arrival of the god, who descends from the heavens or the mountain to the rice paddies of the plain, marks the beginning of a new cycle of cultivation, the renewed fertility of the fields. The *kami* will watch over the growth of seedlings throughout the summer, averting the dangers that threaten it until autumn, when, after the harvest and the feast of thanksgiving (the second *matsuri*), it will leave the sanctuary and return to spend winter elsewhere, in a sphere inaccessible to man, where, like the earth, it will rest and regenerate until the following spring.

Over the centuries, these festivals have become greatly secularized. The culminating moment is still the procession during which the image of the divinity, in a wooden, sumptuously gilt palanquin, is escorted to the temple. The procession has now become a pretext for a great display of carriages and costumes. The musical entertainment and dance are directed no longer towards the god but towards the pleasure of participants, while the offerings of delicious food are now on sale in colorful stalls.

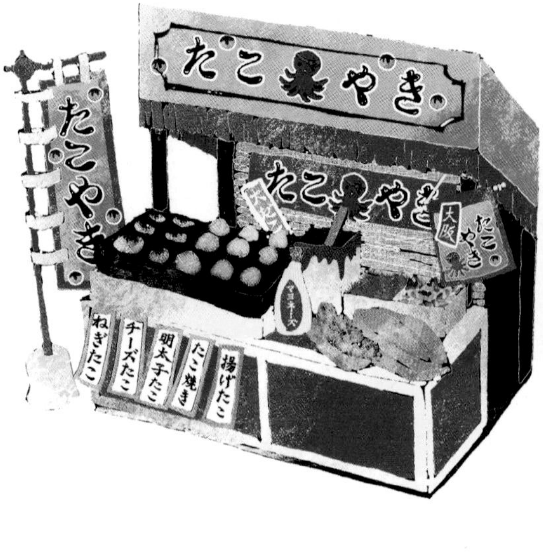
たこやき
たこやき
たこやき
ねぎたこ
チーズたこ
明太子たこ
たこ焼き
揚げたこ

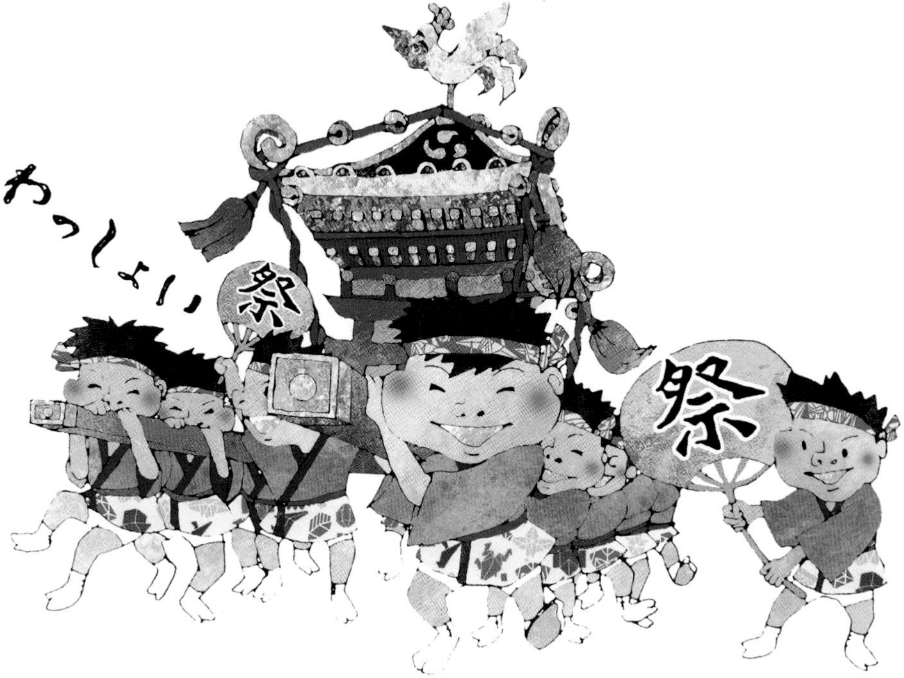
わっしょい
祭
祭

Takoyaki and Yakitori

The *matsuri* cannot exist without the *yatai,* the colorful stalls at which one gets street food. The most common dish is *takoyaki,* a rissole made of octopus, but also popular are *yakitori,* skewered chicken cubes with a special sauce, and *okonomiyaki,* a treat halfway between a pizza and an omelet. *Matsuri* dessert consists of *dango,* large, sweet, rice-flour dumplings.

Kanamara Matsuri

The *matsuri* of Kawasaki reveals the ancient bond between these festivals and the theme of fertility in a highly explicit manner. It is famous, in fact, for the enormous phalluses paraded down the streets. The processions end at the shrine of Kanayama, the destination of couples who pray at it for a happy marriage, painless labor, or because their union has been blessed by a birth. All the candies, candles and decorations made for it are penis-shaped.

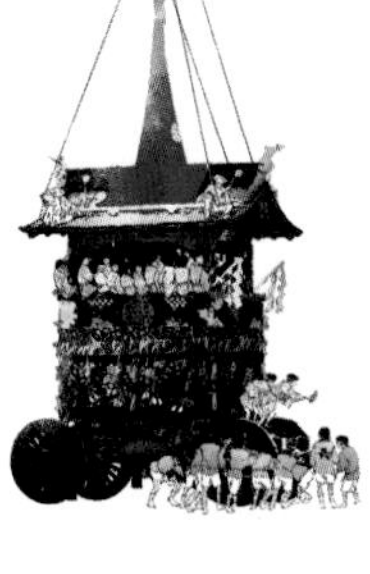

雅

Miyabi

Elegance and Grace

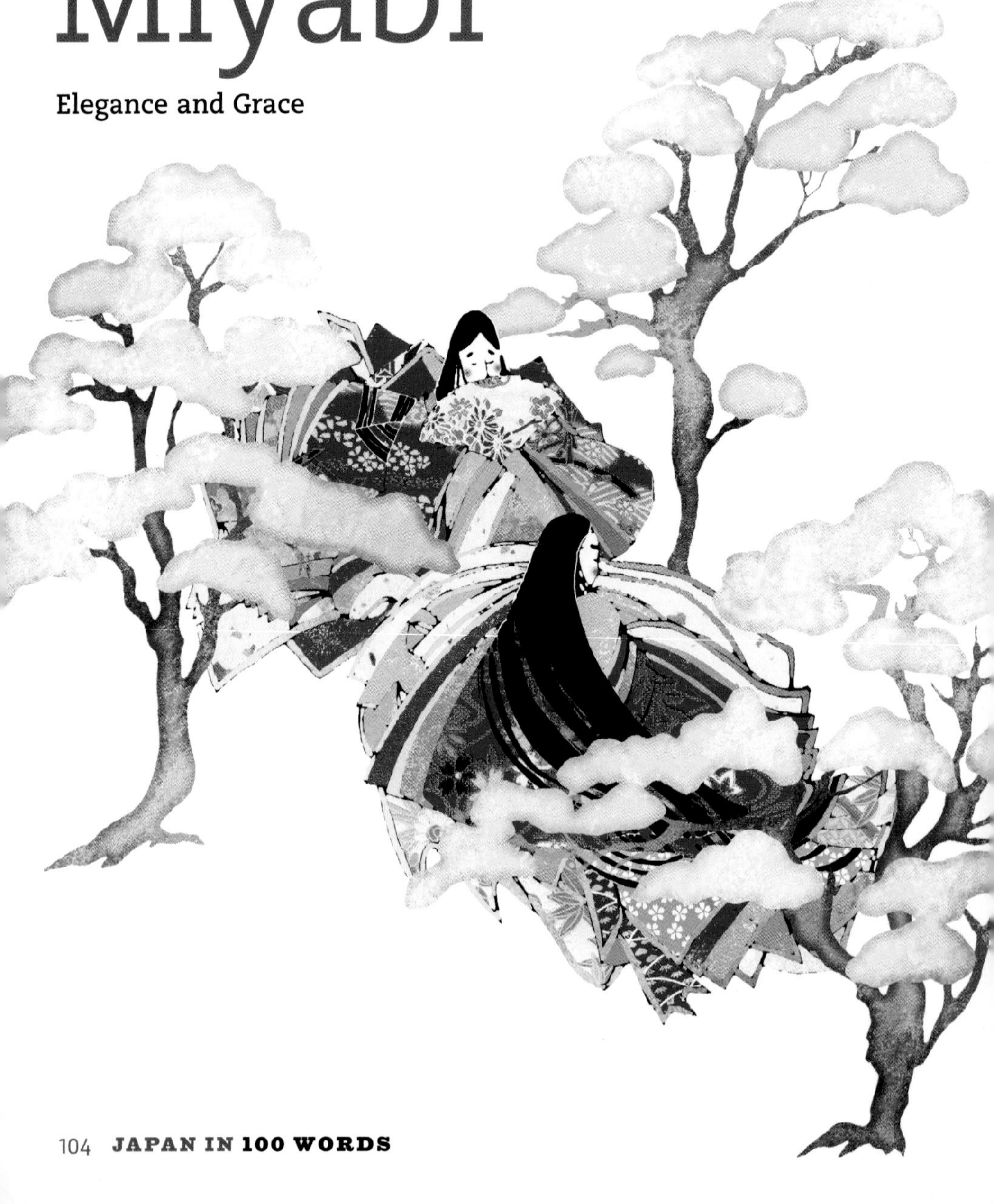

In no period of Japanese history was the search for beauty as all consuming as in the Heian era, in the 8th to 12th centuries, when the aristocratic elites gathered at the imperial court far from the mundane universe of common mortals and spent their days focusing on intellectual pursuits and the amusements of society, and devoting themselves to the exhausting practices of beauty. Every tiny detail of everyday life was governed by a complex of minute and imperative norms: the *miyabi* canon.

The first to submit to this regimen was physical appearance. The female face was made seductive: its mouth repainted to seem smaller, the whiteness of teeth eliminated with black lacquer, the eyebrows redrawn as two short segments far above their natural location. *Miyabi* also meant knowing how to tastefully pair kimono patterns with the season, choose the most suitable perfume and writing paper for any occasion, charm a guest with an improvised poem, have not only elegant but also good-looking servants. In short, beauty was a way of life.

Soradaki

Various types of incense, mixed and creamed with honey, were burned to scent clothing and places (*soradaki*). In addition, competitions were held (*takimono-awase*) in which the participants burned their own blends before a jury that decided the winner.

Musubi-fumi

Of incredible importance among the arts in which *miyabi* was manifest was correspondence: a well-composed letter could lead to a career promotion or a new love. The text often assumed the form of poetry, but calligraphy, the color of the paper as well as the perfume suffusing it also commanded great attention. The sheet was folded into strips and folded (*musubi-fumi*) into a flower or its corresponding branch before being delivered to the recipient.

Uta-awase

Poetry contests (*uta-awase*) were common among the nobility. A judge would ask a question or choose a theme, and two groups of poets facing each other would improvise. A competition could engender several hundred compositions, some of which would find a place in the anthologies commissioned by the emperor.

SORADAKI

水商売
Mizu-shōbai

Hostess Clubs for Corporate Entertaining

It was for many years a proud boast that Japan's total corporate entertainment budget was larger than the national defense budget. Though the largesse of the bubble era of the 1980s is long gone, nighttime entertainment remains a huge industry, and a large chunk of it comes under the umbrella of *mizu-shōbai,* which literally means "the water trade." This describes hostess clubs, *sunakku* (snack bars) and other establishments that revolve around alcohol,

flirtation and companionship, but from which actual sex is essentially absent. The etymology is murky and multiple theories exist, though it may be related to *ukiyo,* the floating world of entertainment portrayed in *ukiyo-e* prints.

Though the décor, personnel, clientele, atmosphere, activities and prices vary across the different types of *mizu-shōbai,* common threads run through them. Customers pay for the time of a hostess, host or *mama-san* via some combination of pricey drinks or other charges. For many, *mizu-shōbai* serves as a form of casual therapy, a release from the rigidity of corporate life or other stresses; a sympathetic ear and a complimentary companion.

Kyabakura

Kyabakura (cabaret clubs, also known as hostess clubs/bars) form the higher end of *mizu-shōbai* and are staffed by *kyabajō* girls, usually decked out in glamorous dinner dresses and sporting big hair. Prices in the top clubs of Tokyo's Ginza are eye-watering, but they retain an important function in sealing business deals. Host clubs, where the gender roles are reversed, can be equally expensive, though many of the best customers are *kyabajō*.

Sunakku

Sunakku emerged as Japan cleaned up the image of its nightlife for the 1964 Olympics, with food being nomi-

nally served to circumvent laws and allow them to stay open late. There are tens of thousands of these reasonably priced watering holes located in back streets and entertainment districts. They are overseen by a *mama-san,* often a retired *kyabajō,* who entertains, pours drinks, lights cigarettes and sings karaoke with the mostly regular clients.

> *The blossoms of the cherry trees fade while beneath this rain, I, with absent soul, watch life escape.*
>
> —Ono no Komachi, 9th century

> *I do not complain about a destiny that I share with flowers, insects and stars. In a universe in which everything passes like a dream, we would not forgive ourselves for lasting forever.*
>
> —Murasaki Shikibu, Genji monogatari, 10th century

物の哀れ

Mono no aware

The Fleeting Nature of Things

If cherry blossoms move the Japanese so deeply, it is in part because their breathtaking beauty lasts no more than two or three days. If autumn leaves inspire many verses, it is also because their splendid nuances are the final outburst before their death brought about by winter. *Mono no aware* is the word for this fleeting charm, this aesthetic ideal that came into being at the turn of the 9th century in the exquisitely refined milieu of the imperial court and provided content for several centuries of poetry and laments. Roughly translated as "the perception of things," it refers to the wise knowledge that the beauty of the world and of nature appears to us in all its splendor only at the moment right before its loss, when it is on the verge of disappearing.

Mono no aware is the subtle, melancholic awe caused by a miracle that has just been recognized as such, but, eternally elusive, has already passed. It embraces the Buddhist awareness of the transience that unites all things, the sense of non-existence that Indian religion introduced into Japanese culture, but also the concept of the annual cyclical transformation of the Whole, which, in the succession of seasons and the metamorphosis of the cosmos also recognizes our fated mortality.

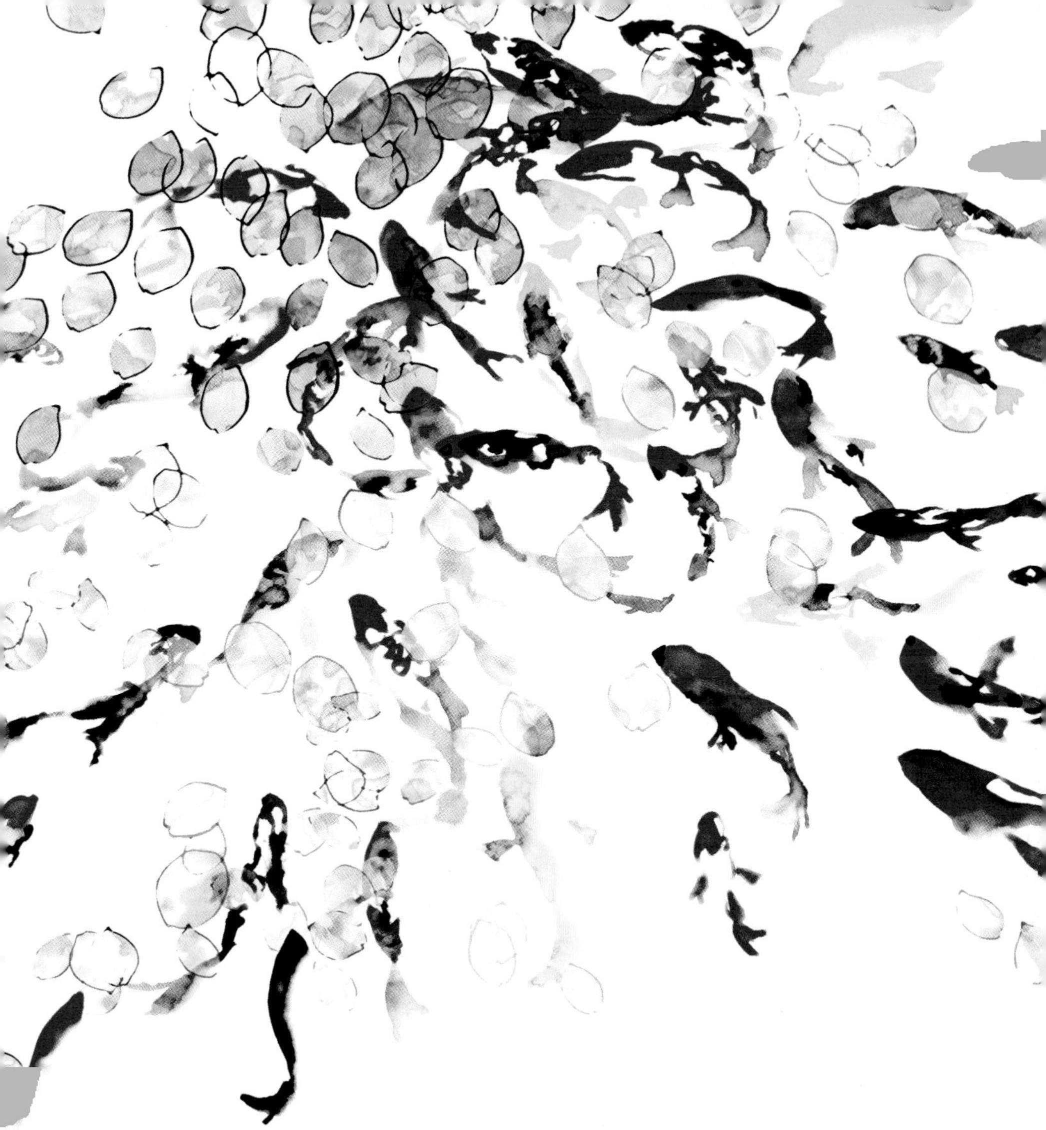

The aesthetic of *aware* did not disappear with the end of court culture but has continued to surface here and there throughout the history of Japanese poetry, reaching a new peak in the 20th-century works of Kawabata Yasunari. Surprisingly, it served as the theme of a poignant animated film that appeared in 2007, Makoto Shinkai's *Five Centimeters Per Second*.

根付

Netsuke

Exquisite Miniature Pouches

These curious small objects, of which there is no equivalent outside of Japan, are miniature sculptures that nonetheless serve a particular practical function. During the Edo period, in the 1600s, men used to keep personal items in tiny bags that they tied to the sash of their kimono with a string bound to a weight, or *netsuke*.

Their practical function did not prevent these accessories, which were initially fairly simple, from soon evolving into veritable works of art, which, thanks to their precious materials and refined craftsmanship revealed the rank of the samurai and merchants who wore them. Although the earliest ones were made from small gourds, shells or simple roots (the name derives from *ne*, "root," and *tsuke*, "apply"), over time they came to be carved out of horn, ivory and other precious substances, such as ebony and sandalwood.

Their subjects are varied and reveal the imagination, powers of observation as well as the humor of Edo craftsmen. In addition to scenes and objects of everyday life depicted with incredible realism, they capture mythological heroes and legendary figures, demons and gods, fantastical animals and monsters, flowers, insects and natural themes, and theatrical masks. Included too are erotic subjects, sometimes rendered with open-minded fantasy. Paired with tobacco sacks, *netsuke* often assume the form of *kagamibuta*, small bowls used as portable ashtrays. In short, they come in a variety that, along with exquisite detail, has made them a highly sought-after article by Japanese antique collectors.

Inrō

The bag is not the only accessory to complete the outfit of the Edo gentleman. Among the *sagemono*, or objects hanging from the belt, was the writing set, the pipe case, the tobacco pouch and the *inrō*, a type of elegantly decorated lacquered box with multiple superimposed compartments that was used to hold seals or sometimes pills.

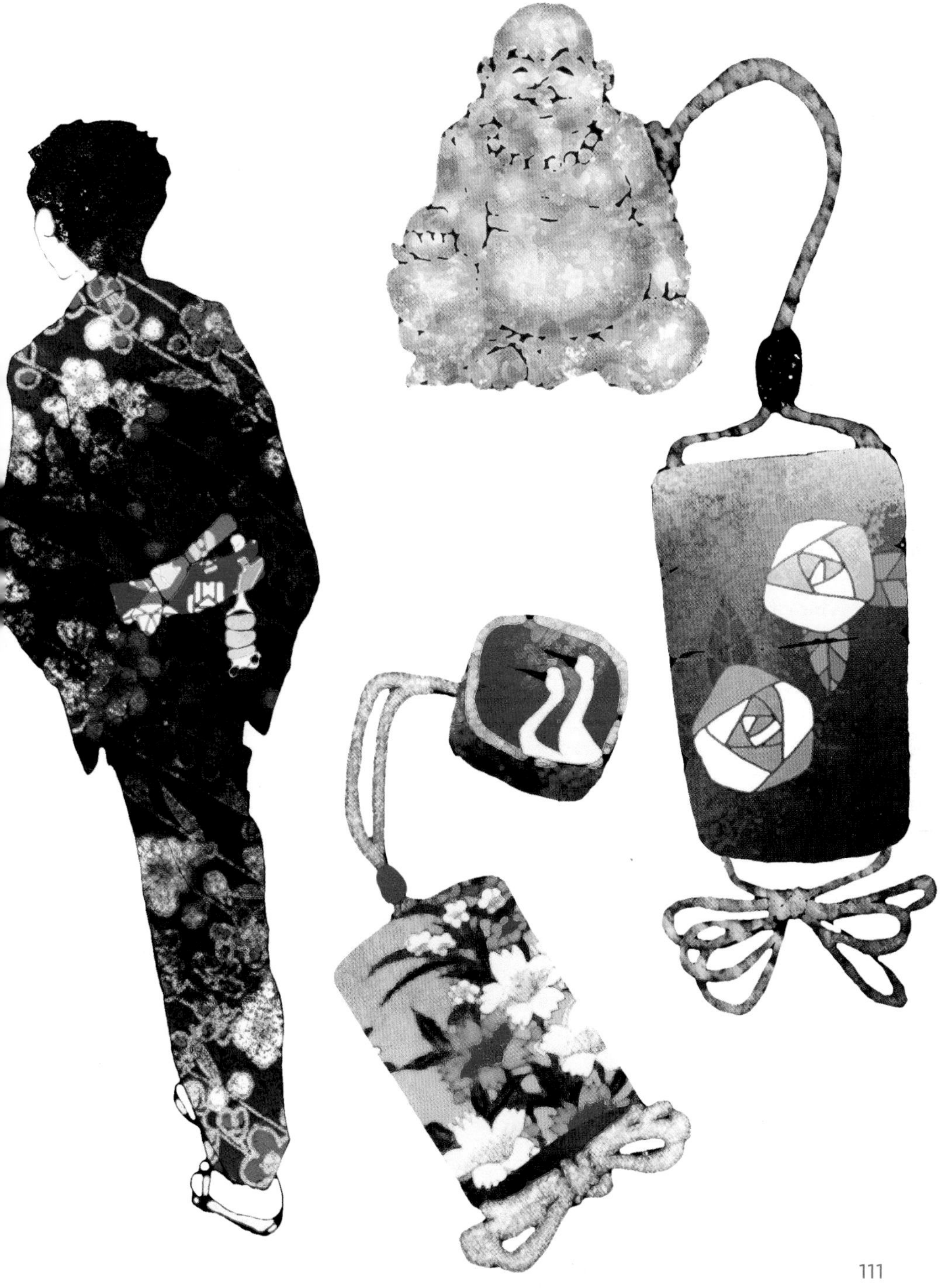

忍者
Ninja

Japanese Men in Black

Mysterious figures clad in black stealing silently across castle rooftops in the dead of night carrying concealed weapons on a mission to assassinate a *daimyō* before vanishing in a puff of smoke—this classic image of the *ninja* is one that has been reinforced and portrayed in stories, films and comics around the globe. If there is a figure from warfare history more mythologized than the samurai, then it is surely their sometime contemporaries, adversaries and allies, the *ninja*. Even the term *ninja* is questionable, coming into use much later. They were referred to contemporaneously as *shinobi*, an alternate reading of the same characters, or *shinobi no mono*. The verb *shinobu* can mean "to conceal" or "to endure."

The origins of *ninja* are unclear, but they may have descended from *yamabushi* mountain priests who developed techniques based on strategies from a Chinese martial text. It has been suggested that *ninja* were recruited from samurai, though they were more likely families of common folk from isolated areas. The two most important clans were from Iga and Koga, mountainous areas where *ninja* undertaking training from a young age in climbing, swimming, running, scouting and survival can be easily imagined.

Shinobi were also said to learn techniques of armed and unarmed combat, explosives, medicine, poison, disguise, subterfuge, psychological warfare and escape. This has collectively come to be known as *ninjutsu*, though most of the written sources related to their techniques dated to the later Edo period. It was the preceding *sengoku* Warring States era that was their heyday, with accounts surviving of them infiltrating castles during sieges and other exploits. But many of their missions are believed to have been spying and information gathering, on which they moved disguised as ordinary people. Like the samurai, their role was largely superfluous in peacetime, and there are reports that some were recruited as guards and policemen at Edo Castle.

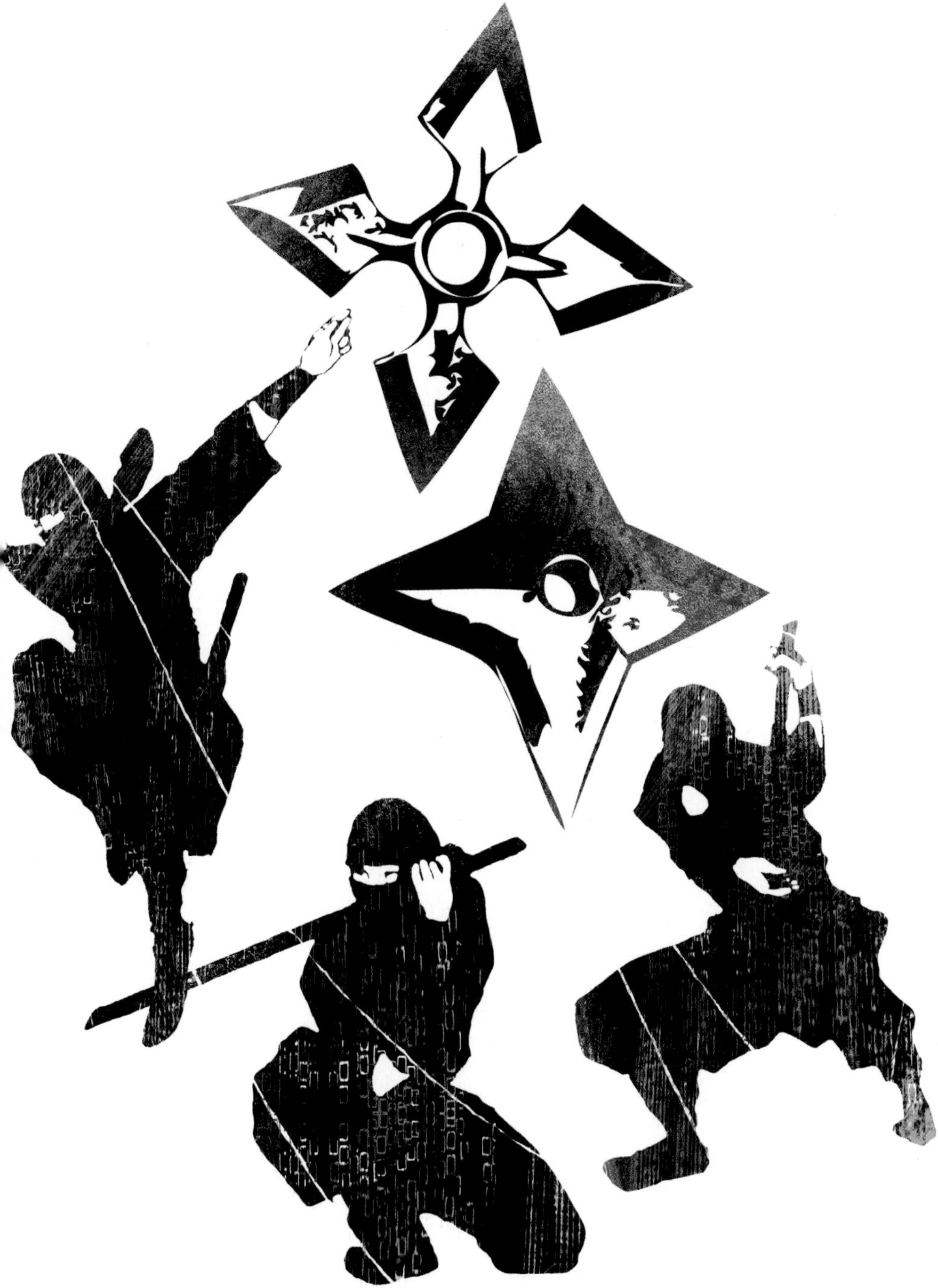

能楽堂
Nō theater

Historic Spiritual Theater

Of all the forms of traditional Japanese theater, *Nō* is the most aristocratic, sophisticated and spiritual. The stories it retells are not meant to entertain and amuse the public but to heal the soul, to open a window into the depths of the psyche.

Nō theater arose from sacred liturgy as a shamanic pantomime with which to represent to men the manifestation of a god or a demon. Even after it left the temple for the theater, its intention remained to cure or illuminate a spirit sickened by remorse, the death of a child, all-consuming and destructive jealousy, a predilection for sin, or unrequited love.

The preliminary condition is always that of an obsession, a dark, nebulous region that torments the protagonist (*shite*) by generating disgrace and disease. The process of liberation is generally triggered by the arrival of a foreign figure (*waki*), often a Buddhist monk, who knows how to empathize with the pain of the other without getting involved. It is he who leads the character to cathar-sis, forcing him to relive the events that precipitated his despair in a sort of psychoanalytical flashback.

Against the background of a stage set reduced to bare essentials, the words in verse, delivered as a song and amplified by the mask, become a sort of musical accompaniment to the vision, while the dance, accompanied by flutes and drums, acts out situations with austere and stylized gestures. Everything is designed to arouse a profound suggestiveness in the viewer and bring him closer to the threshold of the sublime.

Kyōgen

This is the brief humorous interlude that lifts the spirit between the first and second act of a *Nō* drama. It features a comedy in costume, often centered on the stories of lovers, feudal lords, hermits or monks (with an anti-clerical twist). However, the most popular performance is that of the servant Tarō Kaja and his comic misadventures.

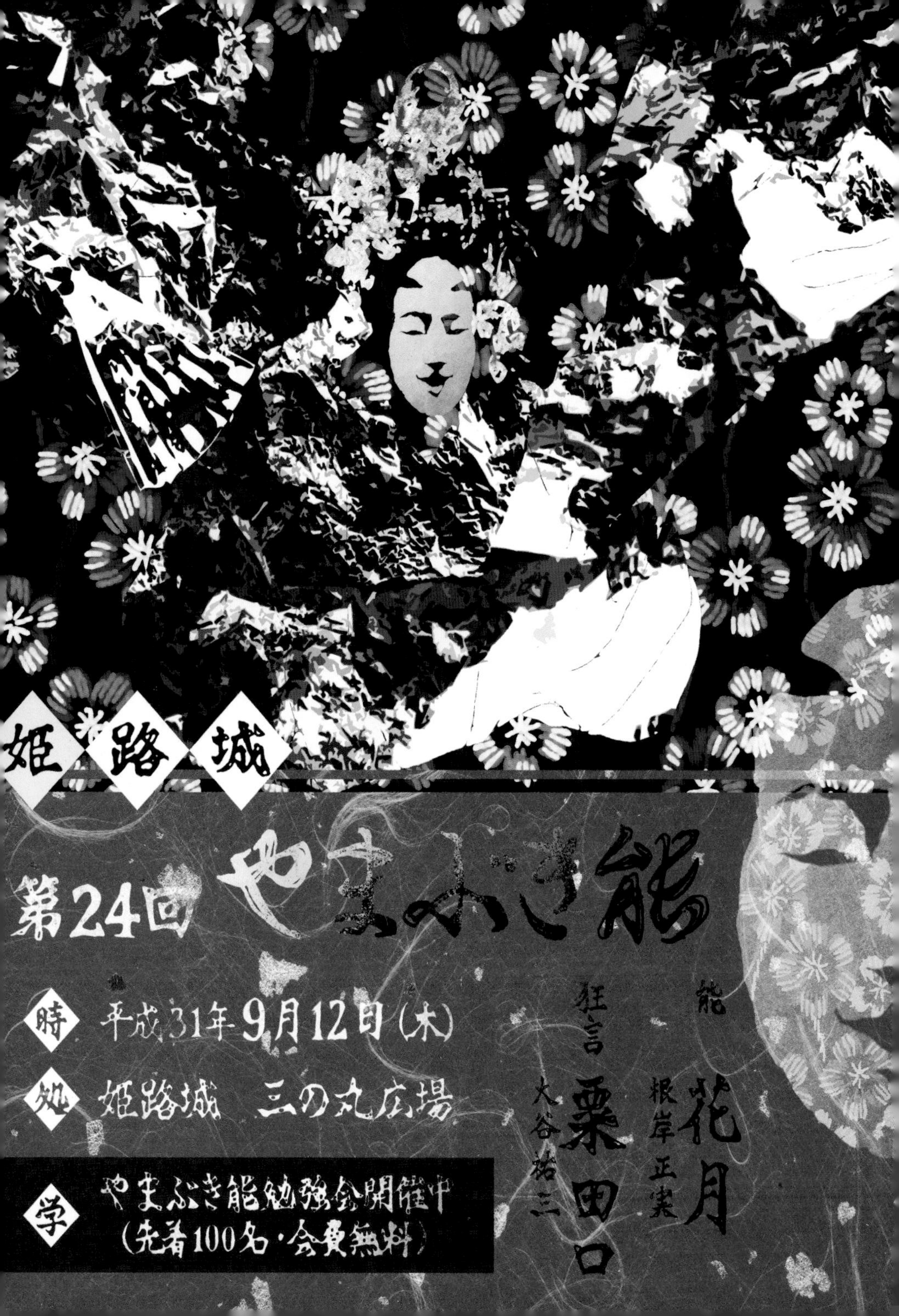
姫路城
第24回 やまぶき能
時 平成31年9月12日(木)
処 姫路城 三の丸広場
学 やまぶき能勉強会開催中
(先着100名・会費無料)
能 花月 根岸正実
狂言 粟田口 大谷裕三

Tokyo Marunouchi Bon-Odori Festival, Summer 2019

東京丸の内
盆踊り大会
2019夏

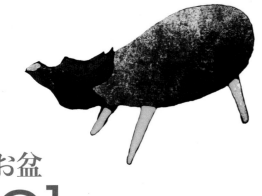

お盆 Obon

A Time to Remember Departed Souls

In Japan, the feast of the ancestors, *Obon*, somewhat resembles Christmas. In mid-July or mid-August, depending on the region, those who work or study far from their parents, return regardless of the length of their journey to their paternal home for three days of festivities, during which each family celebrates its roots and continuity.

Ancestor worship has played a significant role in the structure of Japanese society, which is composed of family clans whose various branches find a source of cohesion and solidarity (even of a military nature) in their descent from a common ancestor. Assimilated to the spirits of nature, transformed into divinities, the ancestors' *kami* watch over the community and establish the sense of identity of its members.

The care with which this festival is prepared is standard. A lit paper lantern is placed on each grave to welcome the spirit of the dead, while a lantern at the entrance of the house invites the dead to visit what was their home during their lifetime. Inside, everything is ready for receiving guests of such importance. Before the domestic altar in the most important room lie offerings to the dead consisting of flowers and tiny portions of an actual meal: rice, fruit, eggplant, pumpkin, sweets, and, of course, the foods that they loved during their lifetime.

Although the people in attendance pray for deceased relatives and friends, the commemoration is not a sad event. It is accompanied by a joyfully celebrated family feast and the performance of a popular crazy dance (*bon-odori*) before a temple or by the sea or river, which attracts flocks of people.

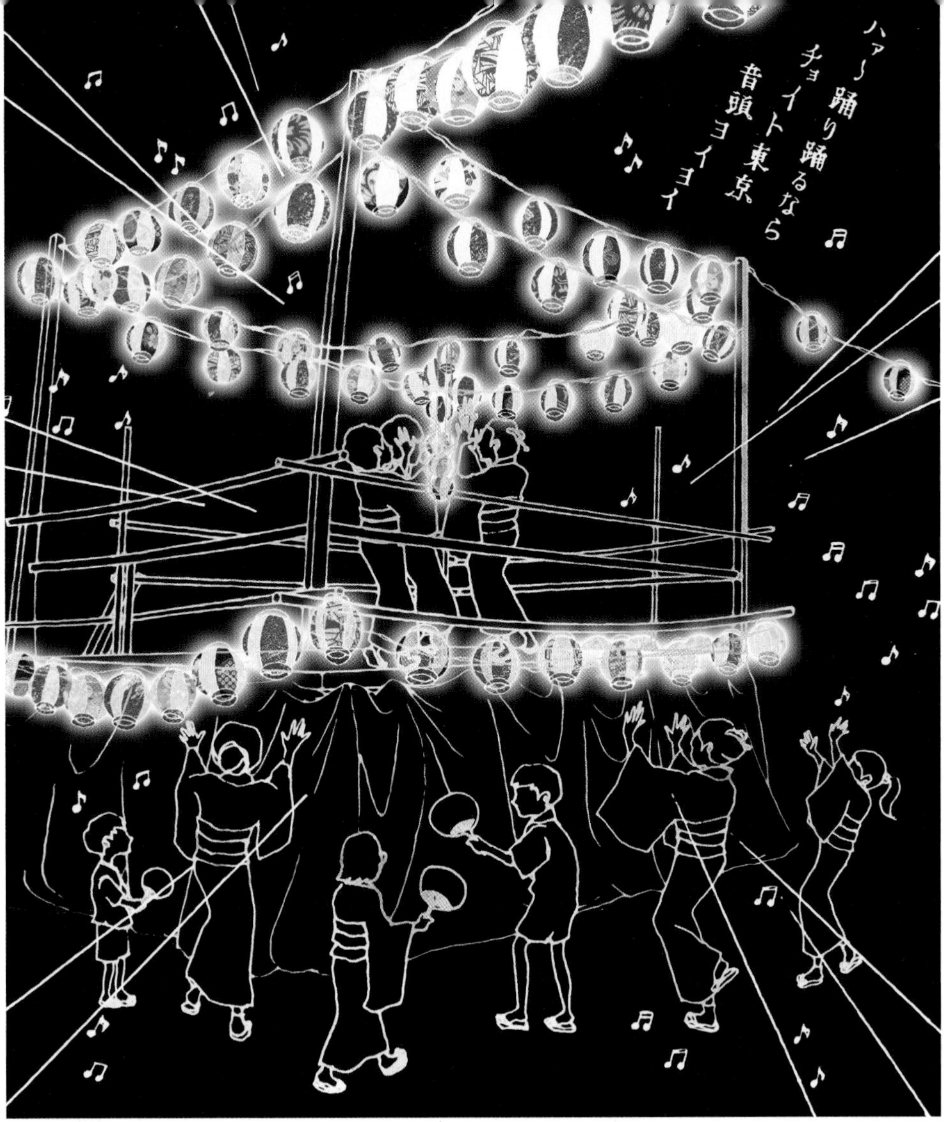
ハァ〜踊り踊るなら
チョイト東京音頭ヨイヨイ

Tōrō Nagashi

One of the symbolic images of *Obon* is that of hundreds of lights floating on the surface of rivers, carried away by the current in the darkness of night. These are the souls of the dead, who, at the end of the party, are sent on tiny straw boats back to the unknown country beyond the sea from where they came. Honoring ancestors, the feast of *Obon* is also responsible for ensuring their return to the afterlife, so that they do not stay behind and disturb the daily life of the living.

踊り
Odori

Popular Folk Dances

Traditional Japanese dances can generally be grouped into two categories: *mai*, which derives from *Nō* theater and the aristocratic traditions of Kyoto, and is characterized by solemn, controlled movements, slow turns and symbolic gestures; and *odori*, which, in contrast, grew out of *Kabuki* theater and is lively and rhythmic, with leaps and beats marked by feet.

This second category includes all the popular folk dances performed in cities and villages during various festivals. The most typical of these is the feast of *Obon*, in which the spirits of the ancestors returning to visit their families are welcomed. With its ancestral rhythms, the *bon-odori* brings together men, women and children in rowdy revelry on the streets of the city. Every location has its own music and gestures, but the strong rhythm accentuated by drum strokes and the beating of hands and feet is common to all. The dancers alternate between spinning and swaying, and at times freeze like statues while performing spectacular choreography.

Awa Odori

This is a particular type of *bon-odori* that has been performed in Tokushima since 1586, when the local *daimyō*, Hachisuka Iemasa, announced a great celebration in honor of the completion of his castle. The dancers move at a march-like pace and sing to the accompaniment of *shamisen*, drums, flutes and bells.

Kaze no Bon

For 300 years, this has been practiced in Toyama between September 1 and 3 for the specific purpose of preventing typhoons. Young men and women (strictly unmarried) dance in the streets until dawn with their faces covered by long straw hair, possibly to make them unrecognizable to the *kami* whose anger they hope to appease.

Suzume Odori

The sparrow dance was apparently improvised by the stonemasons employed to construct the castle of Sendai for the *daimyō* Date Masamune. The two sparrows that appear in Date's heraldic device inspired the fluctuating movements of this dance, which is now performed in Sendai in May, on the occasion of *Aoba matsuri*.

お好み焼き

Okonomiyaki

A Cross between a Pizza and an Omelet

A dish made popular by *manga* and *anime*, even in the West, Akasaka's highly sought after *okonomiyaki* is a giant pancake halfway between a pizza and an omelet, that the protagonist of *Kiss me Licia* cooks in her father's restaurant.

Its name can be roughly translated as "whisk whatever you want in the dish," because the recipe is open to interpretation and can lead to exquisite results, regardless of whether one sticks to the favorite, highly sought after ingredients or throws in leftovers from the fridge.

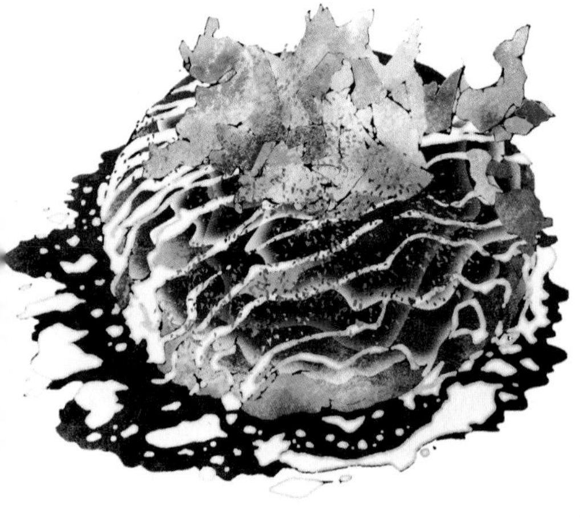

The base is a mixture of flour, water, eggs and an impressive amount of cabbage sliced into very thin strips, which will disintegrate into the dough while cooking. Connoisseurs also add grated *nagaimo*, Chinese potato, which apparently makes the final product exceptionally tender. After that, the imagination can be let loose, though instructions suggest onion, ginger, bean sprouts, bacon or shrimp (or both). Stir all of this in a bowl and pour it over a hotplate. Once the pancake is well cooked on both sides, top it with a double layer of *otafuku*, a thick sweet sauce, and mayonnaise.

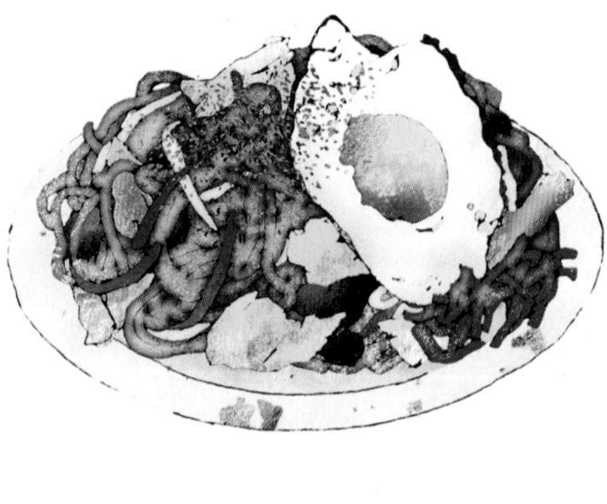

Teppanyaki

Okonomiyaki must be cooked on a special plate, a *teppan*, used for a variety of foods, including the famous *yakitori* skewers, that Japanese cuisine has been borrowing from the Koreans since the early 20th century. Its metal top, heated electrically, is generally placed at the center of the table or on a counter which guests sit around so that they can tinker with the meal.

The most typical type of *teppanyaki* (*yaki* means "to roast") is *nikuyaki*, made with slices of beef, preferably the exquisite marbled Kobe *shimofuri*, accompanied by vegetables such as shiitake mushrooms or leeks cut into thin diagonal slices. Buckwheat noodles (*yakisoba*) can also be sautéed on the plate. The people of Hiroshima like to flip the *okonomiyaki* over and top the whole thing with a grilled egg.

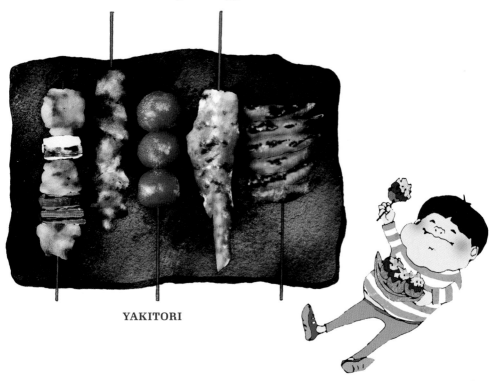

YAKITORI

お見合い
Omiai

Arranged Marriages in Japan

For a long time, marriages were a family affair in Japan. Until a few decades ago, the *omiai*, or arranged marriage, was an almost inevitable choice, and one that even today is made by a good 6 percent of the country's population. Of course, unions based on love have increased in number, but faith persists in a rationally established bond based on a meticulous assessment of the strengths and weaknesses of the two candidates, from the social rank of the family to the level of education, from the stability of employment to physical beauty. All this is based on the notion that the union will be solid and harmonious if the characteristics of husband and wife are balanced. Nonetheless, while over 90 percent of Japanese women claim they want to get married, they do not expect happiness from the marriage. The stability of the parental nucleus is very important for a society that has emerged from a multitude of clans and bases all social relations on the model of the family. And when given such a noble end, a woman does not mind giving up something as frivolous as personal gratification. Statistics confirm this: divorce among married couples who opt for *omiai* are far rarer.

Nakōdo

Like all Japanese institutions, *omiai*, whose supreme officiator is the *nakōdo*, is highly ritualized. Usually the *nakōdo* is a trusted person, either a relative, the boss or a friend of the family, who lends his service as a matchmaker. Before introducing the two candidates to each other, the matchmaker fills out a list of pros and cons, examines the respective family backgrounds, then organizes a meeting between the two candidates and their families. Even after the marriage, the *nakōdo* will remain a point of reference for the couple, who will turn to him in moments of crisis.

Yuinō

The engagement ceremony, or *yuinō*, is a solemn affair and involves the exchange of codified gifts, which differ from region to region. In addition to a cash sum that the groom's family is obliged to give the other party, the tradition includes presenting the woman with a kimono sash, a fan, dried fish and an entire series of symbols of prosperity and longevity, such as the pine, the plum, the crane and the turtle.

名前	山下薫子
年齢	23
職業	会社員

自己紹介	
学歴	東京大学法学部卒
本籍	小樽市
身長	158 cm
趣味	旅行・読書
特技	料理
性格	温和
家族	両親、兄一人
誕生日	8月24日

御神籤

Omikuji

Temple Prophecy Slips

A visit to any Japanese temple, whether Shinto or Buddhist, is not complete without a stop at the place where *omikuji*, slips of fine paper on which prophesies regarding one's future are written in dense writing, are obtained. Consulting such oracles is a fairly serious affair, and though that may be hard to perceive in tourist-packed temples where they are dispensed by machines, it retains its charm in sanctuaries where one still pulls out a bamboo stick with the number that refers to the prophetic slip.

The fortune is written in the form of ancient poetry, but the text beneath explains how things will go and specifies success in the various sectors—heart, work and health—in a more accessible manner. Indeed, even before going into the details, the text discloses the degree of happiness awaiting the recipient in large letters: *Daikichi* (much luck), *Shōkichi* (a little luck), or, on the contrary, *Kyō* (disgrace), *Daikyō* (terrible disgrace) and so forth, including a wide range of intermediate states. Tradition dictates that a negative *omikuji* should not be saved as it will bring bad luck home. Instead, it should be folded repeatedly into a thin strip then firmly knotted to the branch of a pine tree (*matsu*), perhaps because this word also means "to wait." Yet care must be taken, as according to some sources, even an overly auspicious *omikuji* should be tied to a pine tree. Too much good luck generates pride and is nearly always destined to reverse itself.

Ema

In order for the gods to fulfill prayers or wishes, these must be written by hand on special votive tablets, then hung in long rows in temples. Classic *ema* plaques are wooden and pentagonal, with an image of a sacred animal, such as the fox, messenger of the god Inari, often appearing on one side.

Omamori

Inevitable in a purse or bound to a cell phone, the *omamori* is an amulet that protects against illness or failure in love or at school. It is a kind of tiny fabric pouch holding a prayer, but one that should never be opened on pain of losing all its power.

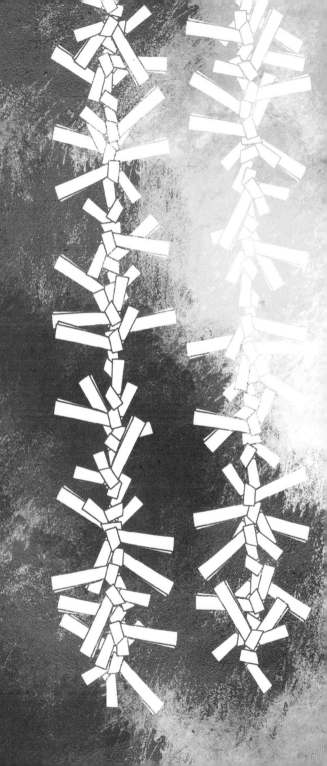

遅勢　大吉

●願望　思ふまゝなり
●待人　おそくとも来る
●失物　末になるべし
●旅行　吉利益のあり
●病行利益をなし
●両行利益をなし
●学業　忽子勉強べし
●方向　東の方よし

●争事　勝分速信ほの
●恋愛　白みを納え大吉
●転居　さはりなし
●お産　やすく心おだやか
●病気　軽くなる
●縁談　たかふり破るゝ恐れあり

おみく

おもてなし
Omotenashi

A Tradition of Impeccable Hospitality

To anticipate the need of a guest before they have realized themselves that it even existed, and to unobtrusively see that the need is met, must surely be the ultimate manifestation of customer service. *Omotenashi* is made up of *omote*, the public face one presents to the world, and *nashi*, or nothing, that is, pure service from the heart, with nothing hidden behind it. *Omotenashi* can be found in interactions with customers and guests everywhere in Japan, but is an art honed for centuries in *ryokan* inns. At traditional establishments, guests return to their rooms to find bedding has been silently laid out or whisked away at the appropriate time, with a table bearing a tea set miraculously appearing in its place. Indeed, the roots of the uniquely Japanese concept of *omotenashi* lie in that most Japanese of rituals, the tea ceremony.

The 16th-century tea master and Zen philosopher Sen no Rikyū is credited with establishing *omotenashi* as an integral element of the "way of tea," or *cha no yu*, as part of the refinements he made to both the rituals of the ceremony and the understanding of its significance. The sacrifice of oneself in the pursuit of perfection is present in the exacting simplicity of the art of tea making, and permeates multiple aspects of traditional Japanese culture.

The Japanese words for guest and customer are one and the same, and the spirit of *omotenashi* makes no distinction between the two. *Omotenashi* encapsulates the notions of hospitality and service, but goes far beyond that to a selfless concern for the peace of mind and comfort of one's guest.

The word has been enjoying a distinct renaissance in Japan, and came to the attention of the world, following its use in a speech in Brazil in 2013 during Tokyo's bid for the 2020 Olympics by French-Japanese TV presenter Christel Takigawa.

If there is criticism of *omotenashi*, it is that a dedication to service beyond the call of duty can push businesses toward inefficiency and low productivity.

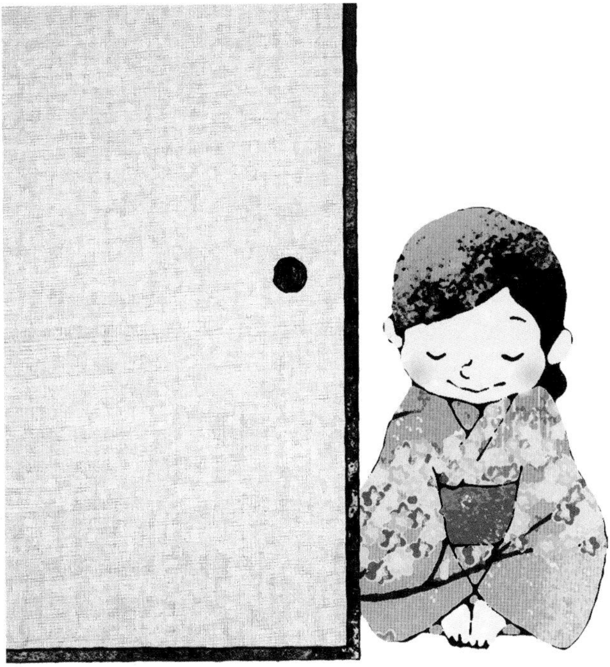
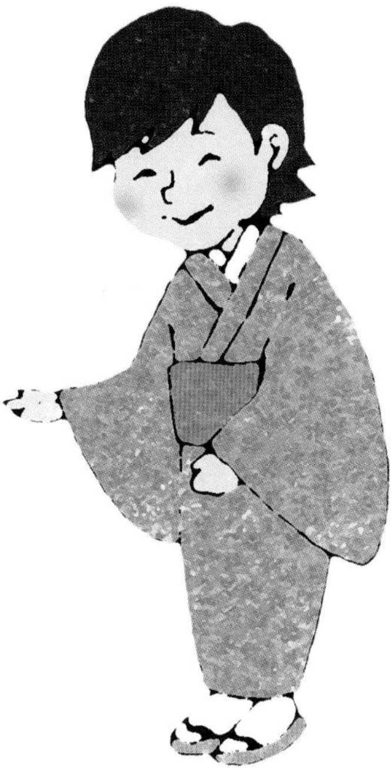
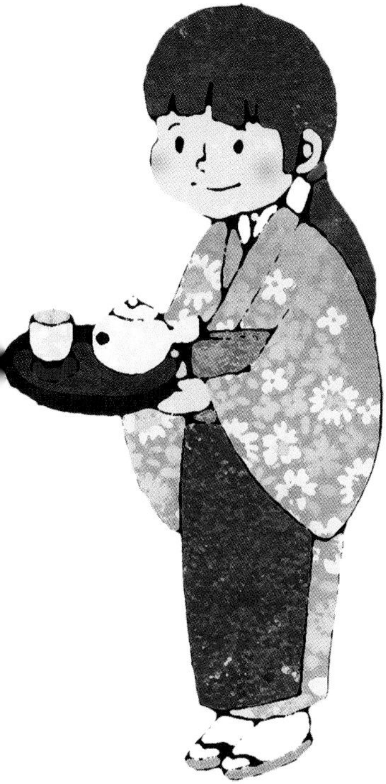
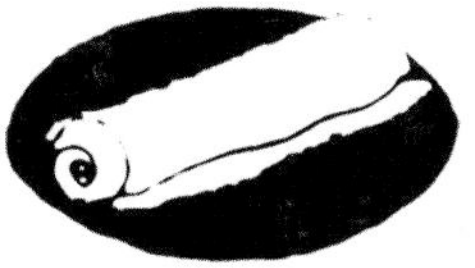
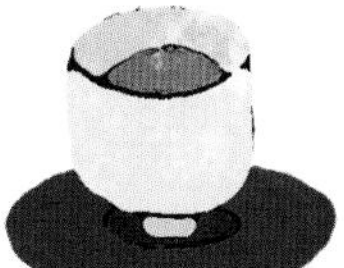
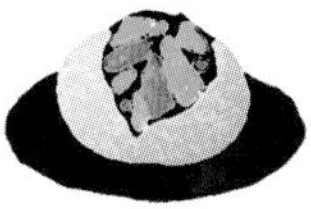
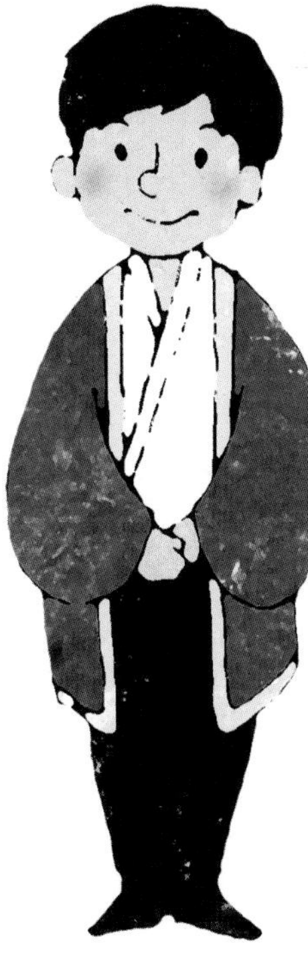

鬼
Oni

Ghosts and Demons

Good or evil demons? Clearly, the physical appearance of *oni*, the powerful fictional humanoids of Japanese mythology, is meant to instill terror.

Folklore depicts them as giant beings of superhuman strength with bestial traits such as horns, claws, thick fur and occasionally fangs. They have more than two eyes, more than ten fingers and red, blue or black skin, and they go around garbed in tiger skins armed with large spiked clubs. Despite all this, they were born good creatures.

Oni originally embodied the forces of nature and the spirit of ancestors: their grim appearance was meant to chase away evil. Only towards the 8th century did they come to be identified with the guardians of Hell, torturers of damned souls. This association

did not serve to their benefit. They began to be regarded as fierce and destructive, as carriers of disease and instigators of disasters, and thus as beings to be kept at a distance.

It is in this capacity that they often appear in *manga* and *anime*, generally as inhabitants of a gloomy, ghostly world, as in Yoshihiro Togashi's *Yū of the Ghosts* but also in the role of the broker in *Wall Street*.

Setsubun

Setsubun takes place on February 3 each year, and corresponds roughly to New Year in the ancient lunar calendar. On that day, rites are celebrated in many Buddhist and Shinto temples as well as in homes in the hope of driving away disease and misfortune in the coming year. Wearing a mask, the head of the family usually assumes the guise of a demon, who is pelted with roasted soy beans by children to the cry of *Oni wa soto, fuku wa uchi!* ("Out with demons, in with fortune!"). To ensure good fortune, each family member must pick up and eat as many beans as his age, plus one for the year that is about to begin.

Kanabō

This is the long wooden club with metal spikes, a heavy and powerful weapon wielded by the *oni*. Unsurprisingly, in Japanese "providing an *oni* with a *kanabō*" means providing those who are already strong with an advantage.

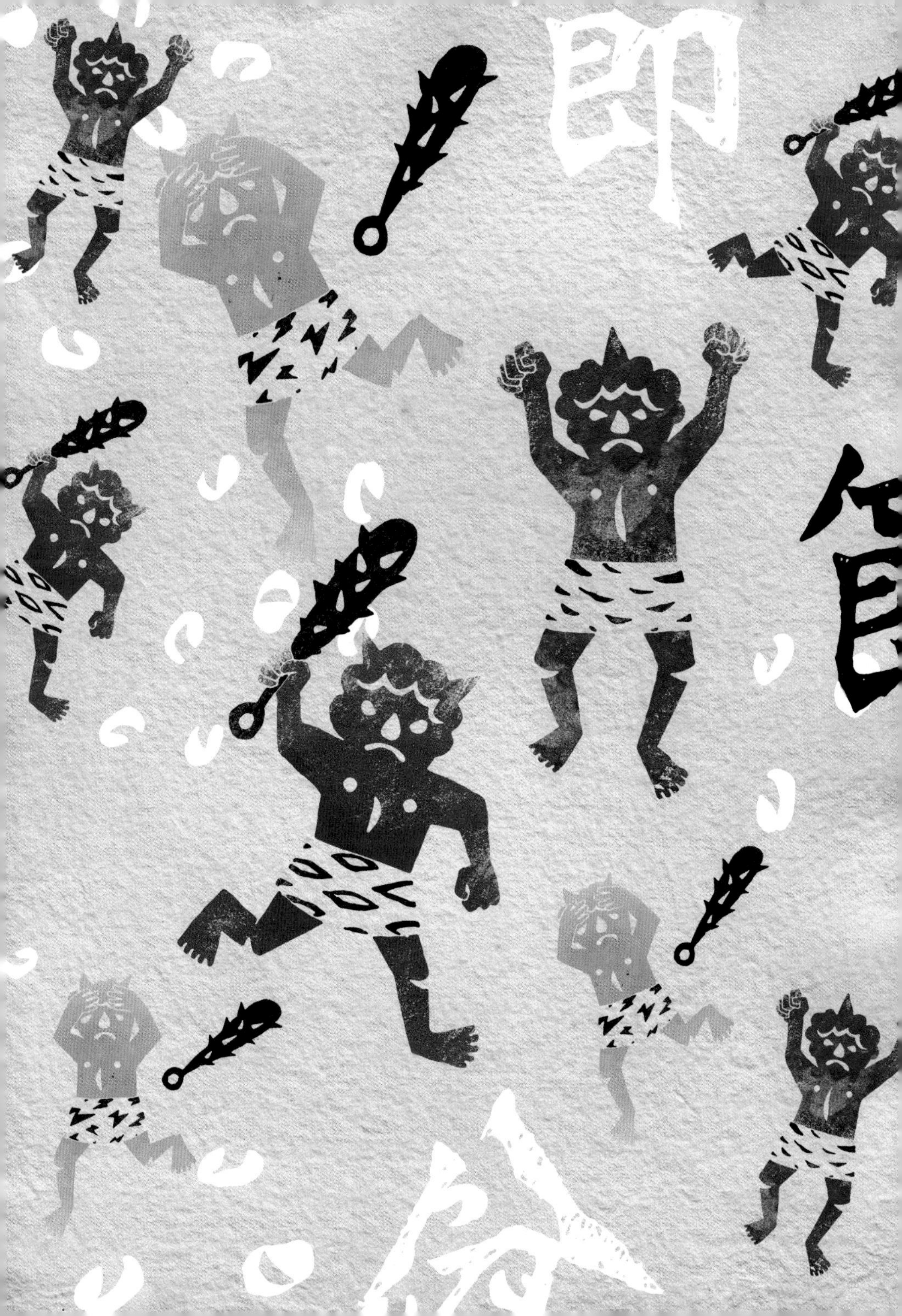
即

折り紙
Origami

The Ancient Art of Paper Folding

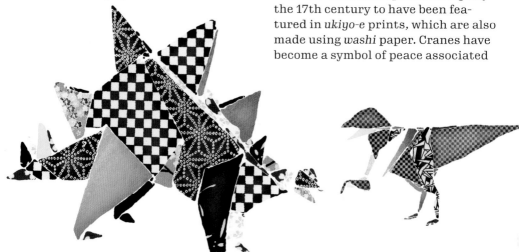

Consisting of the self-explanatory characters *ori* and *kami*, "fold" and "paper," *origami* has been practiced in Japan for around 1,000 years. It blossomed in the imperial court at Kyoto, as did so many cultural pursuits, during the Heian period (794–1185). The durability, pliability and strength of *washi*, literally "Japanese paper," was instrumental in its development. Usually made from the inner bark of the *kōzo* mulberry bush, *washi* production is a laborious process, but one that leads to paper that can last for centuries. Today, regular paper is frequently used for cost reasons, though professionals and serious hobbyists still commonly work with *washi*.

The earliest *origami* were paper ornaments for Shinto religious ceremonies, and similar forms are still used for weddings held at shrines today. The 14th and 15th centuries saw books on *origami* published as its practice spread from the nobility to the wider population. One of the enduring origami designs is the *orizuru* crane, widespread enough by the 17th century to have been featured in *ukiyo-e* prints, which are also made using *washi* paper. Cranes have become a symbol of peace associated

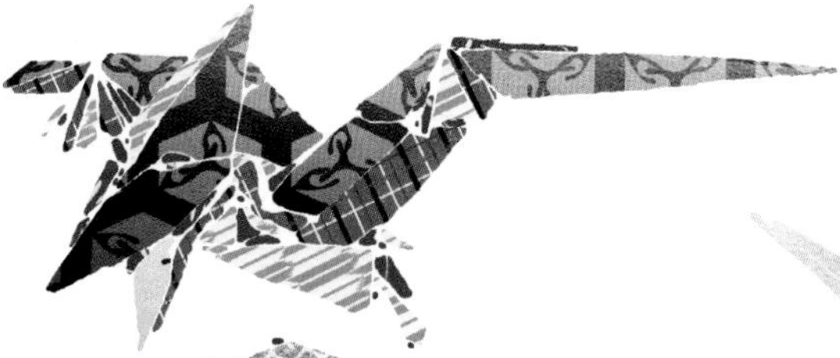

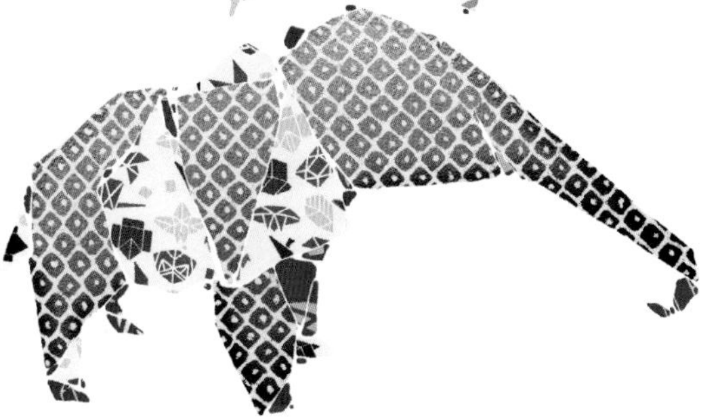

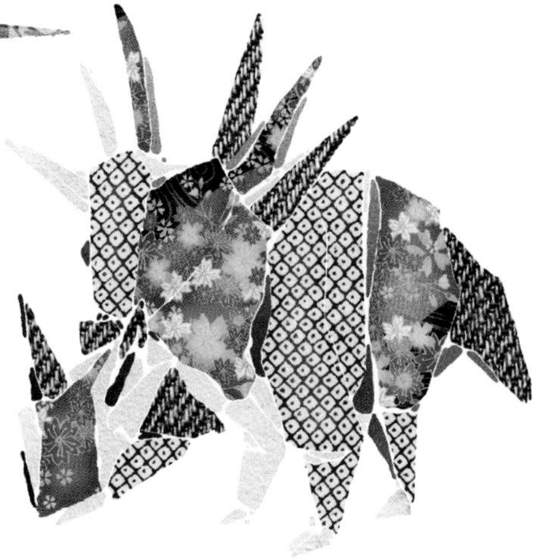

with remembrance of the wartime atomic bombing victims in Hiroshima and Nagasaki, and it would be rare to find a Japanese person today who did not learn to make an *origami orizuru* at school. It was actually a German educator named Friedrich Wilhelm August Fröbel who, in the 19th century promoted the idea of teaching *origami* to Japanese kindergarten students, at the first such school run by the government. This move helped to popularize the art even more widely.

Although the basics of *origami* have remained largely unchanged over the centuries, new techniques such as wetting the paper before folding it have been introduced, along with non-traditional designs. The word *origami* has become accepted in languages around the globe, where the art now has devotees, many of whom find it a cathartic escape from the hectic nature of modern life.

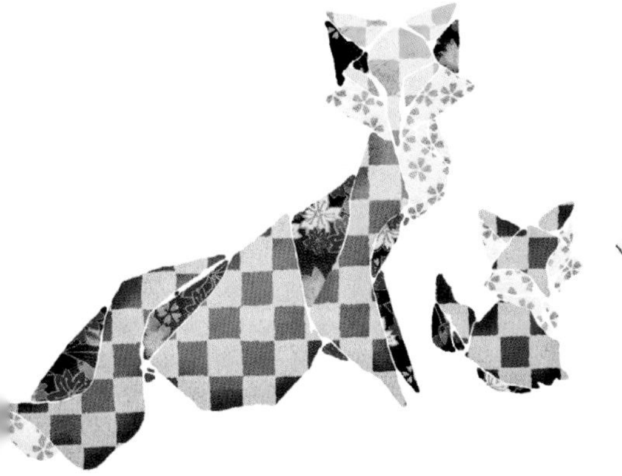

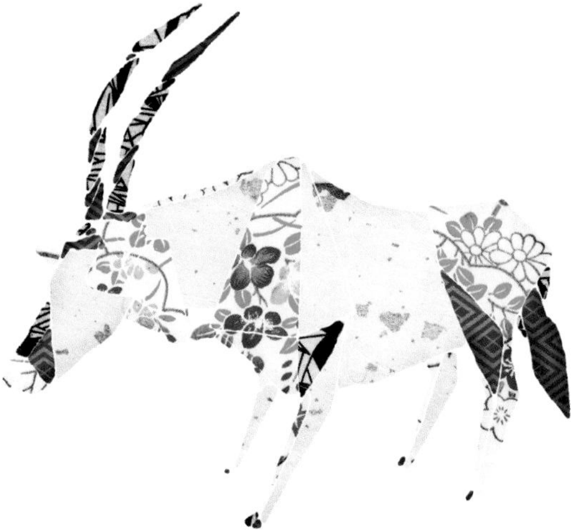

おたく

Otaku

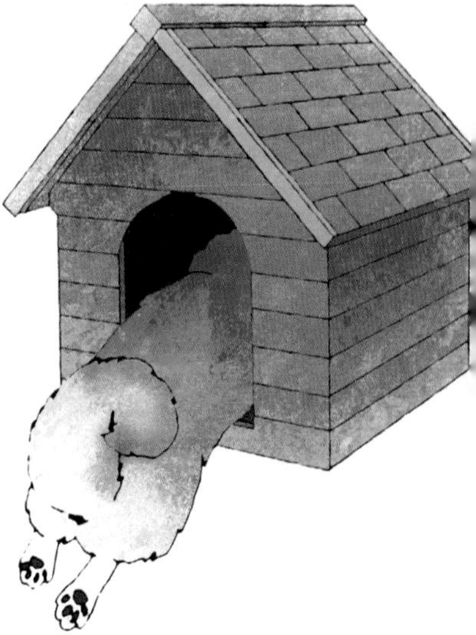

Geeky Fans of Manga, Anime, etc.

One of a number of words and concepts that have made their way from Japanese subcultures into the minds and vocabulary of people around the globe, *otaku* is difficult to define because it means different things to different people. The original meaning of the word is simply "your family/house." It is also used as a formal "you," though in the minefield that is the Japanese language, even referring to yourself or others is rarely straightforward.

One origin story is that *otaku* was used by characters in a 1980s *anime* to address each other, and then adopted by fans who were in turn mocked for social awkwardness in continuing to use the formal term when a more familiar one would have worked. During the 1980s *anime* boom, obsessive fans began to be labeled *otaku*, a use that would spread to fans of *manga*, video games and eventually fields ranging from computers to *aidoru* to collectors in general. Some suggest that *otaku* were nerdy outsiders from Japan's rigid school system, the uncool kids. Lacking social skills, romantically unsuccessful or just uninterested, they fixated on niche aspects of popular culture. The

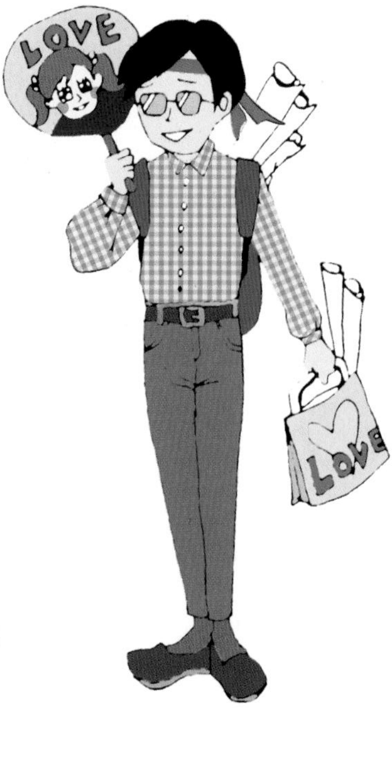
LOVE
LOVE

term acquired infamy in 1989 when a man in his 20s was arrested, and later executed, for a series of sexual murders of young girls. After the police found his huge collection of *anime*, he was dubbed the "Otaku Murderer" by the media, tarnishing the term for years. Today, people will refer to themselves as *otaku* if they have a passionate interest in almost anything, while one of Tokyo's top universities has a course and research department dedicated to the core *otaku* trinity of *anime*, *manga* and games. This trinity also forms the foundation of the government's Cool Japan campaign to promote its pop culture globally.

Hikikomori

Although a somewhat unfair association, obsessive fandom is often linked to *hikiko-mori*, literally "pulling inside" or "confined," the complete social isolation that has afflicted hundreds of thousands of Japanese, usually from better-off families.

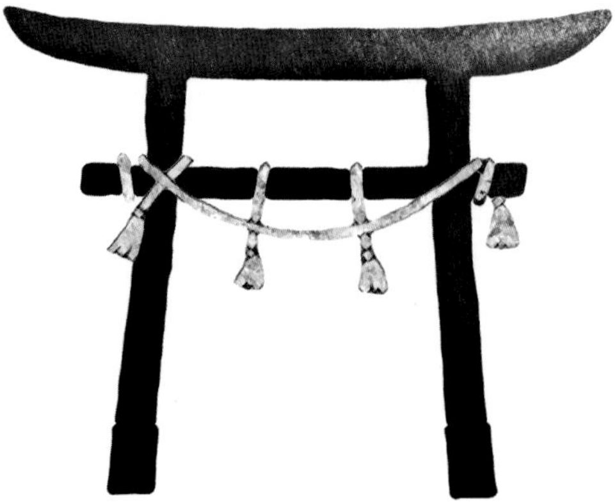

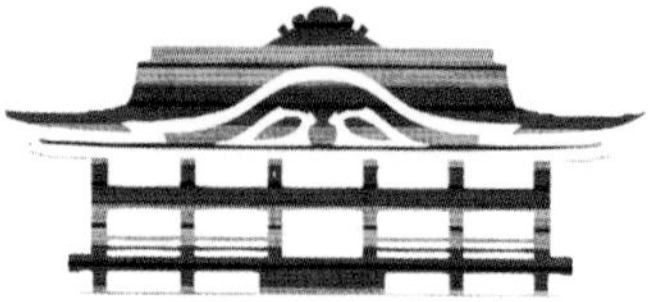

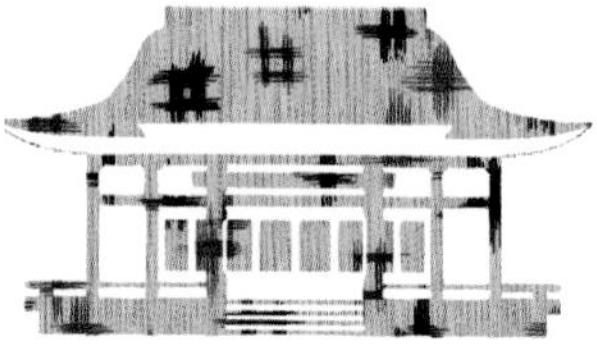

お寺/神社

O-tera and Jinja

Buddhist Temples and Sacred Shinto Shrines

From tiny roadside shrines to huge, magnificent temples, Japan is awash with more than 150,000 sacred structures. Nevertheless, most Japanese take a relaxed view of religion, with families often holding weddings at Shinto *jinja* (shrines) and funerals at Buddhist *o-tera* (temples). The two places of worship can be difficult to distinguish and hybrids that contain characteristics of both can still be found. *O-tera* show more Chinese, and even some Indian, influence than *jinja*, unsurprising given the roots of Buddhism. The easiest way to tell the two apart is their respective entrances. A pair of fierce-looking *nio* statues, one with its mouth open and one with it closed, guard the Buddha from evil at the entrance to temples. Meanwhile, a wooden *torii* gate usually marks the entrance to a shrine of any significant size. The dominant building material of temples and shrines is wood, aside from foundations and some other elements. Between Japan's many earthquakes, fires and wars, many of the most famous temples and shrines have been destroyed and rebuilt multiple times. The sprawling Ise Jingū complex of 125 shrines in Mie Prefecture is the holiest Shintō site in Japan and its two main *jinja* have been torn down and rebuilt every 20 years for more than 1,300 years.

Neither shrines nor temples serve as places of mass worship in the way those of the Christian, Hindu, Muslim or Jewish traditions do. The architecture, interiors and atmosphere of *jinja*, and particularly Zen *o-tera*, also tend to be more subdued than their counterparts elsewhere. That is not to say all are lacking in splendor; the 1,001 golden Kannon statues of Kyoto's Sanjūsangen-dō or Nara's Todai-ji, said to be the world's largest wooden building and home to an immense bronze Buddha, are certainly stunning. Some temples still function as active monasteries for monks to live and train in, though rural depopulation has left others with no priest to watch over them.

楽焼

Rakuyaki

Zen-inspired Irregular Pottery

This particular type of pottery, which is both rustic and extremely refined, is ideally suited for the tea ceremony. In the 16th century, a great master of the ritual, Sen no Rikyū, asked the ceramicist Chōjirō to create for him a type of cup that harmonized with the Zen simplicity of his tearoom and the garden surrounding it. It had to be a crude, opaque cup, with little if any color, random in shape, with nothing of the cool perfection of polished and meticulously adorned, glass-like porcelain made on a lathe. Chōjirō set to work and created something hitherto unseen.

Raku objects are modeled by hand, without the aid of any instruments, and therefore have neither the subtlety nor the regularity or perfect symmetry generally sought by ceramicists. They recall the randomness and spontaneity of nature, and, thanks to the deliberate imperfection of their form, transmit the warmth of the spirit that has created them. Each piece is as unique and unrepeatable as a work of art.

Initially, their finish was monochrome, either black or red. With time, metal oxides were added to the clay to obtain other colors. The pottery is removed from the kiln while it is glowing and placed in a hole in the ground or in a container containing leaves, straw or sawdust. The fumes generated, combined with the oxides, leave behind iridescent and suggestive nuances peculiar to *raku*. Here, too, much is left to chance. Regardless of the ceramicist's expertise, the final effect will always differ and never be altogether predictable.

Today, *raku* pottery is widespread and made all over the world, but the most highly prized and authentic examples are still produced by Chōjirō's great-grandchildren. Raku Kichizaemon, a 15th-generation descendant, continues to work in the founder's laboratory on the western side of the imperial palace of Kyoto, where he produces masterpieces with the same harmonious quality and with equal rigor.

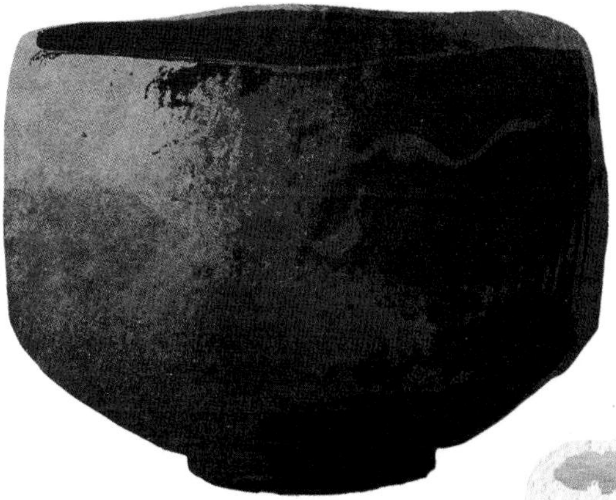

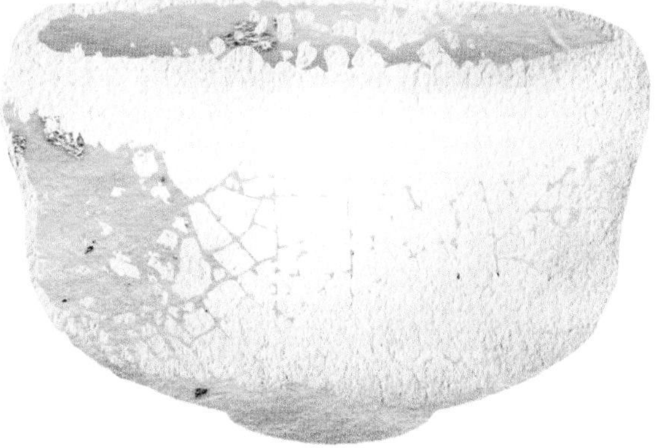

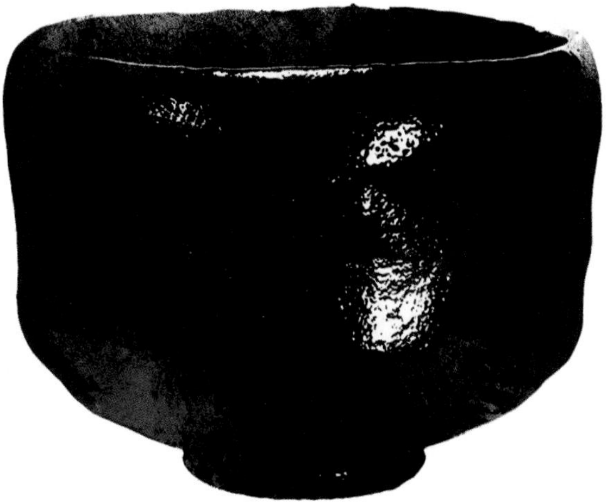

ラーメン
Rāmen

Iconic Japanese Noodle Soup

The best-known Japanese dish in the West after *sushi* is certainly *rāmen*, the noodle soup often shown in *manga*, if for no other reason than because it comes in popular instant versions that can be prepared anywhere in three minutes simply by adding some boiling water. Although no one remembers this anymore, the dish is of Chinese origin, so it has an important place in the tradition of

Nagasaki, which served as a bridge to the continent. The local version is known as *chanpon* and is prepared with a thick pork broth to which are added fried vegetables, chicken and seafood. In Sapporo, people prefer thinner noodles dipped in a *miso* (fermented soybean) broth, while in Tokyo the clear and dark broth is flavored with soy sauce. As for accompanying ingredients, one can say that

anything edible is acceptable, from eggs to vegetables, to sliced pork and seaweed, based on the cook's imagination. *Rāmen* should be eaten by conveying the noodles to the mouth with chopsticks, then drinking the broth directly from the bowl.

It is compulsory to make lots of noise: slurps and smacks are essential to demonstrating one's genuine appreciation.

Udon

These are the long tubular noodles found in the traditional cuisine of Osaka and Kyoto. Eaten mainly in broth, they are available in various types. *Kitsune udon* (fox *udon*) gets its name from the addition of fried tōfu,

which this animal covets. *Tempura udon* is topped with a batter-fried prawn. *Tanuki udon* (badger *udon*) combines broth with fried batter, making it richer and more flavorful.

Soba

Buckwheat noodles, typical of Edo, are eaten with broth but also sautéed with chunks of meat and vegetables (*yakisoba*) or cold noodles (*zaru soba*) and dipped in *mentsuyu* sauce, which is served in a separate bowl. *Soba* also means "near." For this reason, when one moves house, one customarily gifts a packet of this pasta to new neighbors in the hope that the relationship will be long and smooth, just like the noodle.

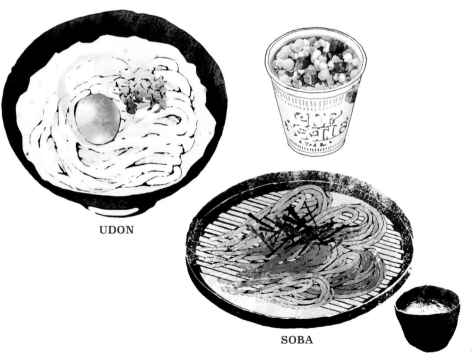

UDON

SOBA

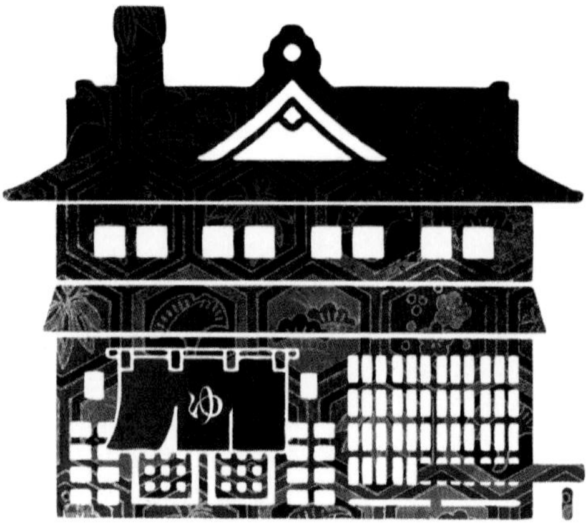

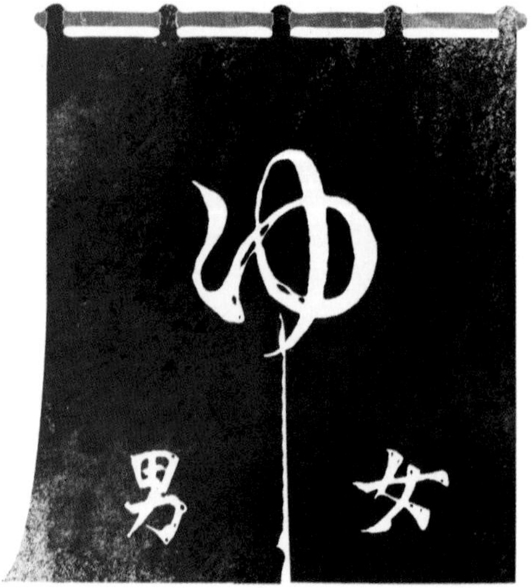
ゆ
男
女

MAKU
curtain

旅館/温泉

Ryokan and Onsen

Traditional Inns and Hot Springs

The world's five oldest companies are Japanese and three of those are *ryokan* inns founded in the early 8th century. *Ryokan* can be found all over the country, but are concentrated in areas with *onsen* hot springs and along old travel routes. They are rare in big cities. The traditional style consists of *tatami* rooms where meals are usually served, sliding doors, relatively large communal bathing facilities and a lobby-like area. Guests sleep on *futons*, which are laid out and cleared by staff, and can wear the casual *yukata kimono* both in the hotel and outside if desired. Food tends to be *kaiseki* courses for dinner and traditional Japanese breakfasts, both served when requested by guests, though generally earlier than at hotels. Much of this has changed little down the centuries, though some *ryokan* have introduced modern interiors or begun to serve Western-style food.

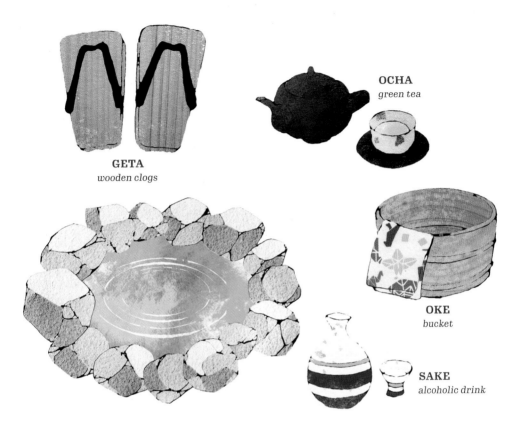

GETA
wooden clogs

OCHA
green tea

OKE
bucket

SAKE
alcoholic drink

Onsen

Onsen are the silver lining to the cloud of Japan being the most seismically active nation on the planet. There are said to be more than 30,000 natural hot springs and more than 3,000 *onsen* resort towns scattered across the archipelago, from Okinawa in the south to the northern island of Hokkaido. While many are attached to *ryokan*, there are also plenty of *onsen* with stand-alone facilities, including some which function as reasonably priced *sentō* public baths. And Japanese-style bathing has always been about more than simply getting bodies clean: it also provides stress relief, opportunities to communicate openly, as well as various health benefits attributed to soaking in *onsen* water containing different kinds of minerals.

Mixed bathing was once commonplace, but in a nod to Western morals during the rush to modernize in the late 19th century after the Meiji Restoration, the number of *onsen* permitting the practice fell sharply.

An unforgettable *onsen* experience is to soak in an outside *roten-buro* in the mountains on a winter evening and watch falling snow melt as it meets the warmth of the water.

料理
Ryōri

Japanese Cuisine

The word for cooking and cuisine in Japanese, *ryōri*, is a suffix used in many food-related terms, but two of the most notable examples are *shōjin-ryōri* and *kaiseki-ryōri*.

Of the numerous types of cuisines that grace tables across the archipelago, *shōjin-ryōri* is one of the more intriguing. A set of small dishes of rice and seasonal vegetables are meticulously prepared, and flavorings are liberally used to bring out the essence of the ingredients. As with many facets of what is known as Japanese culture, *shōjin-ryōri* followed the route of Buddhism from India through China and Korea to Japan, and it is at Buddhist temples where many restaurants selling the genuine article are still found. And, as with most such cultural elements, *shōjin-ryōri* was refined and given sufficient

local twists to make it a cuisine in its own right.

In the 1500s, centuries after *shōjin-ryōri* had developed, Zen monk Sen no Rikyū adapted it for the meals he served at *chadō* tea ceremonies, of which he is regarded as the greatest master. This would go on to inspire *kaiseki-ryōri*, which added more courses, including fish, and made the dishes more lavish. Today, *kaiseki-ryōri*, with typically more than a dozen courses, is regarded as one of the finest haute cuisines in the world. The aesthetics of *kaiseki-ryōri* are almost as important as the taste, and that extends to the décor of the *tatami* rooms in which it is served, which at high-end establishments often have a view out onto a Japanese garden. The center of *kaiseki-ryōri* is Kyoto and the top restaurants there famously declined to be included in the first Michelin guides to the city, though most have since relented.

One feature across nearly every form of *ryōri* is the use of *hashi* (chopsticks); the longer version used for cooking are known as *ryōri-bashi*. They also arrived via China and Korea and were originally folding pieces of bamboo, with other woods such as yew, often with a lacquer covering, coming into use later.

酒

Sake

Japanese Alcoholic Beverages

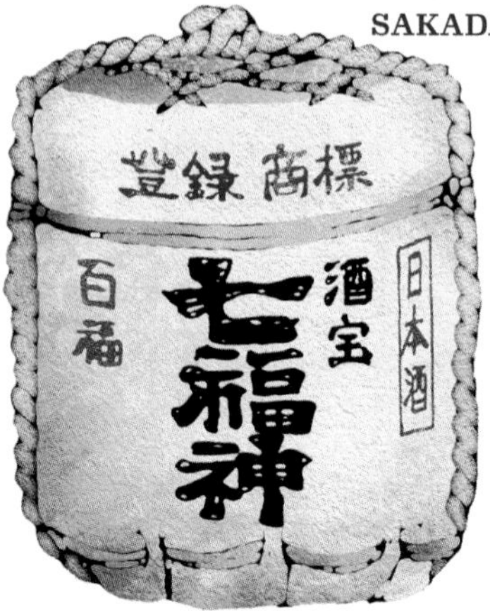
登録商標
七福神
酒宝
百福
日本酒

SAKADARU

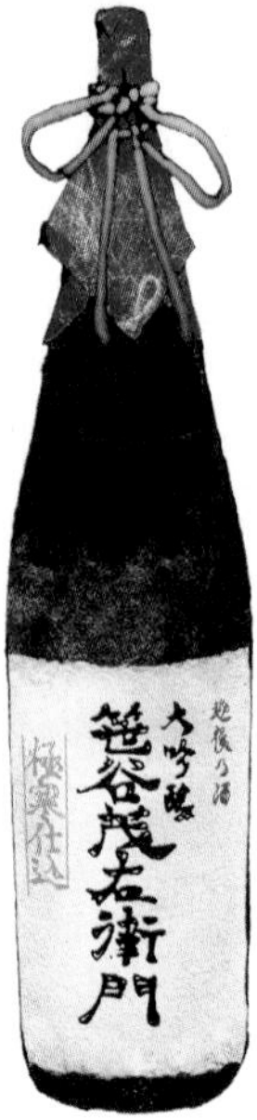
越後乃酒
大吟醸
笹谷茂右衛門
極寒仕込

SAKE

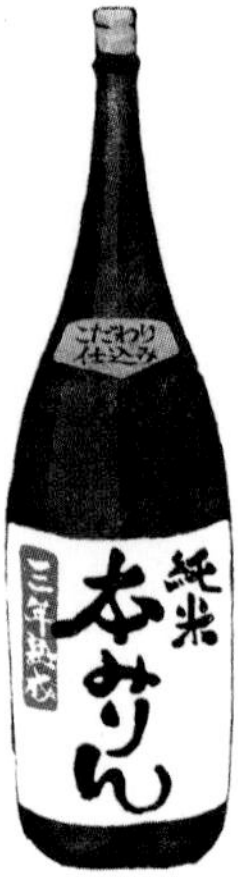
こだわり仕込み
純米
本みりん

MIRIN

Once the only alcohol in Japan, *sake* is these days outsold by beer, spirits and its distilled cousin *shōchū*. But no other alcoholic beverage has the cultural significance of *sake*, as suggested by its other name, *nihon-shu*, meaning "Japanese alcohol." *O-sake* is also used to refer to all kinds of alcoholic beverage.

The earliest written record of *sake* is in a 3rd-century Chinese text which notes the fondness of the Japanese for drinking a rice-based alcohol and dancing, though its history likely predates this. By the 8th century, *nihon-shu* was being fermented using *kōji* mold in a multilayered process that would continue to be refined for hundreds of years. By the 10th century, it was being brewed in Shintō shrines and Buddhist temples, and it is still used for religious ceremonies and other rituals to this day, including weddings, New Year celebrations (the *sake* is called *otoso*) and sumo tournaments.

The quality of *sake* depends on the rice and how finely it is polished, the water used and, of course, the methods and skills of the brewer. The taste ranges from sweetish *ama-kuchi* ("sweet mouth") to the drier *kara-kuchi*, which is slightly stronger due to more of the sugar turning into alcohol. *Sake* is a little stronger than wine and can be drunk in a range from chilled to hot (*atsukan*). Different varieties are best suited to certain temperatures, but high-end *sake* is rarely drunk hot as some subtleties of flavor are lost. The most common

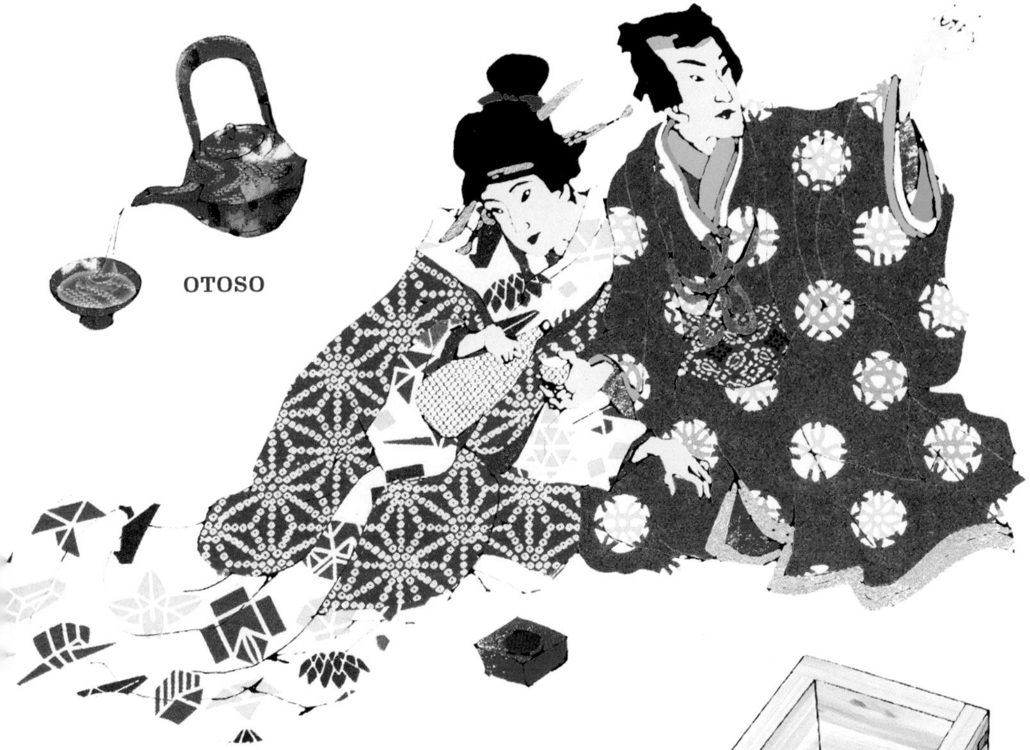

OTOSO

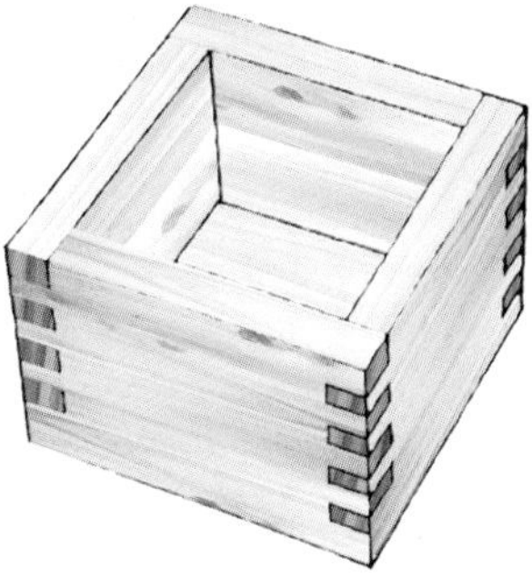

MASU

vessel to drink *sake* from is a small ceramic *o-choko,* poured from a *tokkuri* flask, though glasses are also often used, particularly when the *sake* is chilled. The wooden box-like *masu* is frequently used at ceremonies when large barrels of *sake* are broken open, but also at eateries, often with a glass placed inside them.

Mirin

Mirin is a very sweet variety of *sake,* with a lower alcohol content, employed as a condiment in Japanese cooking for sauces and to flavor the rice on which *sushi* is served.

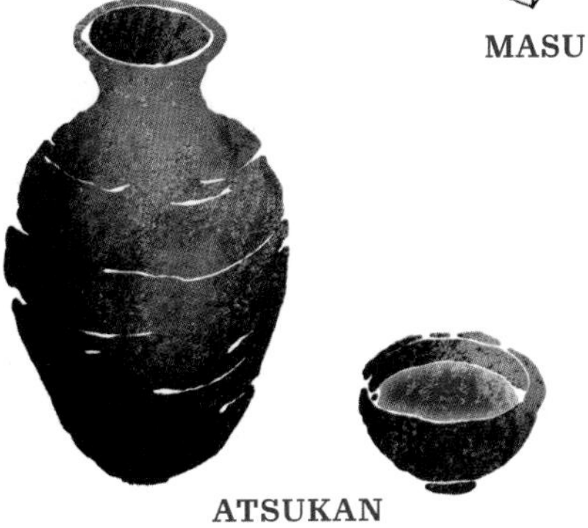

ATSUKAN

侍

Samurai

Highly Skilled Professional Warriors

The Japanese character for samurai means "to serve" and the samurai were indeed originally attendants to landowning lords, employed to protect them and their property. They are also frequently known by the terms *bushi* or *buke* in Japanese, meaning "martial person" and "martial family," respectively.

Although these professional warriors emerged in the 8th and 9th centuries, the term samurai would not be used to refer to them until around the 12th century. In the 900s, the weakness of the imperial court

caused power vacuums which rival regional clans battled to fill, eventually leading to a shogunate system of government that would see samurai rule for 700 years. Two of the most prominent clans, the Taira and the Morimoto, both offshoots of the imperial family, battled for centuries in an ever-shifting melee of alliances, betrayals and bloody violence that saw sides switched and brothers set against each other. Two attempted invasions by Mongol fleets in the second half of the 13th century briefly united the samurai clans, but the thirst for power meant civil wars quickly flared up again. It was during the Warring States era (1467–1600) that samurai came into their own.

When Zen Buddhism spread across Japan, many samurai were attracted to its teachings of self-discipline, austerity, decisiveness and acceptance of death. Along with the new philosophy, many *bushi* also engaged in cultural pursuits such as calligraphy, poetry and the tea ceremony.

Although some samurai were born into noble houses, others began life as peasant farmers and earned their stripes in battle. One such warrior was Toyotomi Hideyoshi, who unified the nation, bringing constant warfare to an end. Ironically, it was Hideyoshi who enforced the four-tier caste system with the samurai at the top, preventing the social mobility that had allowed him to become the most powerful man in the land. By the subsequent Edo period, samurai accounted for around 10 percent of the population, but the need for their martial skills was minimal in the two and a half centuries that followed. Most became bureaucrats, some were impoverished, and not a few turned to crime. The official end of the *bushi* class came with the Meiji Restoration of 1868, but their glory days had already long passed.

Rōnin

Samurai who had lost their lord due to death, betrayal or misfortune were known as *rōnin,* literally "wave man," referring to their rootless existence; it is used today to describe people who have not yet been able to enter university. *Rōnin* existed since the early days of the samurai and were sometimes recruited into the service of other *daimyō,* particularly during the *sengoku* period, when skilled fighters were in great demand. Miyamoto Musashi, known as Japan's greatest swordsman, spent time as a *rōnin,* wandering the country fighting numerous duels. Enter the Edo period, with its peace and rigid caste structure, and the number of *rōnin* grew rapidly, with fewer legitimate uses for their skills. While some provided security and protection to businesses and tradespeople, others worked as enforcers for gangs or became bandits. But this was also the time of the 47 Ronin, one of Japan's most enduring tales. After their lord was forced to commit *seppuku* following a dispute with a court official, the 47 warriors later avenged him, killing the official. They surrendered and were, in turn, sentenced to commit *seppuku.*

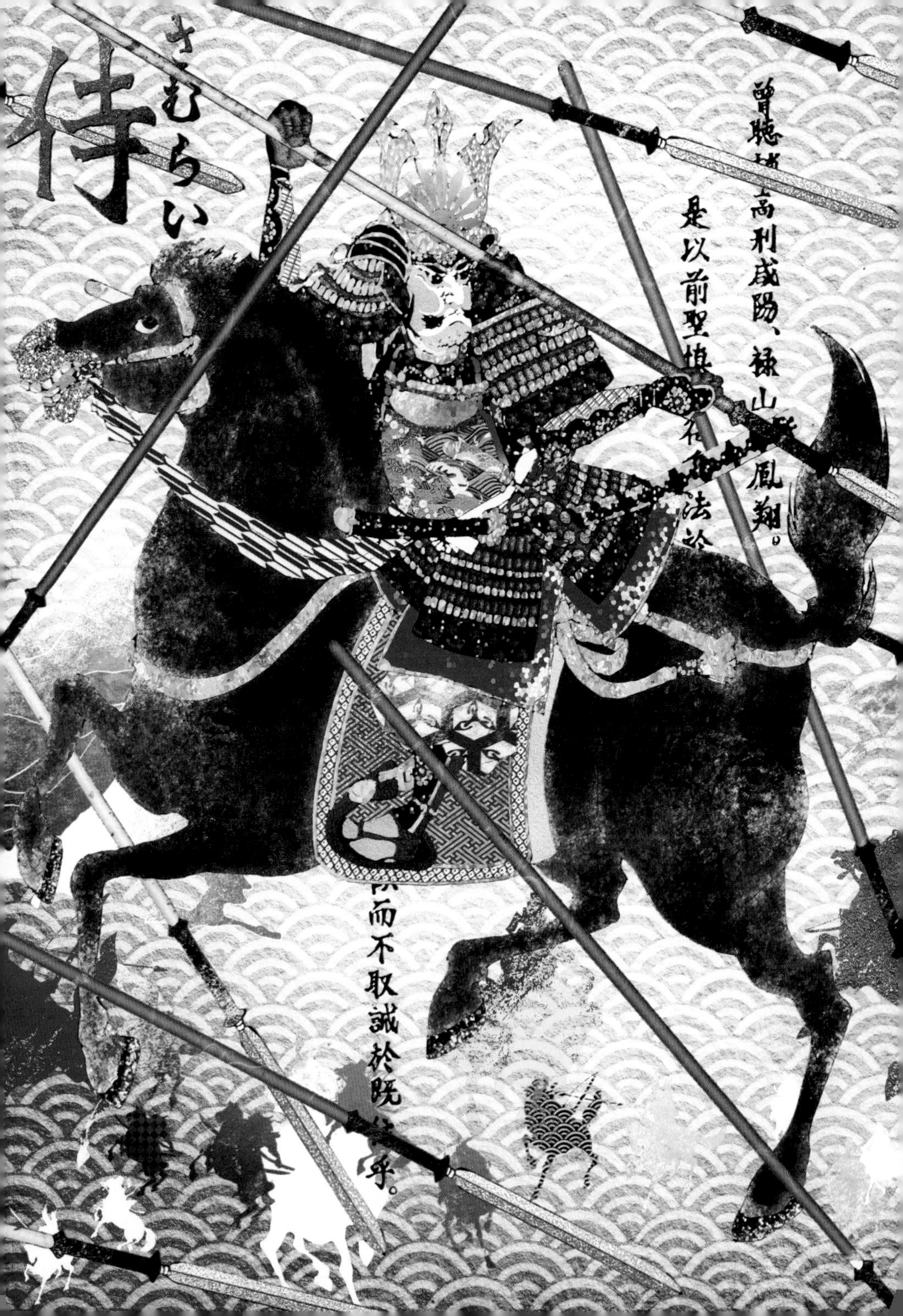

侍
さむらい
曾聴
高利咸陽、禄山
鳳翔。
是以前聖
法於
而不取誠於既
乎。

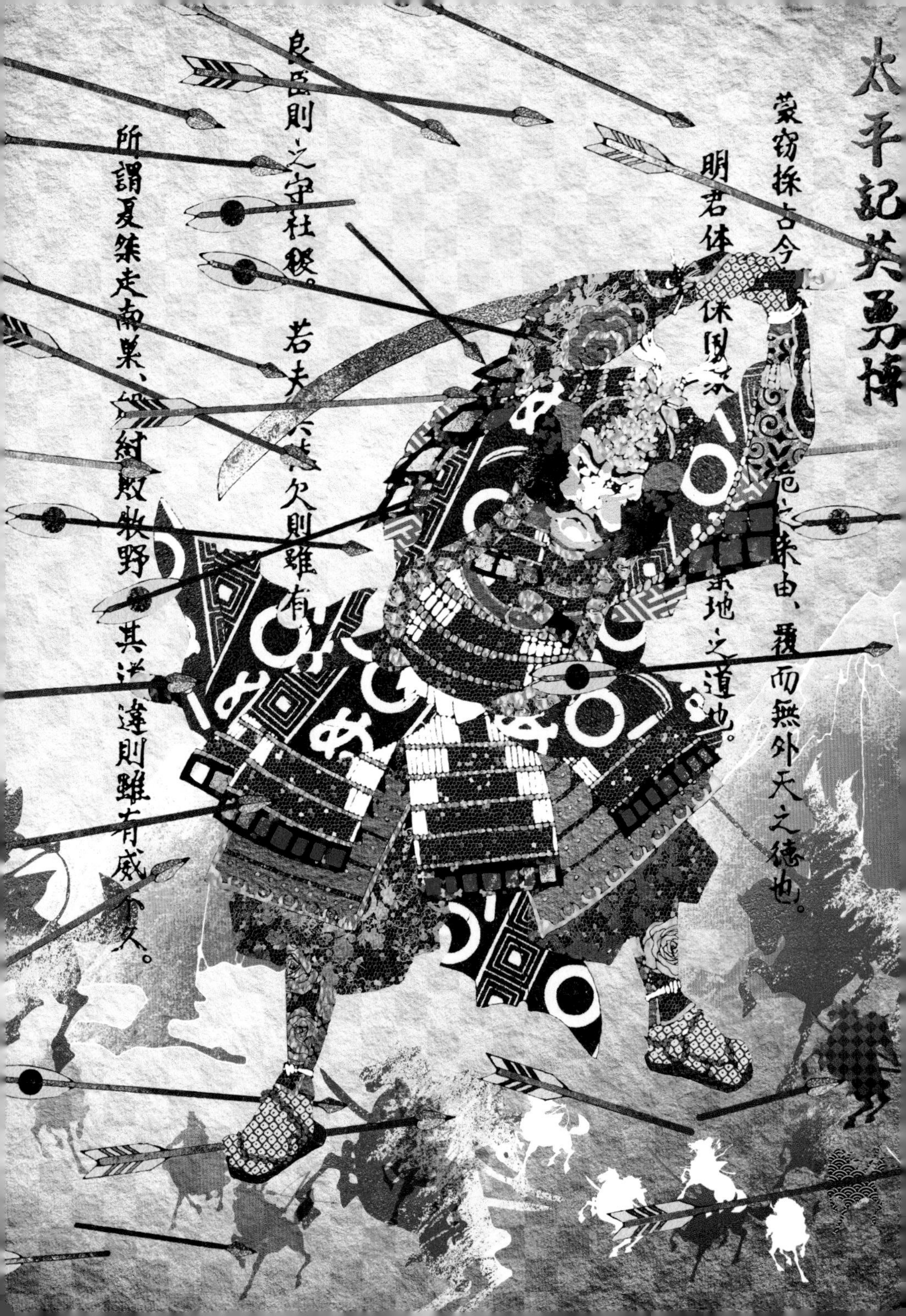

太平記英勇博
蒙窃採古今
危之所由、覆而無外天之徳也。
明君体
保国家
地之道也。
良臣則之守社稷。
若夫
欠則雖有
所謂夏桀走南巢、
紂敗牧野
其
違則雖有威不久。

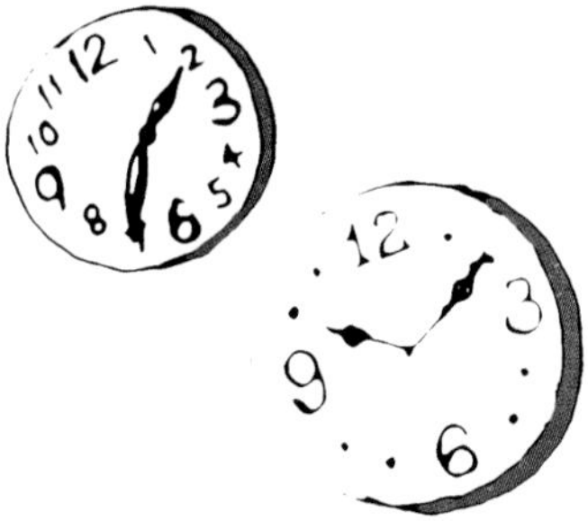

12
1
2
3
4
5
6
8
9
10
11
12
3
6
9

サラリーマン
Sarariiman

The Salaryman

Once seen as an ideal to aspire to for any male university graduate in Japan, the connotation of the *sarari-iman* has shifted somewhat in recent decades. The term is used for white collar workers in private and public organizations, though, for example, movie producers at major studios will also half-jokingly refer to themselves as *sarariiman* to emphasize the fact that they are on set wages and have comparatively little freedom.

Sarariiman, a term originating in the 1930s, for some conjures up images of suited semi-automatons grinding out long hours and dedicating their lives to the company at the expense of themselves and their families. While every April still sees legions of fresh graduates dressed almost identically at *nyūsha-shiki* ceremonies to welcome them into the only company they may ever work for, times are changing. Pointless overtime followed by semi-obligatory drinking parties are less prevalent, as is promotion based solely on age. The phrase "'work–life balance" has been imported from English and the concept is slowly taking hold among younger employees. Nevertheless, putting the collective before self remains a cultural norm in Japan and dozens of *sarariiman* work themselves literally to death in *karōshi* incidents every year. The practice of *tanshin-funin*—relocation to a regional or over-seas office without their family, often at very short notice—also remains common in some corporations.

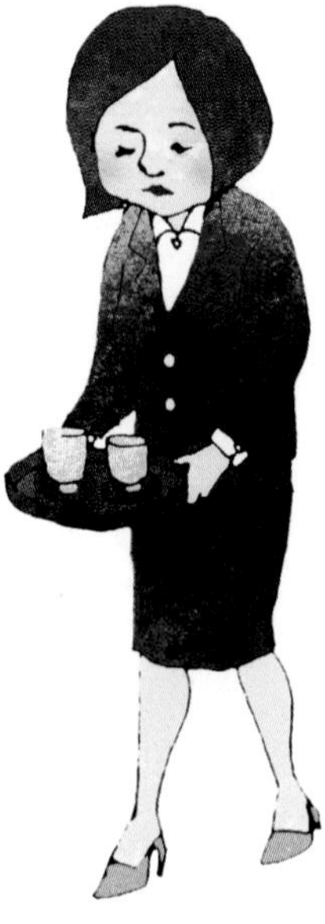

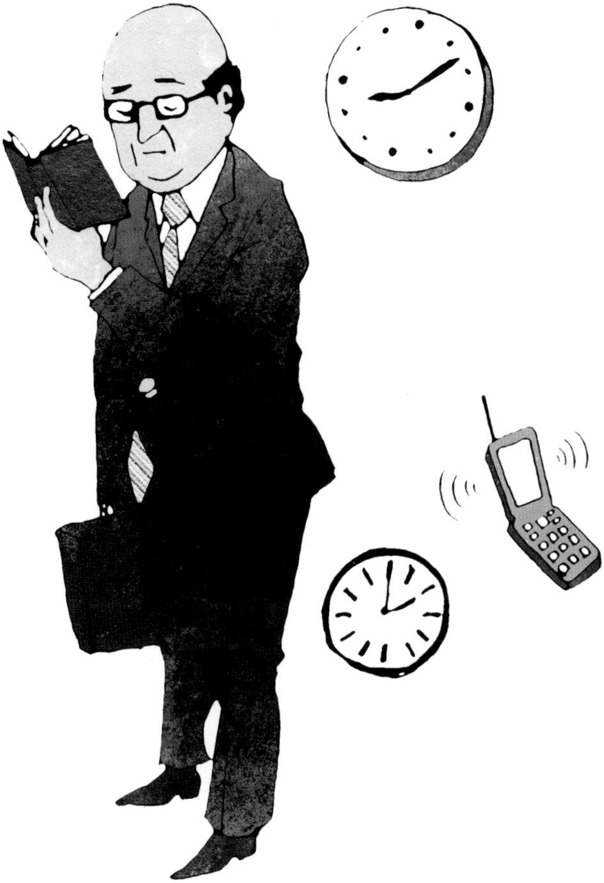

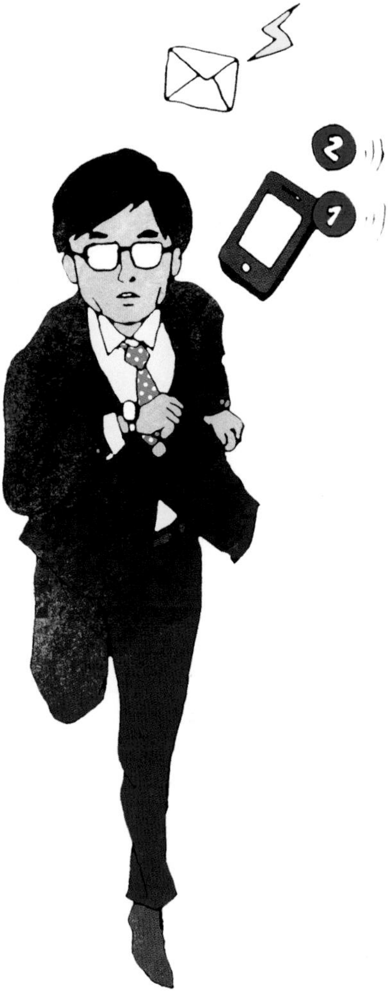

Oeru

Another loanword, "office lady," usually written as *OL* and pronounced *oeru,* is used to describe some female employees in corporations. Once commonly referred to as *shokuba no hana,* or "flowers of the workplace," they were forced to wear uniforms, serve tea and perform basic clerical work, with the expectation they would marry by 30, often to someone from the same company. Despite anti-discrimination laws, opportunities are still far from equal, though fewer women are now officially designated *oeru,* meaning they now have at least some chance of career advancement.

先生
Sensei

Honorable Teacher

The word *sensei* became familiar to many in the West with the global spread of Japanese martial arts, though it is used as an honorific title for a wide variety of instructors, professionals and even *manga* creators. The two characters that make up the word mean "previous/before" and "born," giving a huge clue to the significance of a *sensei* as someone who has much experience and knowledge. In addition to academic teachers and instructors in traditional arts such as *shodō, ikebana* and *chadō,* lawyers, doctors and politicians are also bestowed with the title.

Japan is undoubtedly a *tate-shakai,* or hierarchical society, and the

master–pupil relationship is one of the mechanisms that underpins and reinforces it, whereby students rarely question the opinions, let alone the authority, of their seniors. The merits of such tendencies include an almost unwavering respect and loyalty towards the instructor and dedication to perfecting the skills being taught. Among the disadvantages is the danger of innovation being stifled and a tendency towards unquestioning group-think. However, the concept is not immune to being updated, and these days many people will admit to having learned something from the all-knowing *gūguru-sensei*, otherwise known as Google.

Senpai-kōhai

Another vital relationship in Japan's hierarchical social structure is that of *senpai-kōhai*. The basic meaning is "senior–junior," though the concept encapsulates much more than that. The first character in *senpai* is the same as in *sensei*, though confusingly it is usually pronounced *sempai* and sometimes written as such in the Roman alphabet. The *kō* in *kōhai* simply means "after" and denotes the person joined the school, *dōjo* or company after their *senpai*. The relationship, even one formed in a junior high school sports club, is for life and *kōhai* will continue to address their *senpai* as such and treat them with the proper respect, even if they go on to be far more successful in their career.

銭湯
Sentō

Public Baths

The characters for *sentō* are the self-explanatory "coin/money" and "bath," and their history is believed to date back at least 1,000 years. *Sentō* differ from *onsen* in that they usually use regular water that is heated rather than water from hot springs, though in areas lucky enough to have naturally hot water the two can be one and the same. The number of *sentō* increased rapidly in tandem with the urbanization that took place in the postwar period, leaving millions living in accommodation with no bath. As late as the 1960s, many of the cheaper wooden apartments built had no bath, and *sentō* became community focal points. Against the background of a rule-bound and often formal culture, public bathing is one place where social barriers are broken down and people are more likely to strike up a conversation with someone than when they are clothed.

The fact that the Japanese usually refer to all baths as *o-furo*, adding the honorific "o" prefix, speaks to the important position they hold in the culture. Another commonality across Japanese bathing is the practice of washing the body before entering the water. While this was once done using a small wooden *oke* tub, recently a combination of a shower and plastic *oke* is more common.

Even the most basic *sentō* will often have multiple baths, including cold plunges, some with gentle electricity currents flowing through them, or even saunas. Another characteristic of *sentō* are the hand-painted landscapes of Mount Fuji which can be found above the baths in nearly every facility.

With baths long standard in new homes, the patronage of *sentō* is on the decline and their numbers have fallen rapidly in recent decades. However, new types of so-called *super-sentō* that feature spa-like facilities and often include restaurants and even guest rooms, have been growing in popularity. Japan is yet to fall out of love with *hadaka no tsukiai*, or "naked relationships."

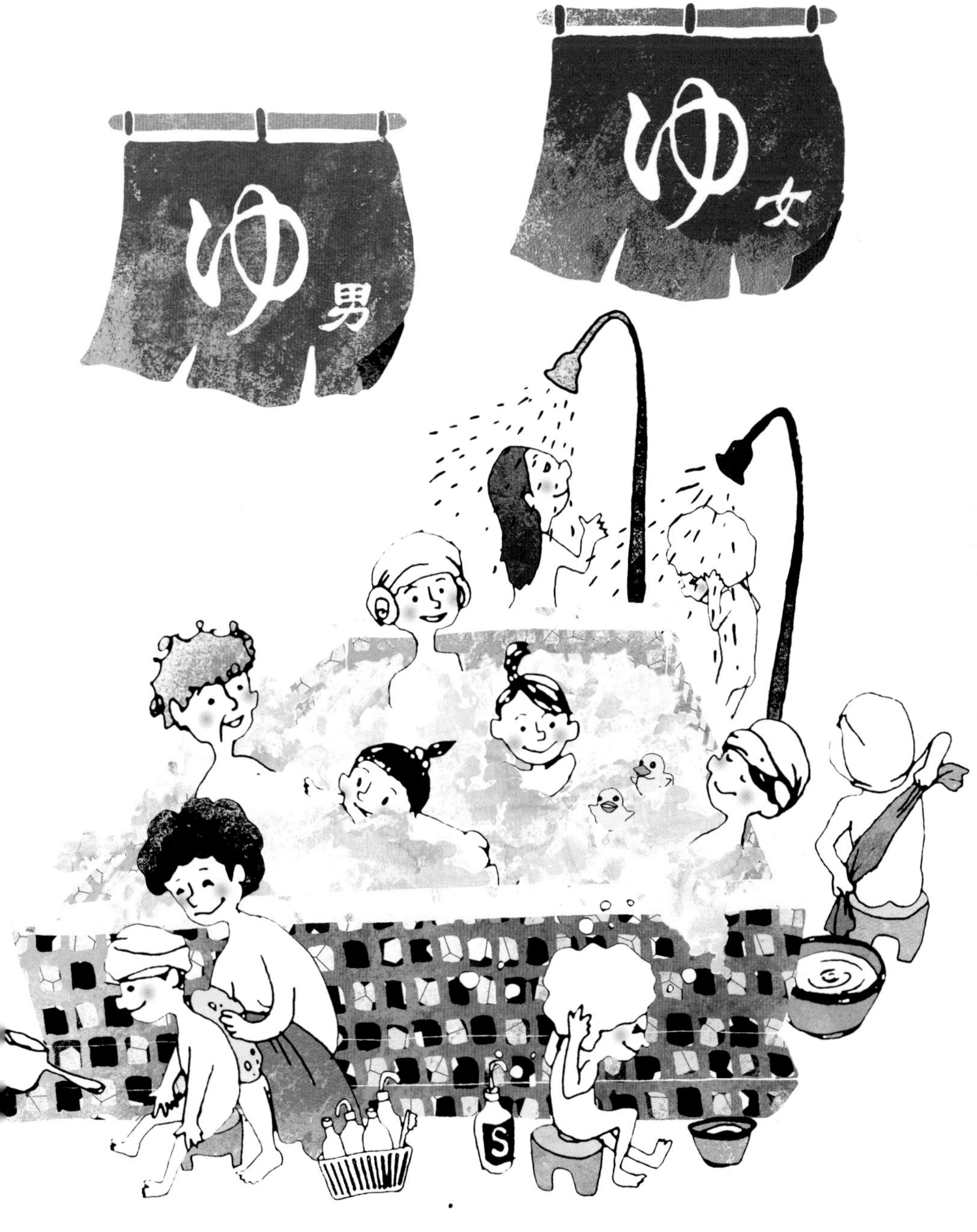
ゆ
男
ゆ
女
S

切腹
Seppuku

Ritual Suicide by Self-disembowelment

Also known by the less formal *hara-kiri*, meaning "stomach-cut," *seppuku* was a horrifically painful death by self-disembowelment using a *tantō* dagger or *wakizashi* short sword.

A samurai who had suffered defeat, whose *daimyō* had died, or who had brought disgrace to their name or clan could elect to commit *seppuku* to restore their honor. Later, the practice developed of *daimyō* or shogun ordering samurai to commit *seppuku* as a judicial punishment.

The origins of *seppuku* are unclear, but the soul was believed to dwell in the *hara,* and as with so much in Japan, the act became highly ritualized. After writing a death poem, the warrior donned a *shini-shōzoku* white kimono, drank a ceremonial cup of *sake* and, gripping his blade with a cloth, cut his abdomen from left to right, while a *kaishaku* (second person) would be on hand to decapitate him with a *katana*. A full *hara-kiri* required further cuts and extraordinary self-control, leading many *kaishaku* to decapitate the samurai early to spare him from the pain. One samurai who elected to perform *seppuku* without a *kaishaku* was reported to have taken an excruciating 18 hours to die of his wounds. The *kaishaku* could be a friend, comrade or even victorious adversary showing respect for his defeated foe. A perfect *daki-kubi* (literally "embrace-neck") cut would, with a single stroke, leave the samurai's head still attached by a small piece of flesh, though theories vary as to the reason for this.

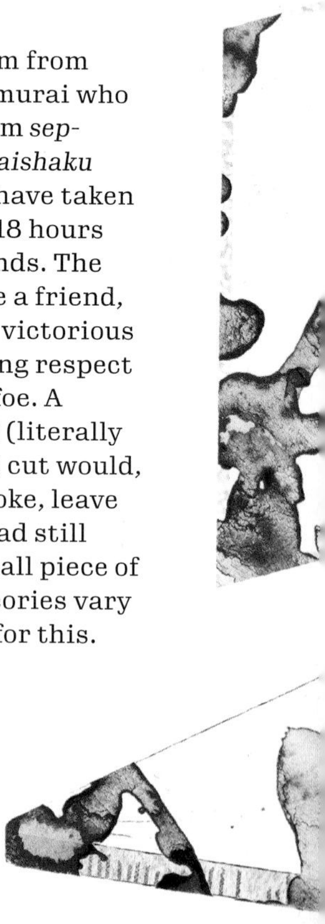

Junshi

The practice of *junshi*, or following a master in death, is believed to predate *seppuku*, with Chinese texts recording the Japanese engaging in it in the 7th century. Performing *junshi* after a lord committed *seppuku* was known as *oibara* or *tsuifuku*, which both use the characters for "follow" and "stomach." The last notable *seppuku* was in 1970 by Nobel Literature Prize nominee Mishima Yukio after a failed coup attempt. Some have suggested that the history of honorable *seppuku* is one reason for Japan's relatively high modern suicide rate.

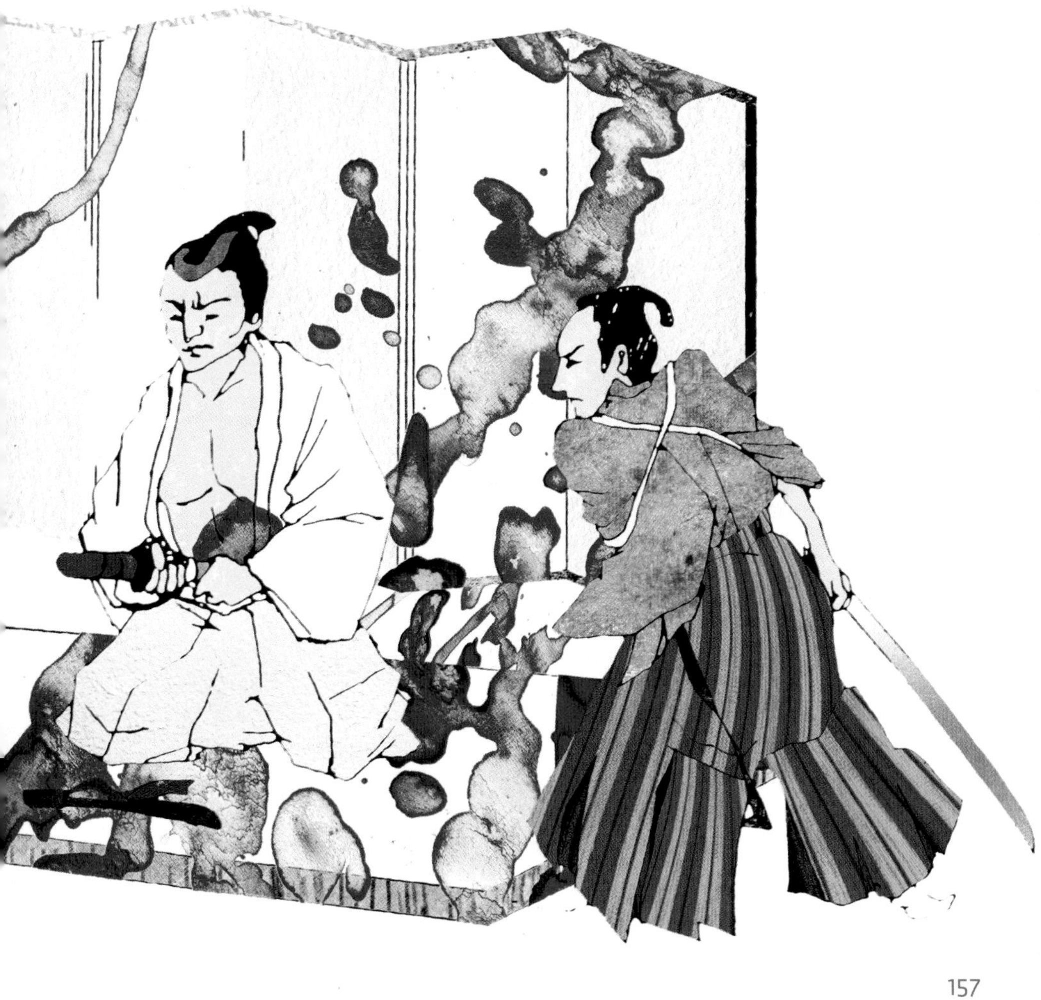

三味線
Shamisen

The Three-stringed Japanese Lute

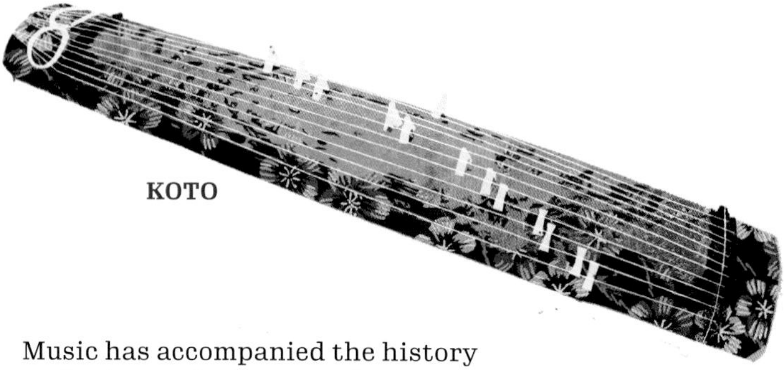

KOTO

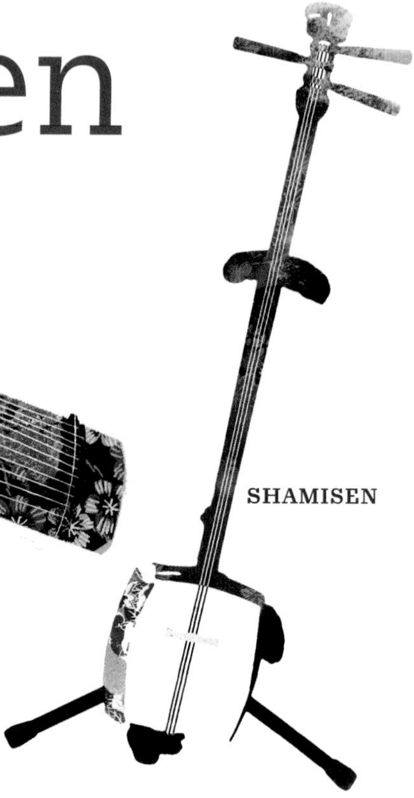

SHAMISEN

Music has accompanied the history and culture of Edo. It was back in the period between the 17th and 19th centuries that this lute of Chinese origin reached the peak of its popularity. It was the *shamisen* that provided the salient notes of the music used in *Kabuki* and *Bunraku,* the tremendously popular puppet theater in the new mercantile cities. And it was once again the *shamisen,* sometimes combined with the flute and the Japanese harp known as the *koto,* that was played by *geisha* to entertain clients at banquets. The instrument consists of a small, square case, attached to which is a long neck fitted with three strings that are plucked with a plectrum.

The case, originally covered with snake skin, was later made out of dog or cat leather. The unavailability of these materials, however, is condemning the instrument to inevitable decline.

Koto

This 13-stringed horizontal harp arrived in Japan from China along with a series of court rituals and amusements around the 7th century. During the Heian period, it was played alone as a background to the recitation of poetry, and continued for a long time to be the instrument of aristocratic ceremony. It was only in the mid-17th century that the great blind composer Yatsuhashi Kengyō came up with a musical repertoire suitable for a broader public.

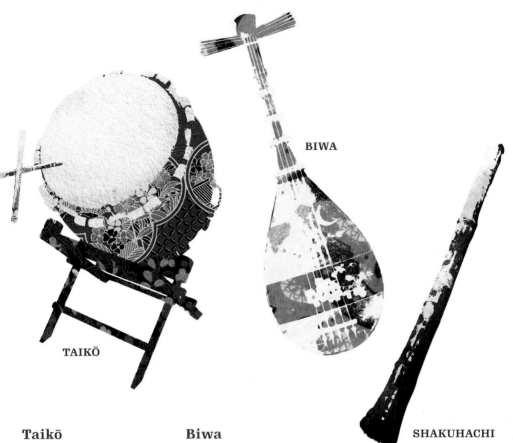

BIWA

TAIKŌ

SHAKUHACHI

Taikō

In Japan, the drum is widely used at religious ceremonies and in the theater and comes in many types. The largest, which is barrel-shaped, is used at folk festivals and for *Bugaku*, or imperial court dances. It is beaten vertically with sticks. The smaller type is slung over the shoulder or by one's side and is beaten by hand.

Biwa

This was the instrument of itinerant blind minstrels (*biwa hōshi*), who began traveling from village to village with this type of mandolin in the 13th century, reciting the exploits of early samurai heroes.

Shakuhachi

Derived from a bamboo cane and played like a clarinet, this is the instrument of Zen monks for whom it is basically a meditation tool. Today, one hears it played around New Year by *komuso*, musicians whose faces are covered with a distinctive basket.

指圧
Shiatsu

Japanese Finger-pressure Therapy

The roots of *shiatsu* lie in the techniques of *anma*, a form of body therapy said to have developed in the early 14th century. *Anma* was itself derived from traditional Chinese medicine and is based on the belief that there is a life force energy that flows through meridians in the body. Known variously as *chi*, *qi* or, in Japan as *ki*, blockages in the energy are said to cause illnesses, injuries and psychological problems. *Anma* was further boosted in the 17th century by a blind acupuncturist, Sugiyama Waichi, who founded schools to teach blind practitioners. Subsequently, the Tokugawa shogunate issued an edict banning sighted people from becoming *anma* practitioners, leaving it the preserve of the blind. Even today, there are many blind massage therapists in Japan.

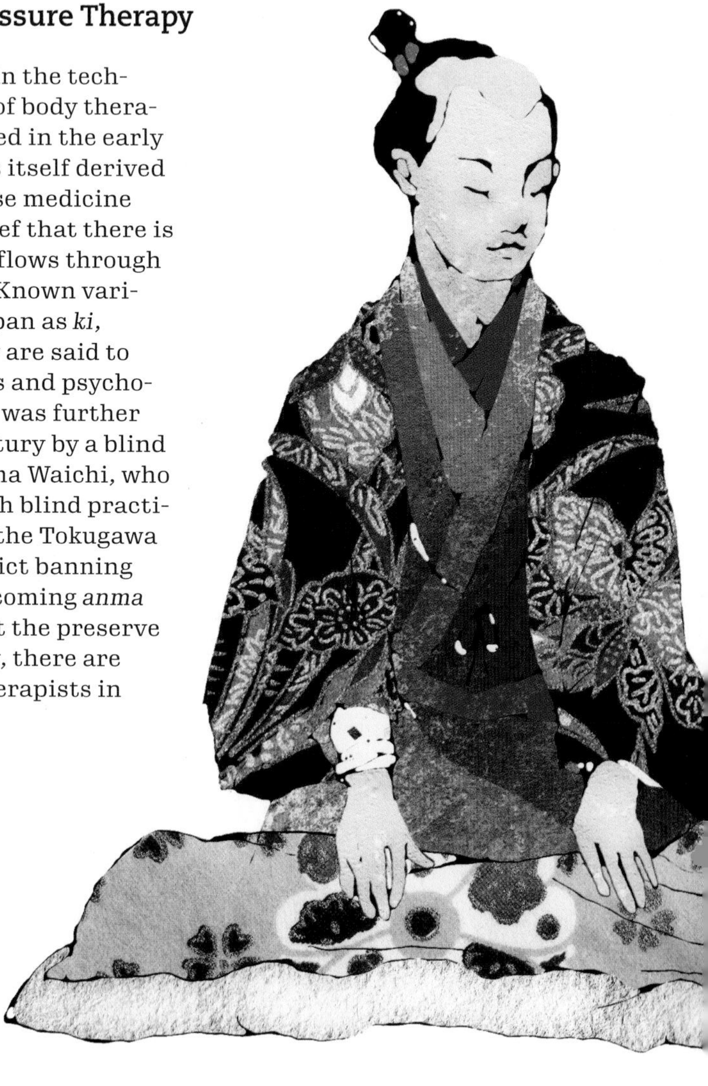

Shiatsu, made up of the characters for "finger" and "pressure," gained recognition by the government in the 1940s mainly due to the efforts of Tokujiro Namikoshi, who pioneered the modern version of the practice. A number of his students went on to establish their own forms of *shiatsu*, including Shizuto Masunaga, who formed a Zen *shiatsu* school. Although the fingers are the main instrument of *shiatsu*, thumbs, palms, feet and elbows are also used by some practitioners.

After the war, the occupying American authorities forbade the practice of *shiatsu*, along with other traditional medicines and various aspects of Japanese culture thought to be associated with nationalist tendencies. American deaf-blind activist Helen Keller lobbied the US government to end the ban on the grounds that it prevented numerous blind practitioners from working. The ban was lifted and Keller went on to be a hero in Japan, where her story is still taught in schools.

Even though *shiatsu* has gained popularity globally, there is no scientific evidence of its effectiveness or of the existence of *ki* power or meridians.

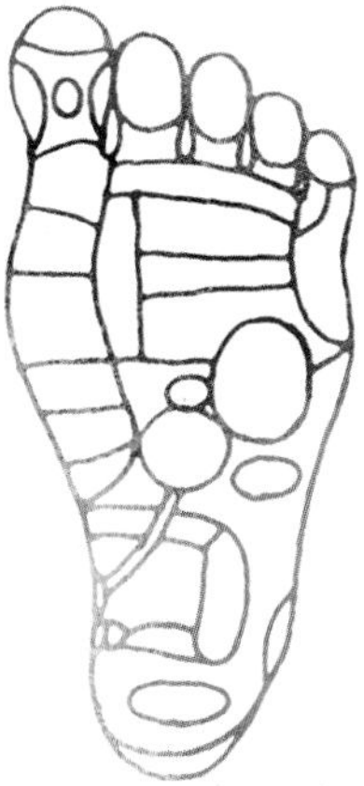

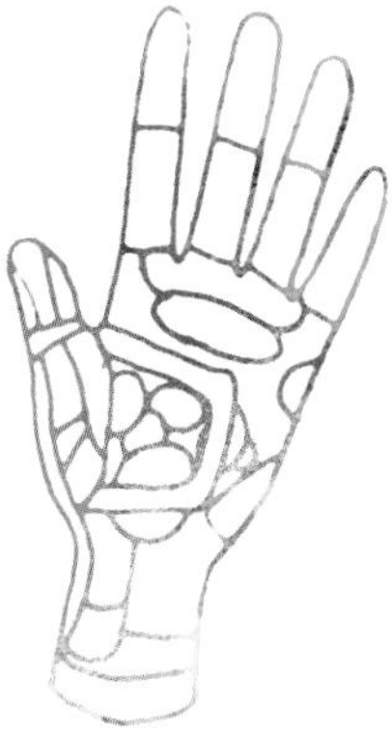

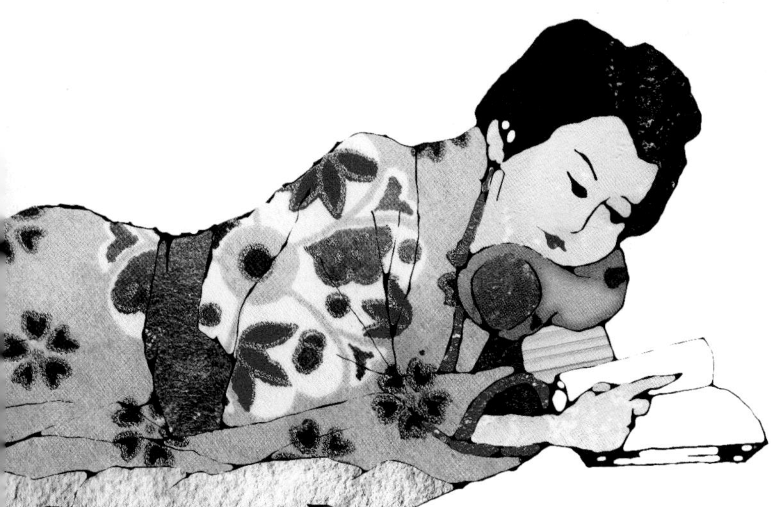

渋い
Shibui

Understated and Elusive Beauty

In Japan, true beauty is *shibui*, that is, "rough and inconspicuous," poised between rusticity and refinement, spontaneity and deliberation. *Shibui* is the vague sweetness with a sour aftertaste of the barely ripe persimmon, far removed from the full, cloying and ultimately boring sweetness known as *amai*.

Already used in the Middle Ages to describe the acrid flavor of certain unripe fruits that sets one's teeth on edge, the term took on aesthetic value during the Edo period. Then it came to be used to describe settings, objects and clothing of a subdued, nearly monastic elegance that eschews ostentation and ornament and can thus be appreciated only by a sharp and cultivated eye. Here we find ourselves at a great distance from the Western concept of beauty, *amai*, which in keeping with its meaning seeks symmetry and perfection of form, favors smooth and flawless surfaces, and lays emphasis on uniqueness and ornamentation.

Shibui is the interior of a traditional Japanese house in which rigid lines are paired with exquisite details and top-quality materials. *Shibui* manifests itself in irregular and asymmetrically shaped pottery that connotes spontaneity, coarse textiles that capture the earthy colors of nature, gardens deliberately designed to appear informal, the unaffected kindness that reigns over a tea ceremony. Generally, *shibui* applies to artifacts and constructions that do not exalt the ego of their maker, but are instead harmoniously and humbly integrated into their surroundings. *shibui* is anything that announces its presence with noble simplicity, that is effective without drawing attention to the effort behind it, that is precious without flaunting its value. The philosopher Yanagi Sōetsu tried to define this fluid and nuanced concept in a series of articles published in Kōgei magazine between 1930 and 1940. But the concept of *shibui* cannot be learned from a book. Like Zen enlightenment, it is something one either has or doesn't have.

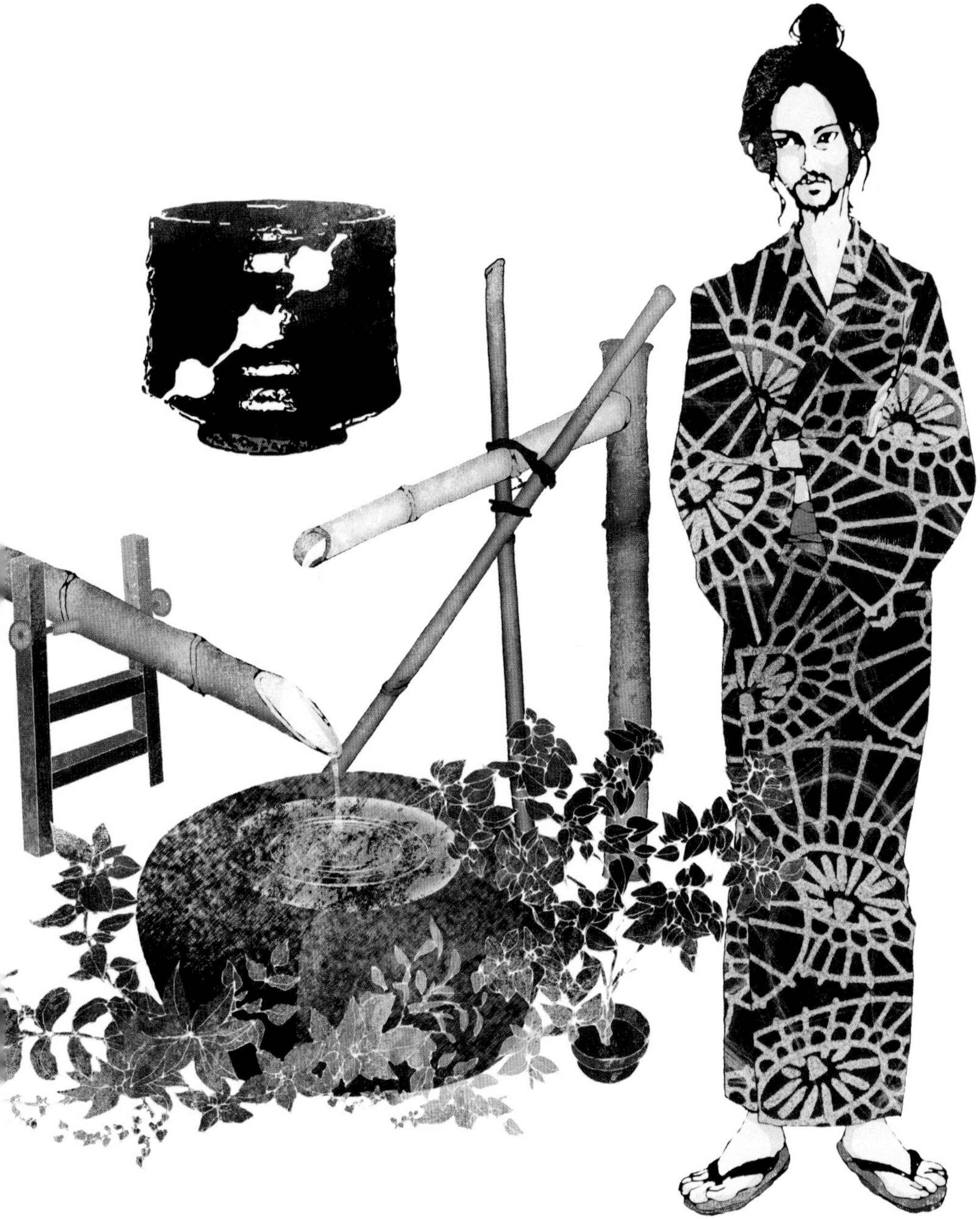

神道
Shintō

The Way of the Gods

The oldest religion in Japan is an animistic one in which ancestral shamanic rituals and a rich mythological tradition continue to survive. Although Shinto means "the way of the gods," the *kami* that it venerates are not divinities in the proper sense, but personifications of the forces of nature, the spirits of ancestors worthy of hallowed respect. Here the important dichotomy is not that of good and evil, but of pure and impure. This is the cult of a people that holds terrestrial and celestial phenomena in awe, that feels it must ingratiate itself with the powers that be in order not to succumb to them but instead to enjoy prosperity and fertility. Indeed, the great annual festivals known as *matsuri,* as well as the rites generally celebrated by Shinto priests, revolve around purification ceremonies, exorcisms or the presentation of votive offerings to appease and extol the *kami*. The liturgy, once linked to the annual cycle of rice cultivation, has by now adapted itself to the realities of modern modes of production, but even today no company celebrates its foundation without inviting a Shinto priest to perform the appropriate propitiatory rite.

Jinja

One approaches the Shinto shrine (*jinja*) through a tall, unusual trestle-shaped portal (*torii*) that leads to the sacred enclosure. The site also usually includes a fountain at which one can purify one's hands and mouth prior to prayer. The most important Shinto sanctuary is that of Ise, which is dedicated to the sun goddess.

Kami

Thousands of these exist. Some, such as the sun goddess Amaterasu Ōmikami, from whom the imperial family supposedly descends, are proper divinities. Others are spirits associated with natural phenomena: mountains, waterfalls, trees or particularly impressive stones.

Ashiwade

This is the term for a double clap performed before the sanctuary in order to draw the attention of the *kami* to whom a prayer is being directed.

Shimenawa

This is a large rope from which hang long tufts of straw and strips of white paper folded into zigzags. It may be bound around a tree or rock, for example, as it delimits or marks sacred space.

Kamidana

Every home contains an altar for holding amulets that symbolize the most highly revered *kami*, as well as offerings of flowers, fruit and *sake* to ancestors so that these may bless the house and protect the family.

書道
Shodō

The Spiritual Art of Calligraphy

In Japan, calligraphy can become a spiritual exercise. *Shodō*, "the way of writing," developed into a mode of meditation in Zen circles in the 12th and 13th centuries before becoming an art form. Its meaning can be fully gleaned from the image of a monk kneeling on a *tatami* while slowly grating a stick of black charcoal into water until it has turned into ink of the desired shade, then, holding a long brush or letting it drip, completing a mark with absolute concentration. A unique, perfect stroke, as definitive as a ritual, that will leave a trace of his soul on the paper.

It is difficult for the layman to imagine the long and painstaking training needed to execute that mark, which seems so spontaneous. Calligraphy is as demanding an art as painting, of which it is considered a fundamental complement. In the East, a good painter must first and foremost be a good calligrapher. It is from ideograms rather than landscapes that he learns about the pressure of the brush, the rhythm of positive and negative space, and above all how to make deliberate strokes appear spontaneous. Whatever the content of the written word or sentence, the important thing is that it communicates the spirit of him who executes it, not only through its meaning, but also through the quality of the sign, just as painting does.

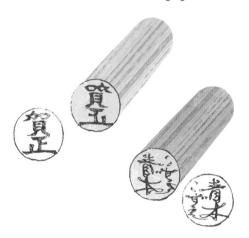

Kanji and kana

Japanese writing consists of ideograms (*kanji*) and phonetic characters (*kana*), which are used together. Both can be the subject of an exercise in calligraphy.

Hanko

In Japan, a seal (*hanko*), usually square in form, with the ideogram of the name engraved on it, is used in place of a signature. The inevitable red dot that adds vitality to calligraphy is provided by the seal.

Washi

Calligraphy is done on thin and extremely absorbent traditional paper, hand crafted out of fibers of a type of mulberry. It is called *washi*, which simply means "Japanese paper," and has been included in the list of UNESCO Cultural Heritage items since 2014.

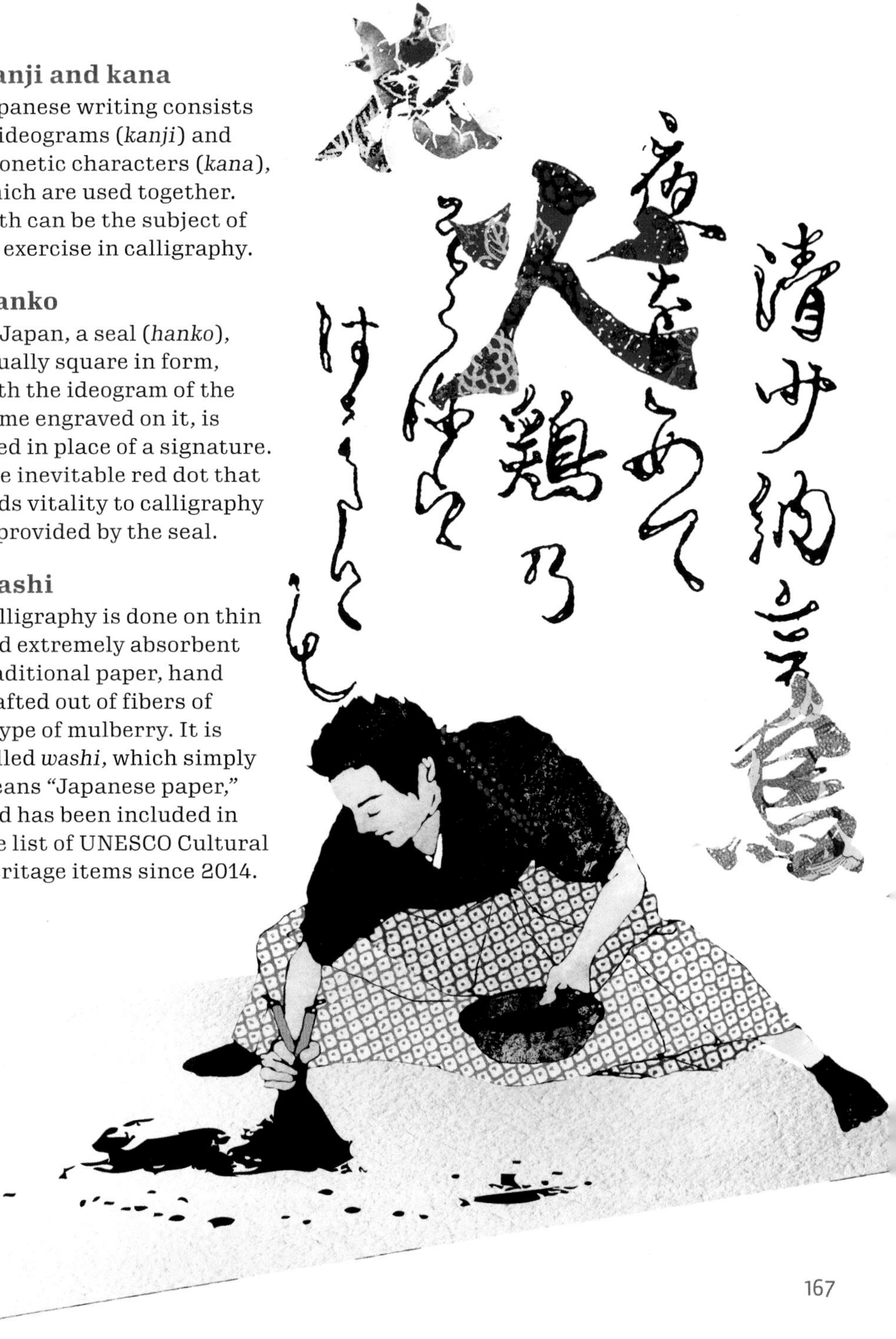

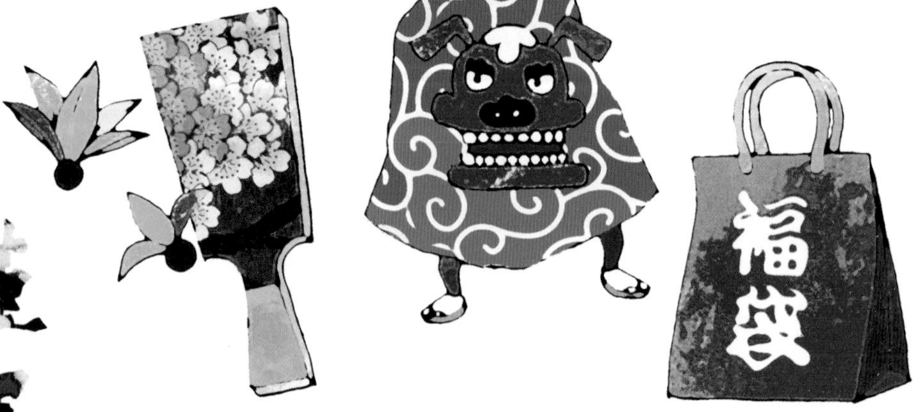
福袋

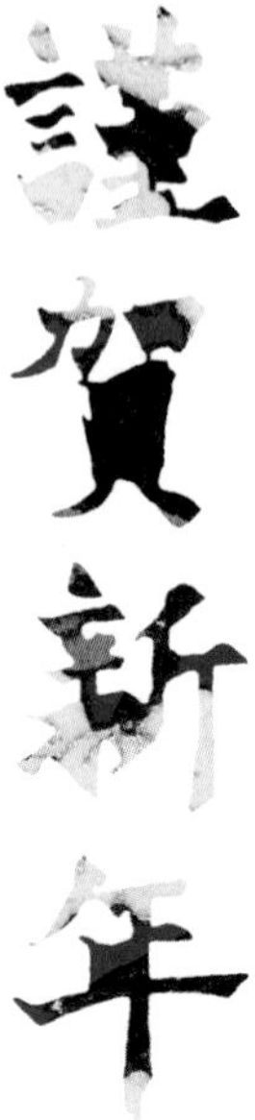
謹賀新年

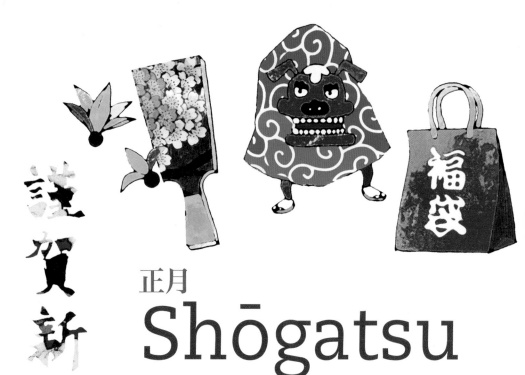

正月

Shōgatsu

The New Year's Celebrations

New Year is a crucial event, underscored by the length of its celebration which begins several days prior with a thorough house cleaning, the decoration of the interior, as well as the preparation of special dishes, and does not end before mid-January. The high point occurs at midnight on December 31 when people pour into the streets to reach the temple of their choice before the bell tolls 108 times and banishes as many bad memories, so that everyone can begin the year in a state of absolute purity as though embarking on a new life. No one sleeps that night, as tradition dictates that people continue dropping by temples until dawn, warming up between visits with a good bowl of *toshikoshi soba*, the noodles "of the new year," which are as long and smooth as the future they wish to each other.

Oseichi

The elaborate New Year's dishes, *oseichi ryōri*, are prepared in the days leading up to the holiday and are carefully arranged in a *jūbako*, a stack of tiered lacquered boxes, each one fitted into the one above, and sealed with a finely decorated lid. Each of the ingredients is prescribed by tradition and corresponds to an auspicious symbol. The menu always includes beans, *kamaboko* (white and red fish paste), chestnuts, certain types of fish and, above all, *mochi*, a sticky rice paste used to prepare a special soup known as *ozōni*.

Kadomatsu

The most common decoration is the *kadomatsu*, an auspicious *ikebana* composed of branches of pine (longevity), plum (courage and success) and bamboo (strength and resistance), and placed on either side of the entrance to the home.

Nengajō

Exchanging greeting cards is imperative. Stationery shops and department stores are full of postcards with good luck images, ranging from Mount Fuji to the crane, as well as signs of the Chinese zodiac.

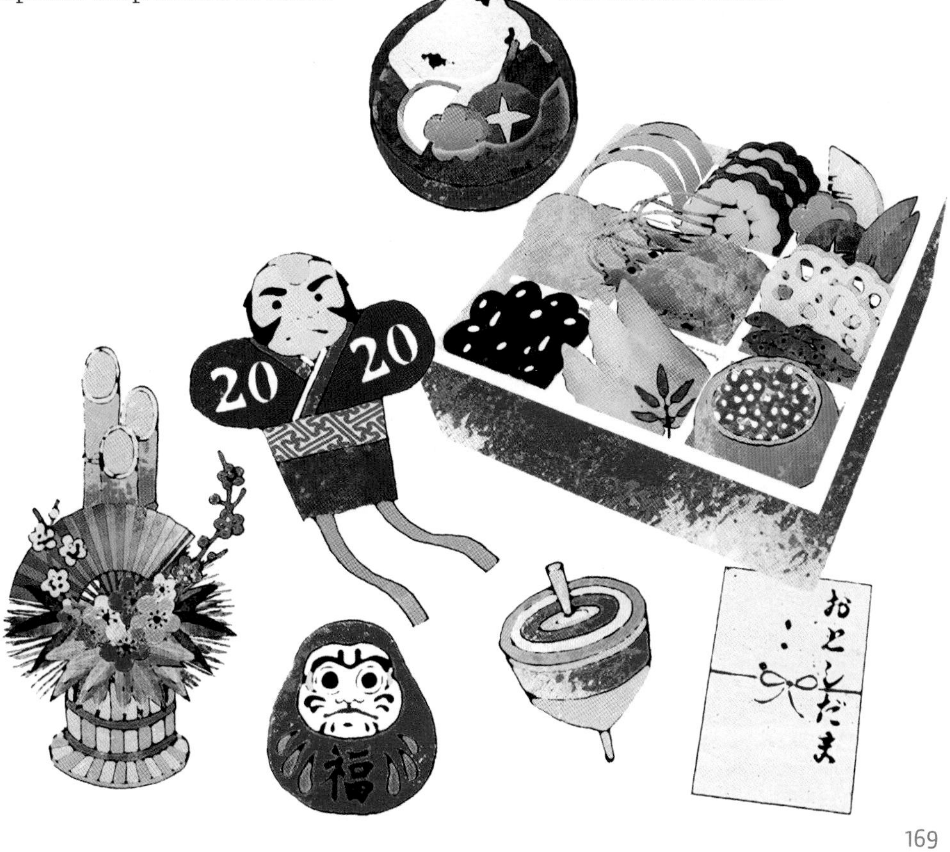
20
20
福
おとしだま

将軍
Shōgun

The Military Overlord

The 10th emperor, Sujin, whose reign is variously estimated to have been between the 1st century BC and the turn of the 3rd century AD, may have been the first to bestow the title shogun. Meaning something akin to "commander-in-chief" or generalissimo, it is believed to have been given to four military commanders who led armies to the four quarters of the nation. Centuries later, the title *sei-i taishogun*, meaning "commander-in-chief to quell barbarians," was given to generals who had successfully fought the *emishi* peoples of northern Japan. In the late 12th century,

Minamoto no Yoritomo became the first shogun as it is understood today, warlords who ruled in the emperor's name. The position was hereditary, though there was continual intriguing and power games among those desiring to influence and rule. The emperor was a mere figurehead during the reigns of most shogun, though many of them, particularly during the Kamakura and Ashikaga shogunates, became little more than puppets themselves. In 1333, the Emperor Go-Daigo overthrew the Kamakura shogunate and restored imperial rule. Three years later, he himself was overthrown by the Ashikagas. Preceding Japan's unification at the dawn of the 17th century, the warlords Oda Nobunaga and Toyotomi Hideyoshi did not take the shogun title, but wielded more power than most who had. Following Tokugawa Ieyasu's victory at the huge and bloody Battle of Sekigahara in 1600, he was awarded the title of shogun in 1603, establishing a shogunate in his family's name that would rule for 250 years. Even the Tokugawa shoguns were not always truly in control, with groups of senior figures from the clan branches sometimes pulling the strings from the shadows. Tokugawa Yoshinobu was the 15th of his line and last shogun, resigning to make way for the Meiji Restoration. The clan still exists and Tokugawa Iehiro, heir to the house, stood for election in 2019 for the main opposition party.

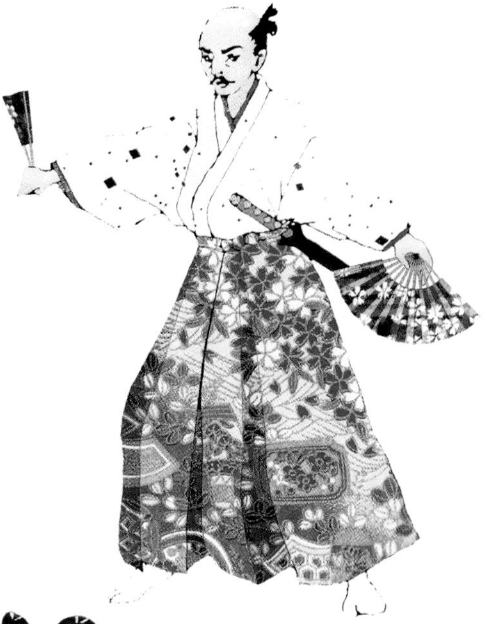

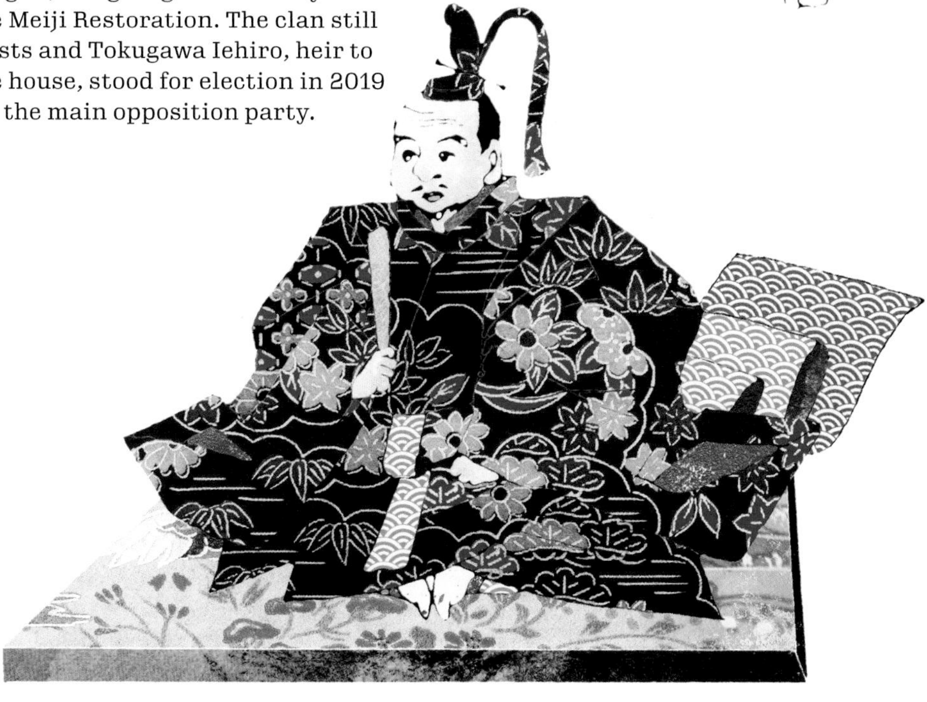

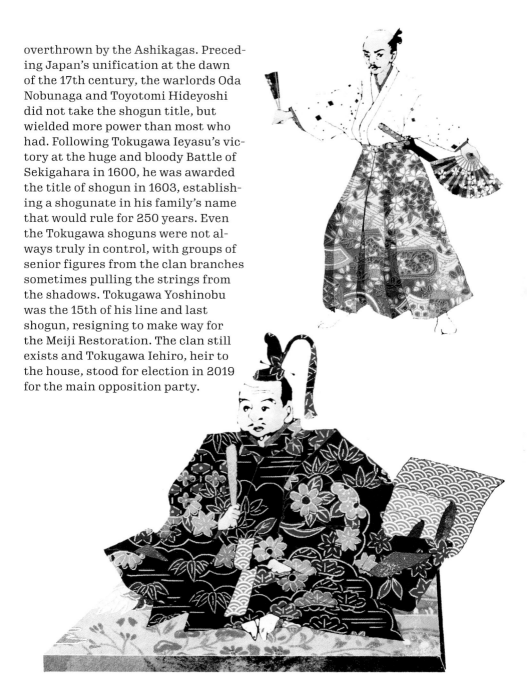

障子
Shōji

Papered Sliding Panels

The traditional Japanese house appears to be of Polynesian origins. The incredible humidity of the region inspired a wooden structure resting on low piles, with large sliding doors to the outside. The most authentic house has neither side walls nor internal partitions. What serves as its walls are *shōji*: sliding panels comprised of a wooden lattice covered with translucent paper. Rooms are created and dissolved by opening or shutting these. When necessary, the entire house can be transformed into a single ceremonial space or subdivided into many tiny rooms.

Even the sliding doors leading outside can be removed to turn the garden into a sort of extension of the house. In old prints, one often sees languid courtesans looking up at an autumn landscape from the alcove in which they are writing or flirting. Penetrating and mirroring each other, interior and exterior speak of the constant search for communion and harmony with nature that animates the Japanese.

Fusuma

According to the great novelist Junichirō Tanizaki, the virtue of *shōji* is to introduce a soft and suffused light into the room, of a kind that no glass can generate. Sometimes, however, the sliding doors are opaque, fully covered with paper or heavy silk, in which case they are called *fusuma*. In the austere Japanese home, virtually devoid of ornamentation, *fusuma* offer a precious support for decorative paintings, usually of landscapes, birds or details of plants and flowers.

Engawa

Outside the *shōji* and along the entire perimeter of the house runs the *engawa*, a sort of veranda that is slightly elevated above the garden and usually paved in wood. Sliding open the *shōji* doors is enough to make the veranda part of the room, a place sheltered by the eaves, in which it is pleasant to sit while silently contemplating the garden.

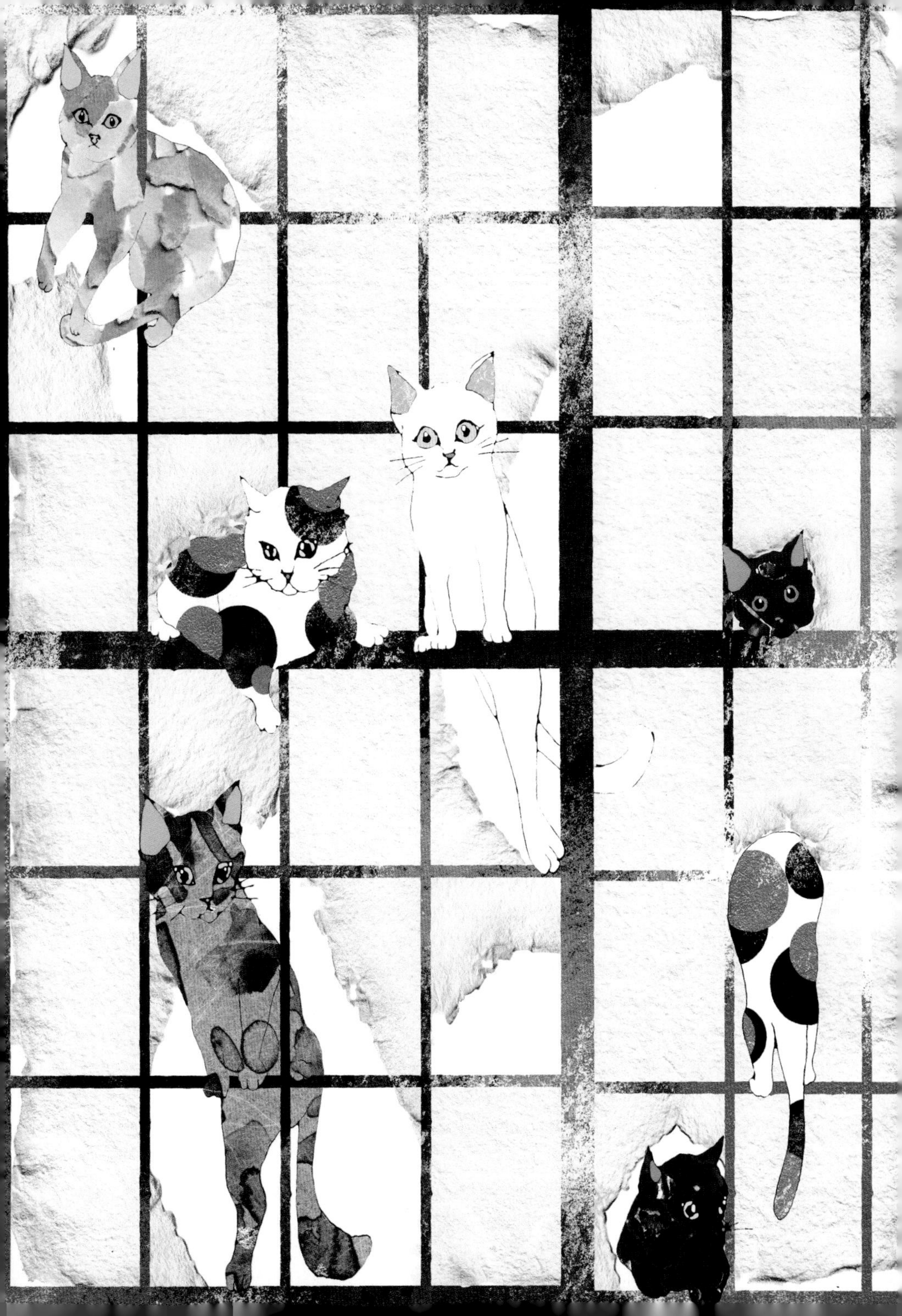

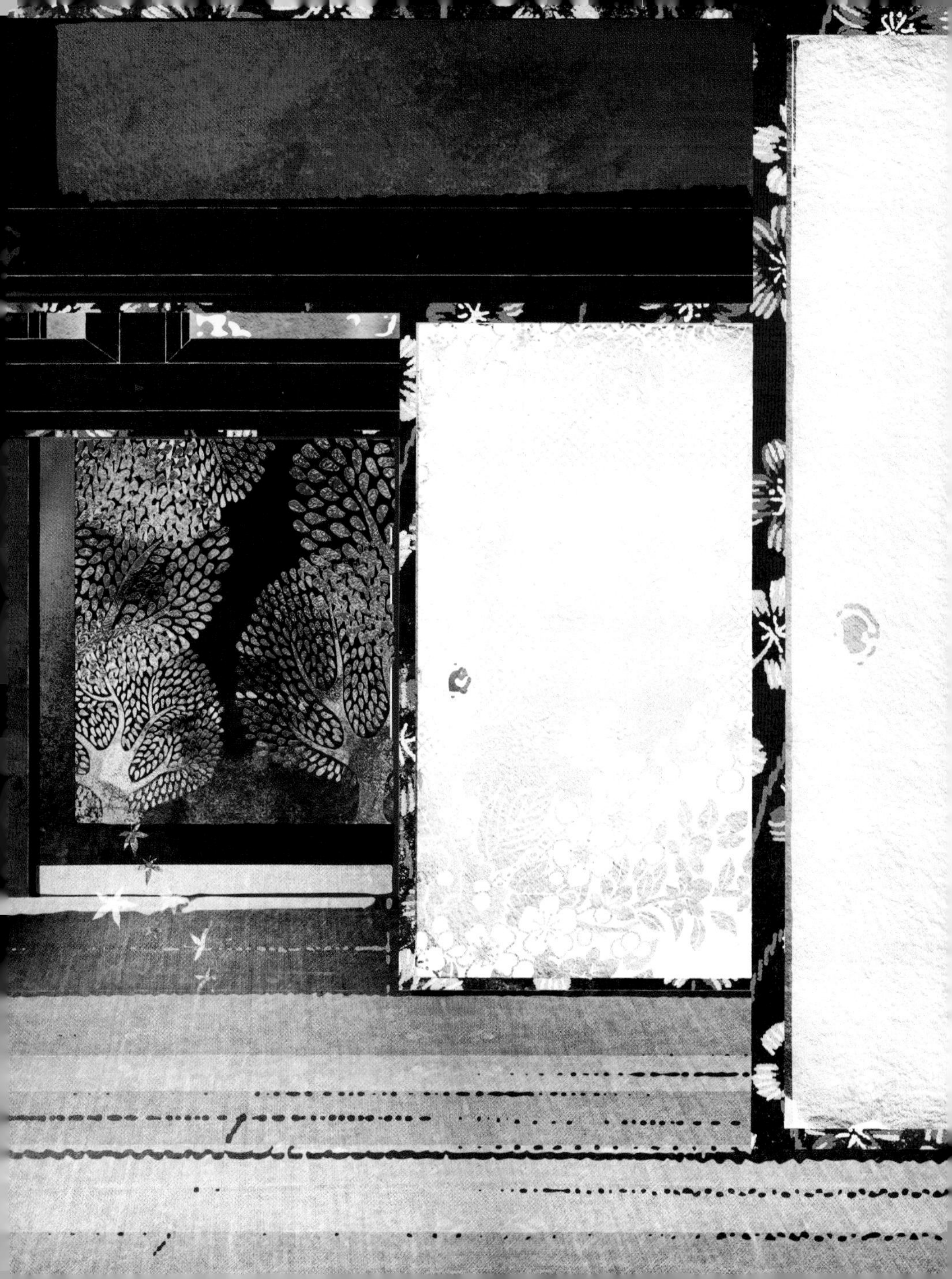

墨絵

Sumi-e

Zen-inspired Ink Paintings

This is the term for monochrome painting done in a particular type of ink known as *sumi*, which is made out of soot and pine resin that have been congealed in a stick. To use *sumi*, one needs to dissolve it in water while patiently rubbing the stick against the bottom of a type of stone inkwell. This slow and repetitive action serves an important function as it calls for a break from the hectic activities of everyday life and a moment of silence and concentration in which one becomes that which one paints. Like calligraphy, *sumi-e* emerged from the shadow of Zen and incorporates all the attributes of that spiritual discipline. For Zen, knowledge is sudden illumination, a lightning-quick flash of intuition unconnected to any logical and discursive process. In order to ignite the mind and open it to truth, art too must not describe things but make their profound essence beam forth.

Thus, while Zen gradually spread throughout Japan, the allusive quality of traditional Chinese black ink made inroads alongside the vivid colors of Heian's didactic and narrative paintings. Between the 15th and late 16th centuries, great artists such as Shūbun, Sesshū and Sesson laid the foundations of an art, still vital today, that reduces things to their essence. At times it is nearly abstract; a few faint brushstrokes can suggest an entire universe.

Favorite themes include landscapes, plants and flowers which convey the Zen ideal of a communion with nature, as well as portraits in which the features of the doctrine's great masters are rendered in a singularly spontaneous and expressive style. Sometimes, however, the center of the painting is devoted to a simple object referring to the decision to lead an ascetic life—a bowl, a saddlebag, a pilgrim's staff—possibly paired with some calligraphy. Exhibited in the *tokonoma*, the ink assumes the role of icon, becoming in its turn an object of meditation.

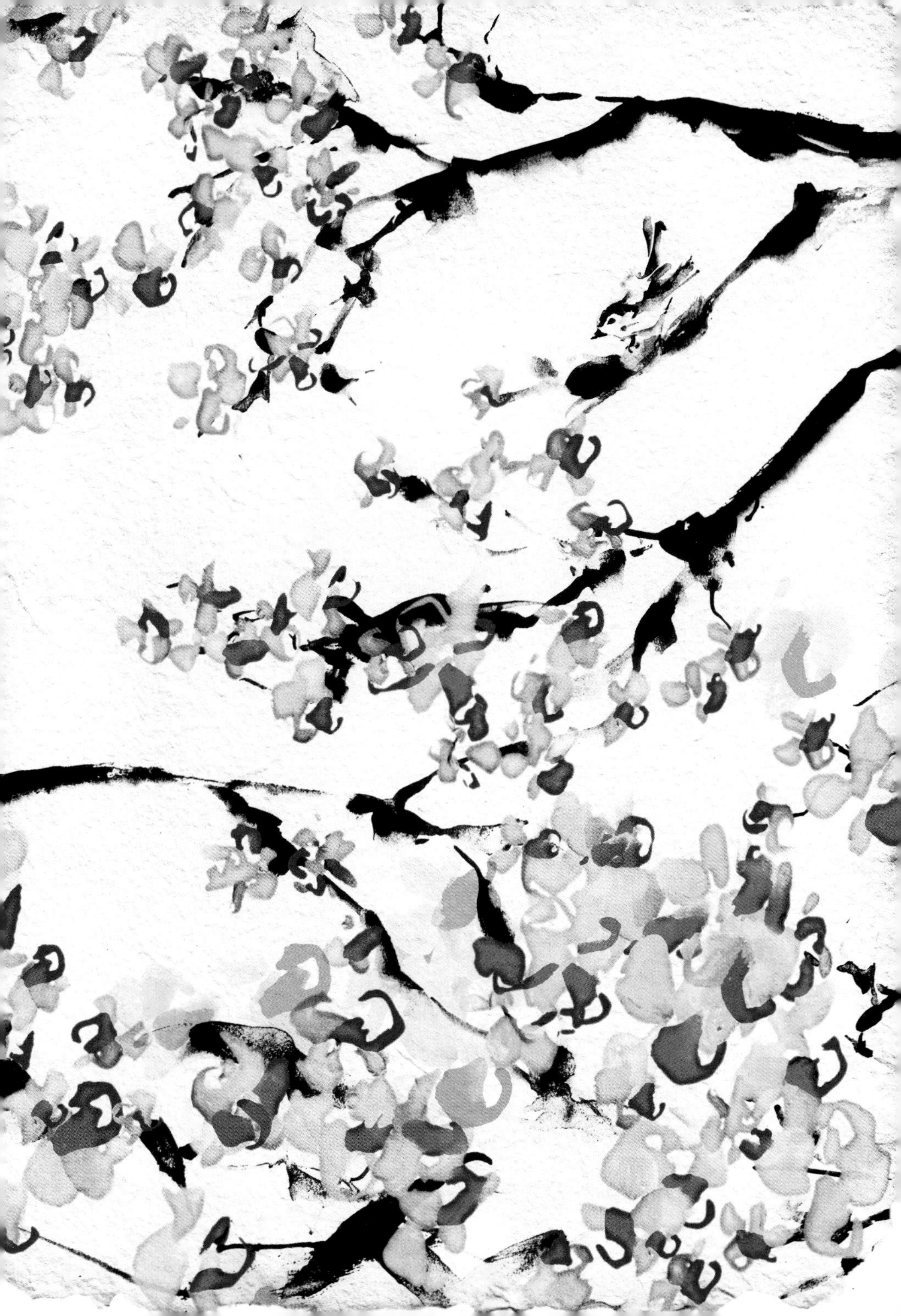

相撲

Sumō

Sumo Wrestlers

There are few sights in sport as viscerally engaging as the moment of impact when two top-knotted giants come together at full speed after minutes of slow, tense build-up. The characters for sumo can be read as "mutual-strike," a simple explanation for a fighting art with more than 70 recognized winning techniques, including shoves, throws, trips, slaps and drags. The rules are straightforward: the first combatant to touch the floor with any part of their body except the foot, or to step out of the ring, loses. Sumo is Japan's official national sport, and though baseball has more fans, the grappling art holds a special place in the country's psyche and culture. The highest-ranked *yokozuna* are revered in ways other sports figures simply aren't.

The history of sumo is hazy, but some form of it has existed for more than a millennium, with Shinto gods being practitioners according to one legend, and it remains steeped in the rituals of the indigenous religion. A Shinto shrine roof sits above the clay *dohyō* ring and referees dress like priests. *Rikishi* (wrestlers) sip sacred water, throw purifying salt and clap to call the gods before a fight. Women may not participate in sumo as their presence on the *dohyō* is said to defile it, causing a number of controversies over the years, including a female mayor prevented from handing out prizes at a tournament.

The life of a *rikishi* is harsh, particularly for the lower ranks. All live in *heya* stables, where they sleep, train and eat huge *chanko-nabe* stews and drink copious amounts of beer to put on weight. Though brutal hazing is largely a thing of the past, fewer young Japanese are willing to endure such hardships, and foreigners have dominated the *yokozuna* ranks in recent decades, with Mongolians holding the title from 2003 to 2017. The promotion of Kisenosato to *yokozuna* in 2017, the first Japanese *rikishi* to be promoted to the top rank since 1998, revived flagging interest, but the popular champion retired in January 2019 due to injury.

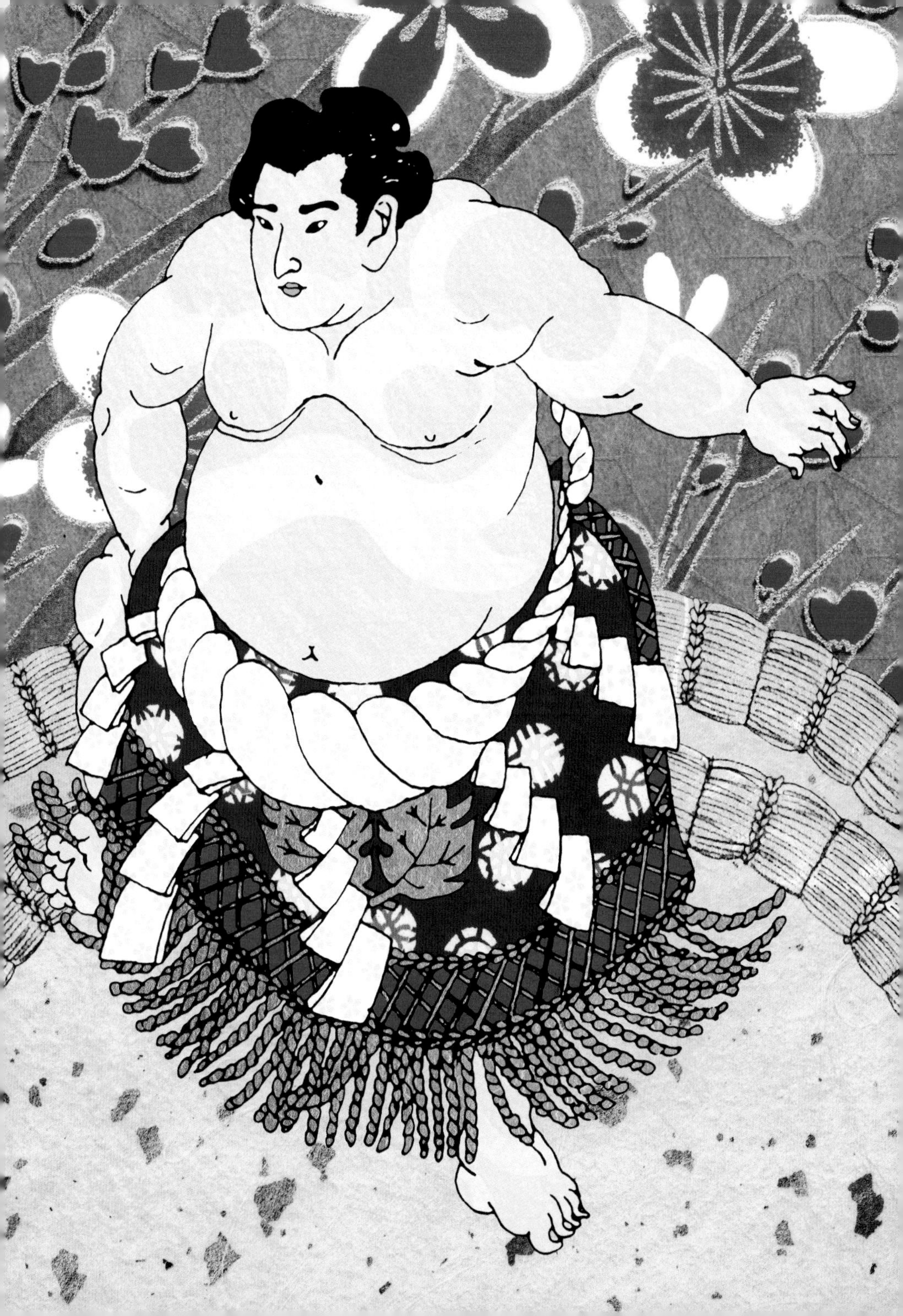

寿司
Sushi

Vinegared Rice with Toppings

Sushi shares a quality with traditional Japanese arts from calligraphy to *ikebana*: an ostensible simplicity obtained through a complex process that involves a great deal of training.

The idea of combining two economic mainstays, rice cultivation and fishing, is ancient and probably derived from practical necessity. Layering cooked rice with salted fish ferments the rice and generates an acid that preserves the fish. In the early 19th century, Hanaya Yohei, a famous chef from Edo, came up with the idea of preparing the dish in bite-sized pieces, thus inventing the refined *nigiri-zushi* that we know today.

The fresh and light *sappari* quality that the neatly arranged pieces on the tray emanate actually entails a difficult technique of filleting and slicing fish, and even a personal knowledge of little secret tricks for cooking and seasoning the rice, because, as Japanese gourmets tell us, it is by the rice and not the fish that the excellence of *sushi* is judged.

Sashimi

Deba, yanagiba and *maguro bōchō* are some of the special, super sharp and carefully calibrated knives needed to prepare the principal item of the formal Japanese lunch. *Sashimi,* composed of slices of artfully prepared raw fish garnished with *daikon* and *shiso* leaves, is based on the perfection of the cut, which is performed with various techniques depending on the type of fish. Once deboned, the fillets must be sectioned on a bias in the opposite direction from the veins to obtain small, uniform slices. These are around a centimeter thick, unless one chooses thinly sliced *usu-zukuri* (suitable for gilthead or plaice), cubed *kaku-zukuri* or strips of *ito-zukuri*.

In any case, this is a delicate operation, learned at special schools, which until a few decades ago admitted no women. In Japan, the handling of fish is by tradition a strictly male affair.

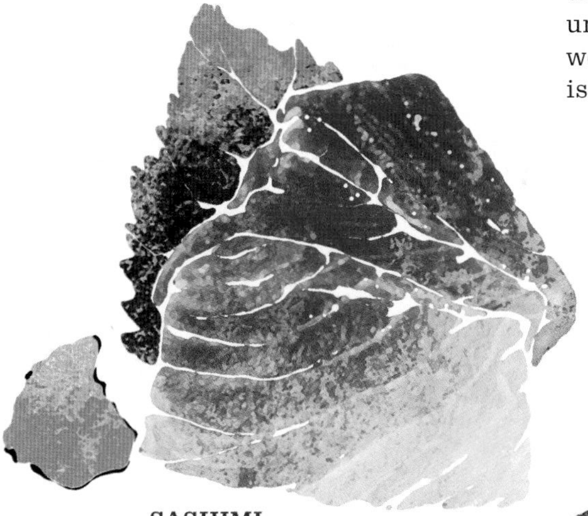

SASHIMI

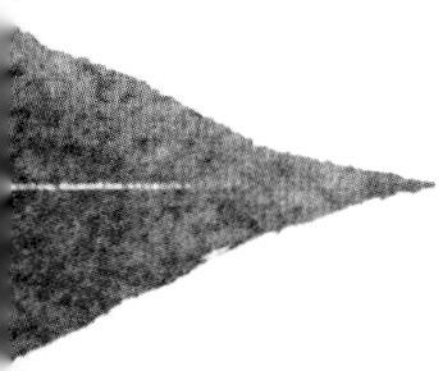

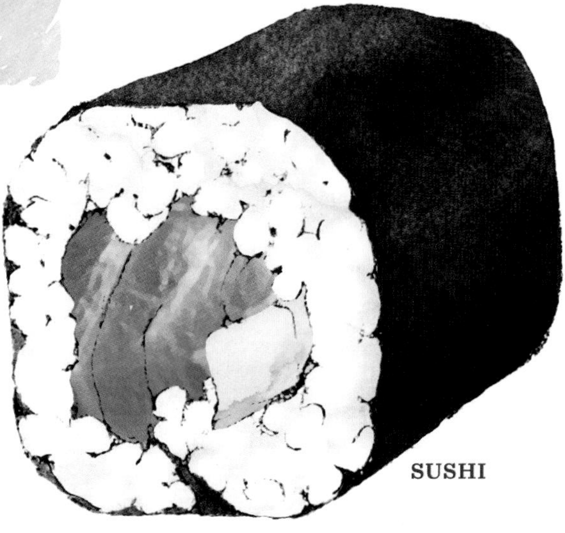

SUSHI

握り寿司

NIGIRI-ZUSHI

hand-formed sushi

まぐろ

MAGURO

tuna

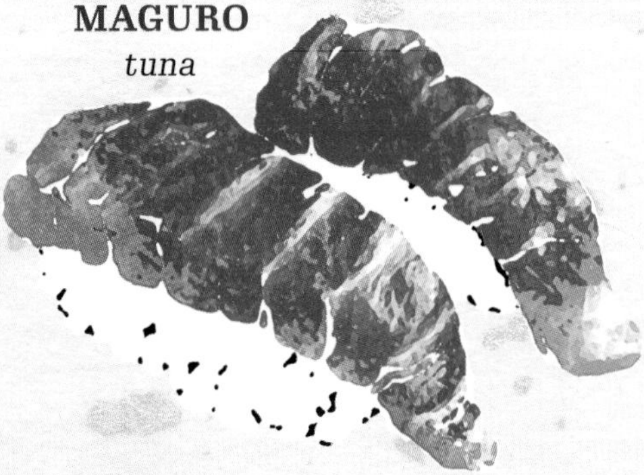

うに

UNI

sea urchin roe

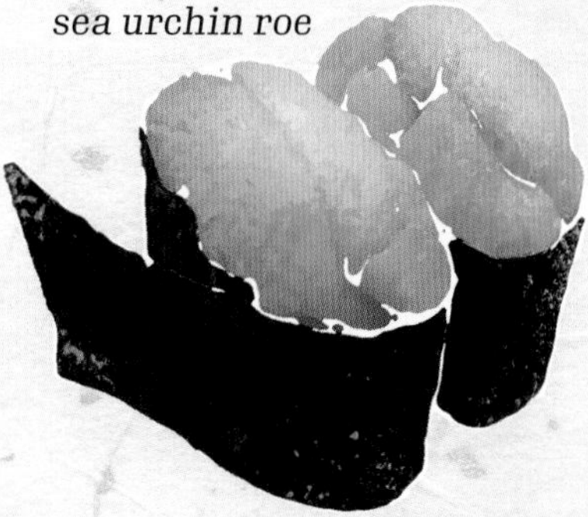

はまち

HAMACHI

rock salmon

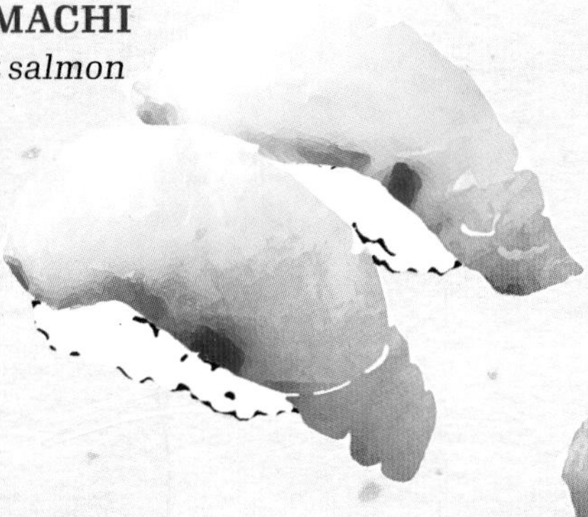

たまご

TAMAGO

egg

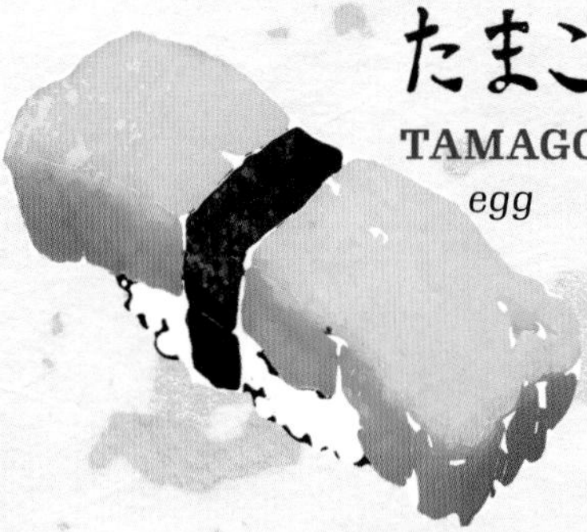

甘えび

AMAEBI

shrimp

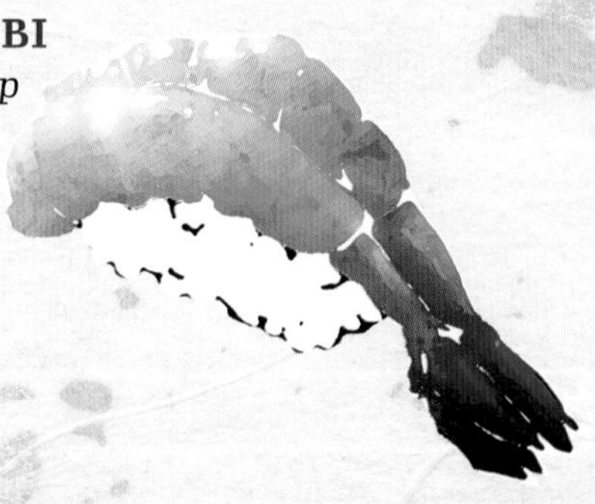

How to prepare "good luck sushi" 恵方巻つくり方

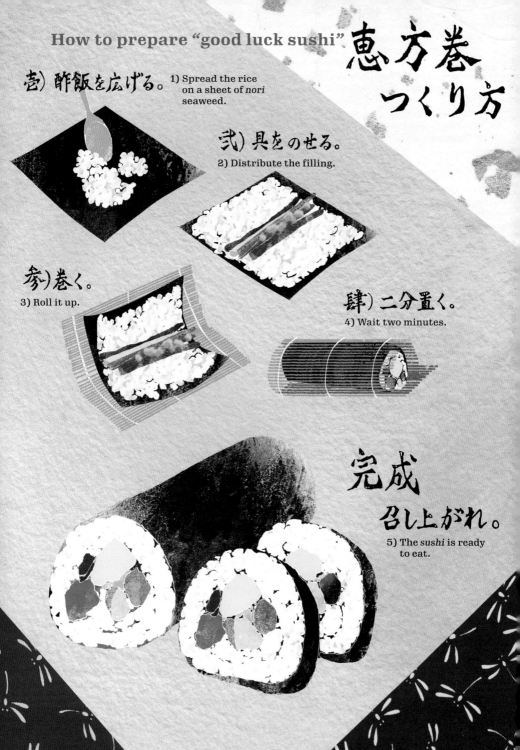

壱）酢飯を広げる。

1) Spread the rice on a sheet of *nori* seaweed.

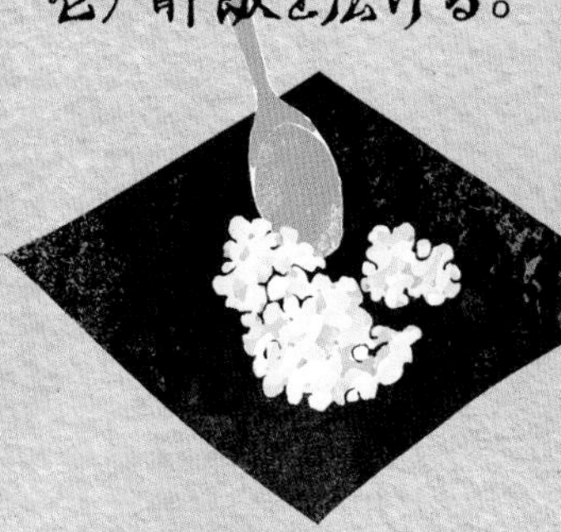

弐）具をのせる。

2) Distribute the filling.

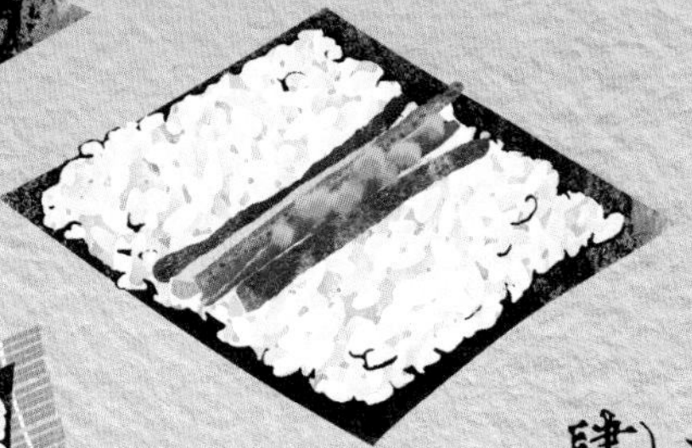

参）巻く。

3) Roll it up.

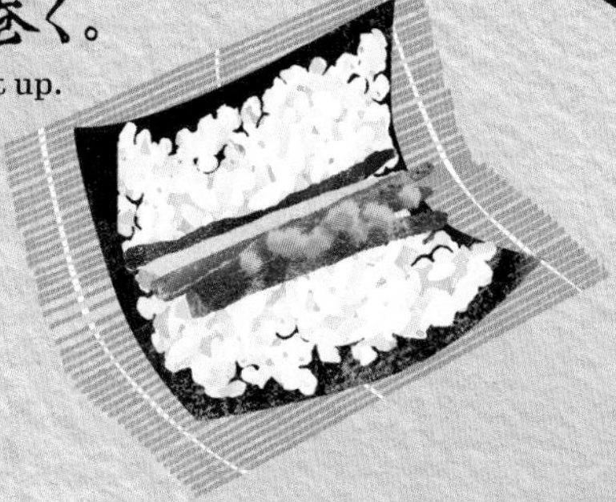

肆）二分置く。

4) Wait two minutes.

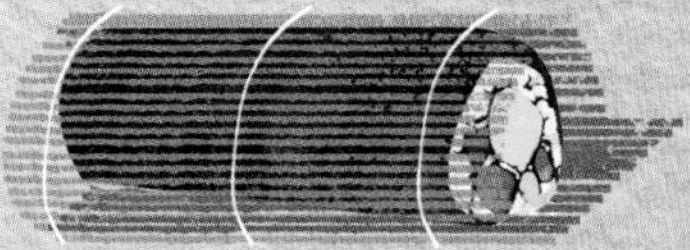

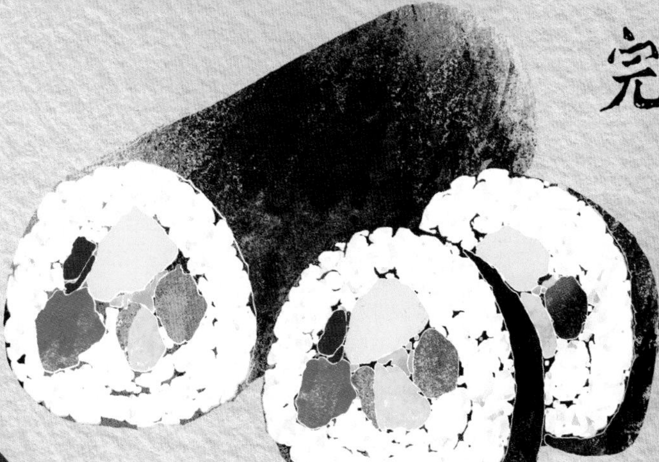

完成

召し上がれ。

5) The *sushi* is ready to eat.

七夕
Tanabata

Festival of the Weaver and the Herdsman

The feast day of *Tanabata*, or the seventh night, remains one of Japan's most poignant holidays. It is a celebration of a legend known to every Japanese child, that of the Weaver and the Herdsman, personifications, in fact, of the stars Vega and Altair.

Simply put, kept apart by gods envious of their love, the weaver Orihime and the herdsman Hikoboshi are permitted to meet only once a year, on the seventh day of the seventh lunar month, that is, July/August 7. On that magical day, a flock of magpies arrives and arranges itself into a chain in order to create a bridge over which the two lovers can cross the celestial river that separates them. This is, in fact, the time of the year when Vega and Altair become visible on either side of the Milky Way. This astronomically oriented legend arrived in Japan from China around the 8th century and merged with an older Shintō ceremony in which a female shaman wove a robe for the gods so that they would protect the rice crop. The literal meaning of *Tanabata* is "loom."

Many Japanese cities, but above all Sendai, hold impressive celebrations on this feast day that include the extensive decoration of streets with huge, streamer-bearing colored orbs, or *kusudama*, as well as food stalls and parades. The most highly anticipated moment, however, is the formulation of one's heart's desire in the hope that like Orihime and Hikoboshi's it will be fulfilled.

Tanzaku

Tradition has it that on the night of *Tanabata*, one should make a wish and write it down, possibly in poetic form, on a small strip of colored paper, or *tanzaku*, and tie it to a branch of bamboo.

Fukinashi

These are the streamers hung everywhere on the feast day. Floating in the wind, they symbolize the threads woven by Orihime.

Kamigoromo

These special paper kimonos, offered as a prayer to the gods, promise to improve sewing skills and protect against disease and misfortune.

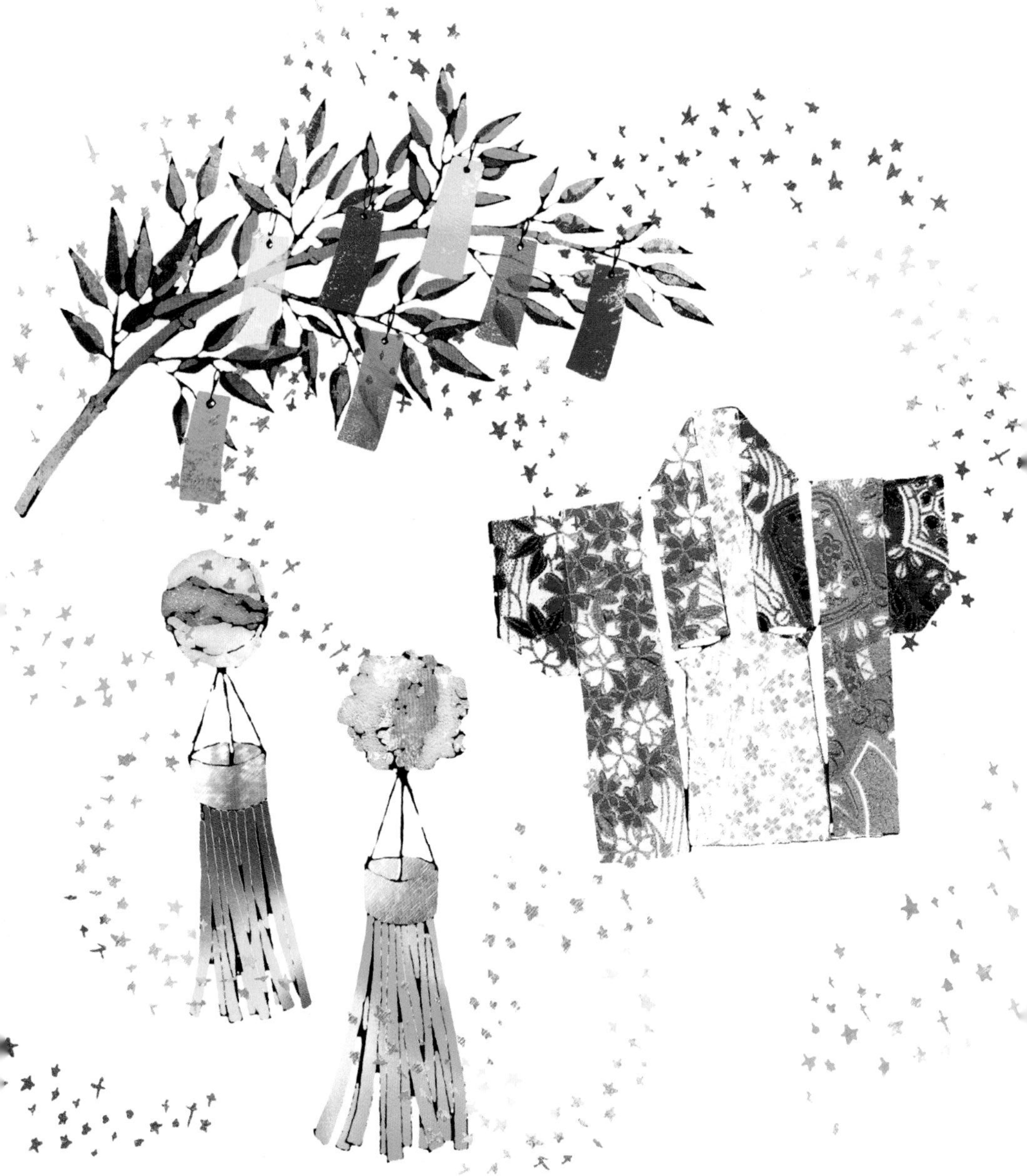

畳

Tatami

Soft Straw-woven Floor Mats

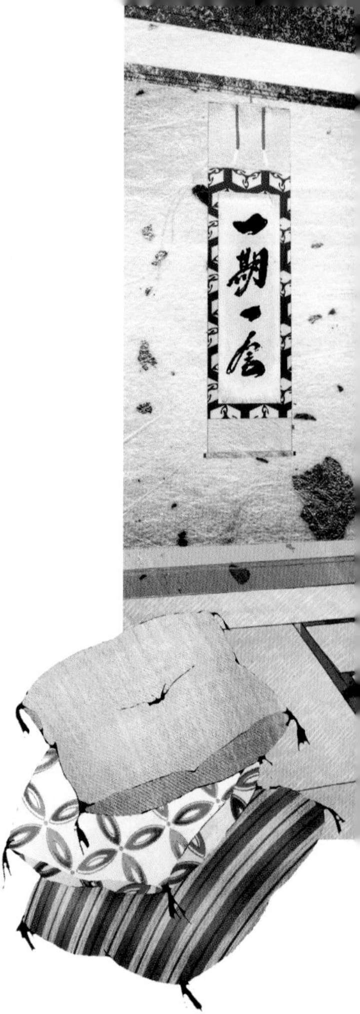
一期一会

What immediately identifies a house as Japanese is a particular type of soft, straw-scented flooring material known as *tatami*. It consists of woven mats, typically 90 cm x 180 cm (3 ft x 6 ft), edged in fabric and placed side by side to cover the entire floor of a room. Below these is a layer of coarser straw padding that makes the floor elastic, so that one can sit comfortably either cross-legged or kneeling on ones legs. These are so inseparable from the image of a home that the dimensions of an interior are usually expressed in *tatami*, as if they were units of measurement.

Washitsu

Even the most modern house usually has one traditional room, known as the *washitsu* ("Japanese room"), with *tatami* and *tokonoma*. The most important room in the home, it houses the altar with offerings for gods and ancestors.

Tokonoma

According to the rigorous rules governing the Japanese house, the only legitimate place to place an ornament is the *tokonoma*, a wide niche, raised slightly above the rest of the room, in which examples of calligraphy and *ikebana*, always in keeping with the current season, are on display. The guest of honor sits before the *tokonoma*, with his or her shoulders turned towards the niche.

Futon and Zabuton

A traditional Japanese house has no fixed furniture. Each room can serve as a dining room, living room or bedroom according to need. The furniture required is stored in large closets. Thus, for example, when it is time to sleep, a mattress, or *futon*, is unrolled on the *tatami*, while a quilt serves as a blanket. When it is time to eat, large square

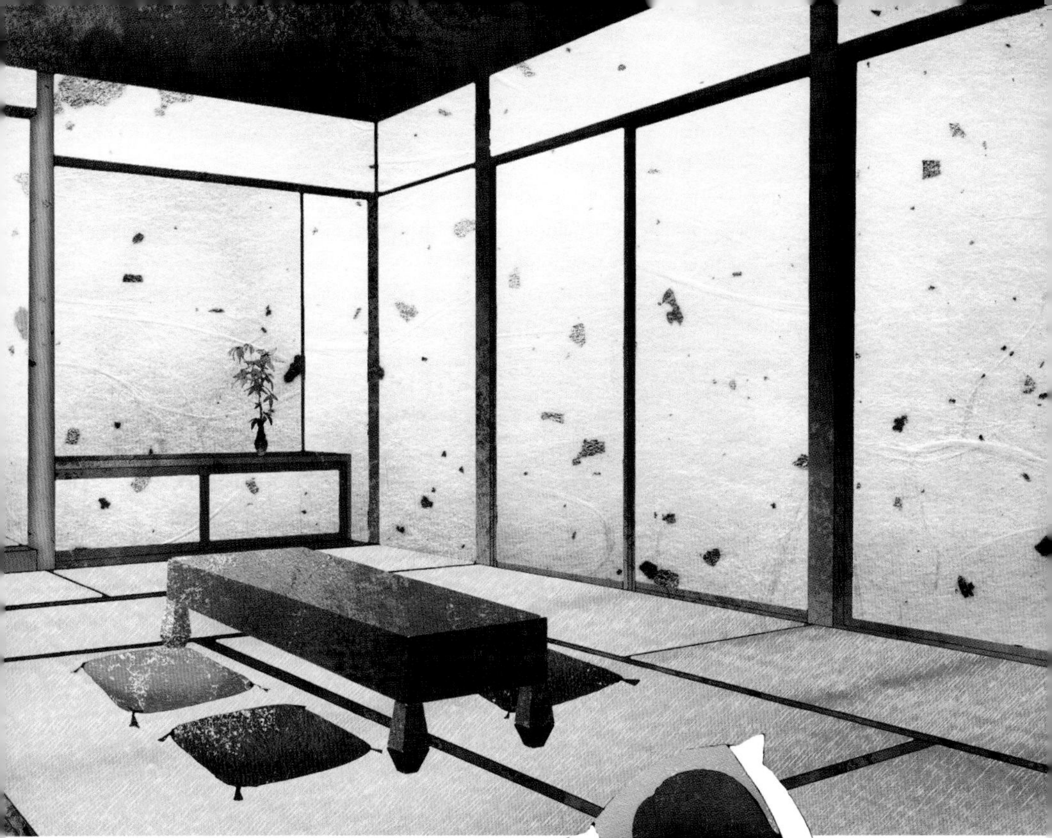

cushions (*zabuton*) are placed around a low table at which diners sit with their legs folded beneath them.

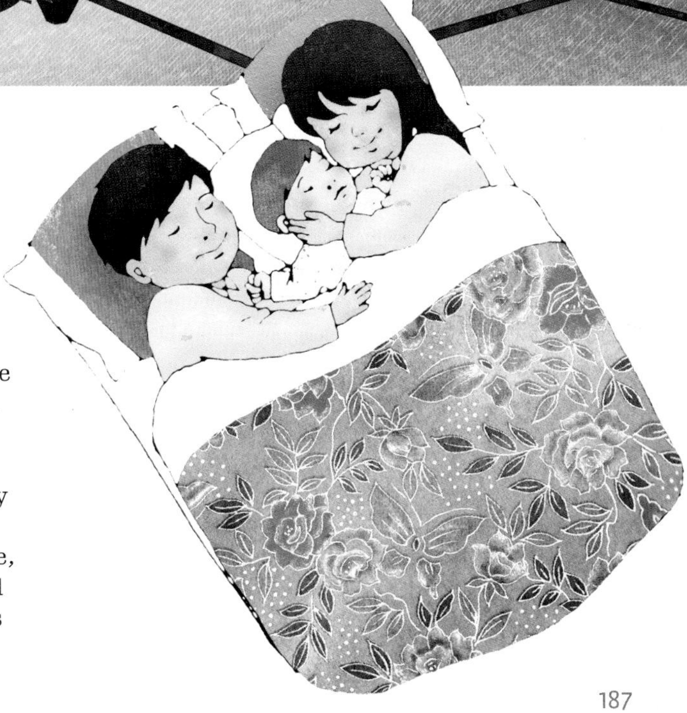

Genkan

It is mandatory to remove one's shoes at the entrance in order not to soil or ruin the *tatami*. Typical of the Japanese house is the *genkan*, a vestibule usually paved in stone, one step below the rest of the house, in which shoes are slipped off and left with their toes facing the outside.

① 切る
cut

天ぷら
Tempura

② 混ぜる
mix

Crunchy Deep-fried Delicacies

This super light way of deep-frying food in batter is, after *sushi*, perhaps the best-known Japanese dish. Few are aware that Japanese cooks learned it from the Portuguese, the first Westerners to land on the coasts of the archipelago. Despite sounding Japanese, the word *tempura* probably derives from *tempora*, the term used by Portuguese missionaries to indicate the fasting periods in the Catholic calendar, when meat was forbidden and replaced by fish and vegetables. Although the dish was a bit *aburakkoi* ("too oily") for the Japanese palate, it soon became popular in a lighter and crunchier version. By the 17th century, every street corner had

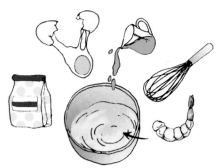

a cart with an oil cauldron that supplied passersby with a piping hot dish to consume on the go. The inhabitants of Edo were crazy about it: some even say that the shogun Tokugawa Ieyasu died of indigestion caused by *tempura* made with carp.

天ぷらつくりかた

③まぶす
coat
④浸す
dip
⑤まぶす
coat
⑥揚げる
fry

Koromo
Koroma, or *tempura* batter, is peculiar in that it should never be perfectly uniform but remain a bit lumpy. It must be stirred lightly and used immediately, while it is still aerated. To add texture and crunch, some people add chopped *sōmen* noodles to the egg and flour. When fried, these result in the dish's characteristic *matsuba-age* ("pine needles") crust.

Tentsuyu
The sauce into which *tempura* is dipped is called *tentsuyu* and is prepared from soy sauce, *sake* and *dashi,* fish broth and seaweed. Real gourmets, however, reject any seasoning as they prefer to retain the flavor of the fish and vegetables and not reduce the batter's crunchiness.

Kuruma-ebi
Kuruma-ebi, king prawn, is *tempura*'s main and most common ingredient. But the dish can also be made with *ika* (calamari), *yamame* (young trout), *ayu* (sweetfish), sweets, and vegetables such as shiitake mushrooms, *ginnan* (ginkgo nuts), *aotōgarashi* (green peppers), *shiso* leaves and potatoes.

盛りつける
serve

完成

天狗
Tengu

Mountain Goblins and Other Supernatural Beings

In its most ancient version, the *karasu tengu* ("*tengu* crow"), a type of mountain sprite, which dwells in the thick of the forest, often on top of very tall trees, is depicted as a hybrid human-bird with feathers, claws, large wings and a big beak. It embodies the essence of the mountain as it must have appeared to the earliest Japanese communities, a wild and violent universe impervious to human control and the opposite of the orderly and domestic world of the village and rice paddy.

For this reason, the *karasu tengu* was regarded as an evil and dangerous being, an emissary of war, fire and disease. To Buddhist monks of the 9th or 10th century, it represented a sort of seductive demon that did everything possible to obstruct their spiritual path, rousing their vanity with promises of supernatural powers, and at times even possessing or kidnapping them.

At some point, however, this symbol of evil began to take on positive

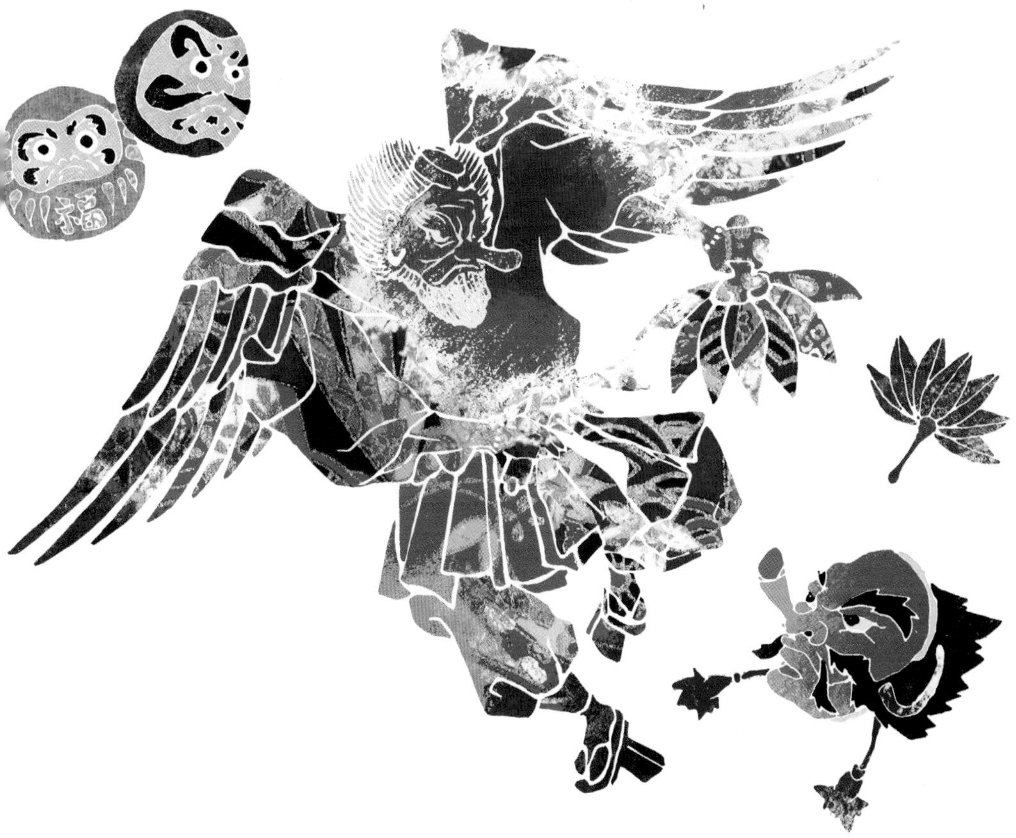

connotations. As institutionalized religion colluded with political power and sunk little by little into corruption, a longing for purity and reform found expression in the *yamabushi*, ascetics who retired alone to the mountains where they submitted themselves to harsh initiatory practices. For hermits of this kind, the mountains were not a hostile world but a school, while the *tengu*, the enemy of institutional monks, was their ally and protector. Even the creature's appearance underwent a transformation. It came to look more human, acquiring its characteristic purple face, with a nose in place of its beak, and its body clad in a *yamabushi* cassock. The sprite of the mountain taught the monks magic and granted them supernatural powers, such as the ability to speak without moving their mouths, or to transport themselves from one place to another, Above all, it provided them with the secrets of the martial arts, so much so that tradition tells us that many illustrious warriors, such as Takeda Shingen, were trained in the art of the sword by no other than the *tengu*.

天皇
Tennō

The Japanese Emperor, Sovereign of Heaven

Japanese emperors have been given the title of Tenno, Sovereign of Heaven, since the 17th century. It was then that the 40th king of Yamato, Tenmu, resorting to a prudent political strategy, legitimized the power of the ruling family by establishing its link to Shinto gods. The *Kojiki* ("Chronicles of ancient events"), which the king commissioned for this purpose, narrates the origin myths, tracing the direct descent of the imperial lineage from the sun goddess Amaterasu *ikmikami*, the principal *kami* of the Shinto pantheon. The goddess supposedly sent her nephew Ninigi no Mikoto to pacify Japan and entrusted him with the Three Sacred Treasures: the Jewel, the Sword and the Mirror, that are transmitted by each sovereign to his successor and remain the symbols of imperial power to this day. The Japanese dynasty is the only one to survive continuously until the present, and the current ruler, Naruhito, who ascended the throne on May 1, 2019, is now the only active emperor in the world. Although the Tenno initially held political power, his primary function is as head of religion.

Today, the Tenno's divine nature is not recognized by the Japanese

Constitution, although the emperor's role as a supreme priest remains undisputed and is expressed through scrupulously handed down ancestral court ceremonies that have remained unaltered over the centuries. The figure of the emperor is the strongest and most influential symbol of the unity of the Japanese people and the basis of every Japanese citizen's sense of identity and belonging.

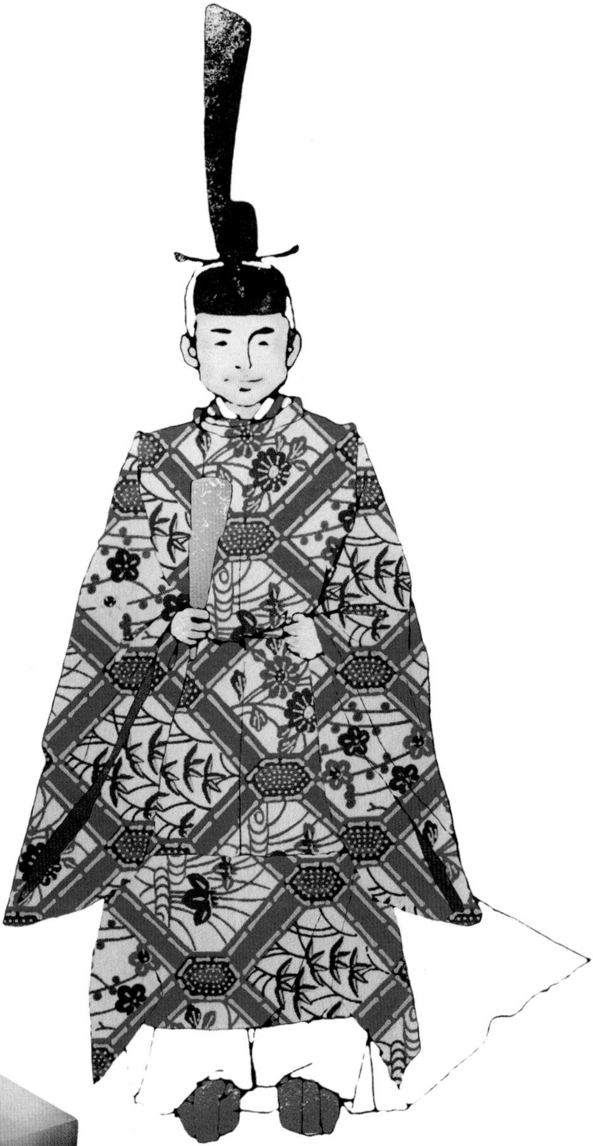

Kikumon

The emblem of the imperial house is a stylized drawing of a yellow or golden 16 petalled chrysanthemum (*kiku* literally means "chrysanthemum"), which also recalls the sun, from which, according to myth, the dynasty descends. It appears that Go Toba, who reigned from 1183 to 1198, was the first to adopt this emblem of the imperial state.

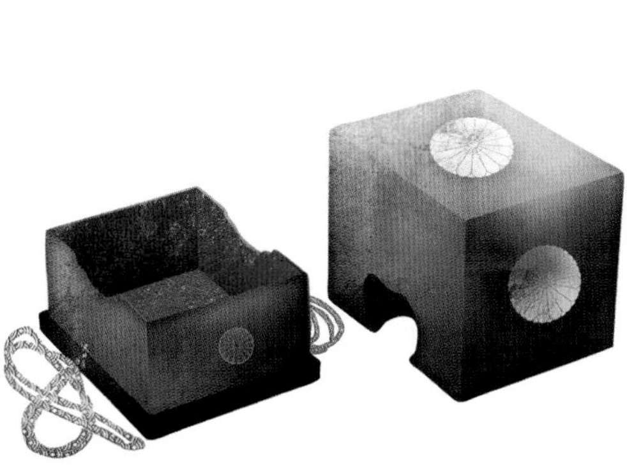

漬物
Tsukemono

Japanese Pickled Vegetables

Today, *tsukemono* refers to the crunchy pickled vegetables that inevitably accompany the Japanese meal, usually served in individual saucers with a variety of samples. But the word is actually a generic term for "preserved food" that once also included meat, fish, eggs, seaweed and fruit marinated in salt or *sake*. Even cherry blossoms were preserved and afterwards served in hot water on the occasion of an engagement or wedding.

The simplest method of preparing *tsukemono*, which is over 1,200 years old and done only in Japan, is to place layers of chosen vegetables in a wooden barrel and sprinkle salt between each layer. Once the barrel is full, it is sealed with a wooden lid weighted down by a large stone. The weight causes the salt to penetrate the vegetables and release water. It is this marinade that gives *tsukemono* its particular flavor.

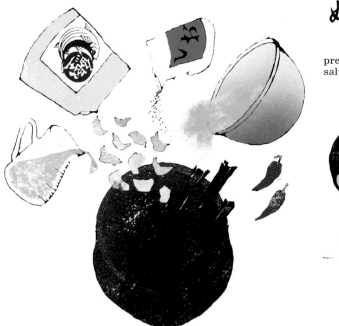

ぬか床を
つくる

prepare layers of vegetables, salt and rice bran

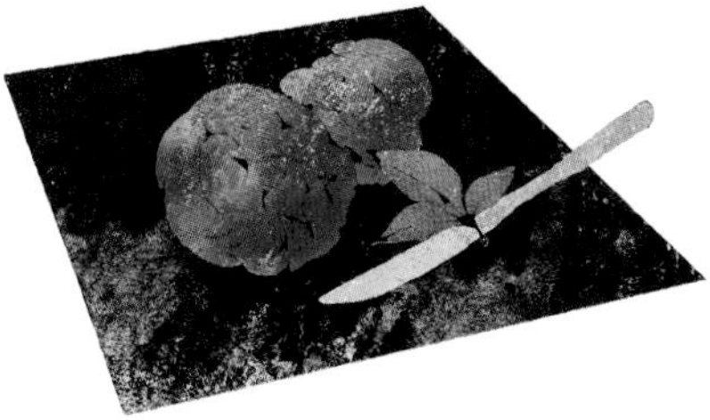

野菜を漬ける

let the vegetables marinate

できあがり

the *tsukemono* are ready

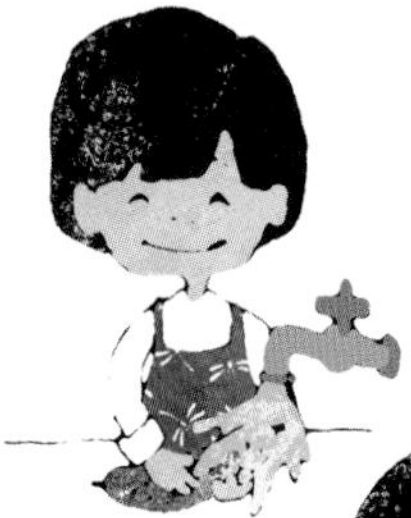

By replacing salt with other seasonings, such as rice bran, *miso* and *sake* sediment, and by combining different types of vegetables, one can create an infinite variety of *tsukemono*. There are apparently 4,000 different types in the archipelago, with each town boasting its own specialty. Among the best known are *narazuke,* with its characteristic sweet flavor from the region of Nara; Shizuoka's *wasabizuke,* prepared with salted horseradish in salt; *takuanzuke,* which contains dried *daikon* marinated in rice bran; and *shōgazuke,* the pickled ginger often served with *sushi*.

待つ

wait

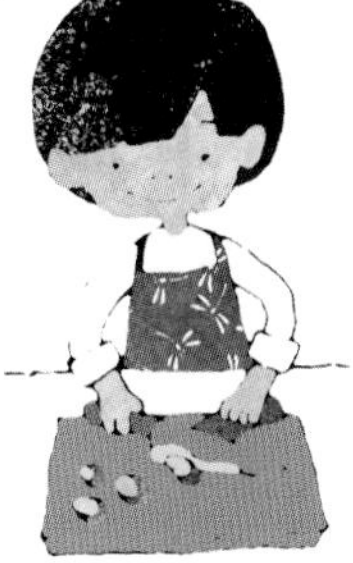

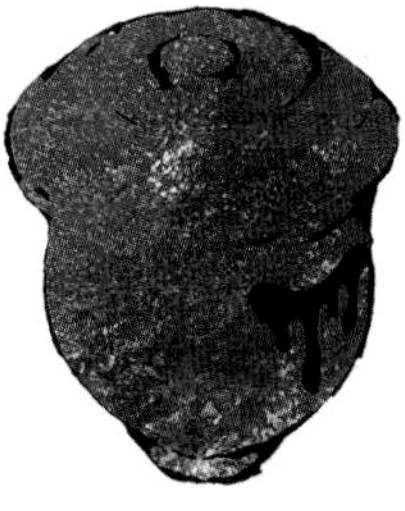

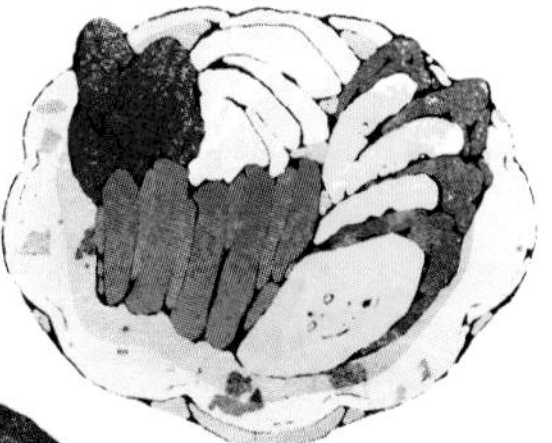

Umeboshi

The most traditional type of Japanese fast food is a white rice ball stuffed with *umeboshi*. This condiment has a strong sour and salty flavor and is made by fermenting a particular type of plum, which is harvested before it is ripe, then salted and dried. Used for medicinal purposes during the 10th century, it is still prepared at home by very old housewives.

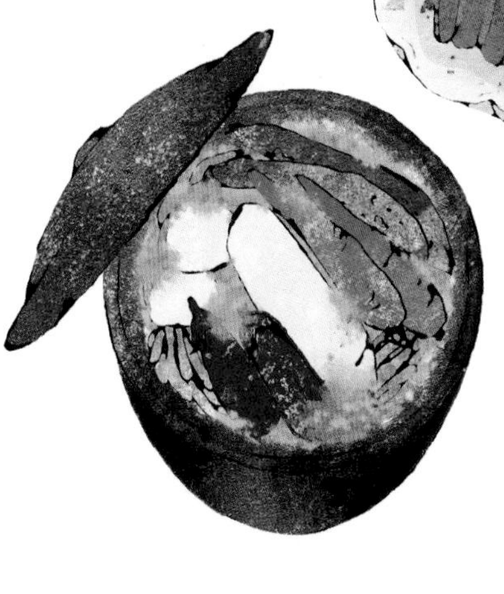

月見
Tsukimi

Moon-viewing Parties

The full moon is the iconic image of Japanese autumn. In no other month does the moon have the poignancy and beauty that it does in September, when the days are still warm but the evening is swept by a refreshing breeze that clears the sky and makes the air crystal clear. In that limpid sky, the full moon of the equinox shines huge and bright, calming the spirit. Stopping to contemplate it, is an irresistible pleasure. Crowds gather to do so in public parks and temple gardens, for example, in the Hyakkaen in Tokyo, or the boat pond in Kyoto's Daikakuji, with eyes turned up while listening to traditional music and poetry. Generally, however, *tsukimi* is celebrated with friends or family. Preparations begin at dusk. A low table is placed at that point of the veranda where the moon is most visible, and covered with offerings in its honor: first, 15 *dango*, the spherical rice flour dumplings that through their shape recall the full moon (15 because the feast is also known as

jūgoya, the 15th night), then seasonal fruit and vegetables, preferably round ones such as chestnuts, grapes and *nashi* pears, and finally the simple "seven herbs of autumn" tart.

When the moon is high in the sky, people sit around the table and spend several hours together, chatting and listening to crickets chirping in the garden while children try to distinguish amid the light and shadows of the silver disk the shape of the legendary "lunar rabbit" that prepares *mochi*.

Nanakusa

The "seven herbs" are comprised of willow bell, Chinese silver grass, prayer plant with small white or yellow flowers, valerian, wild carnation, hemp with racemes and Japanese clover with its poetic cascades of white or rose blossoms. Along with maple and chrysanthemum, these evoke the melancholy and nostalgia that accompany autumn and are symbols of the transience of existence.

The clouds come and go
bringing rest to the
contemplators of the
moon

—Bashō

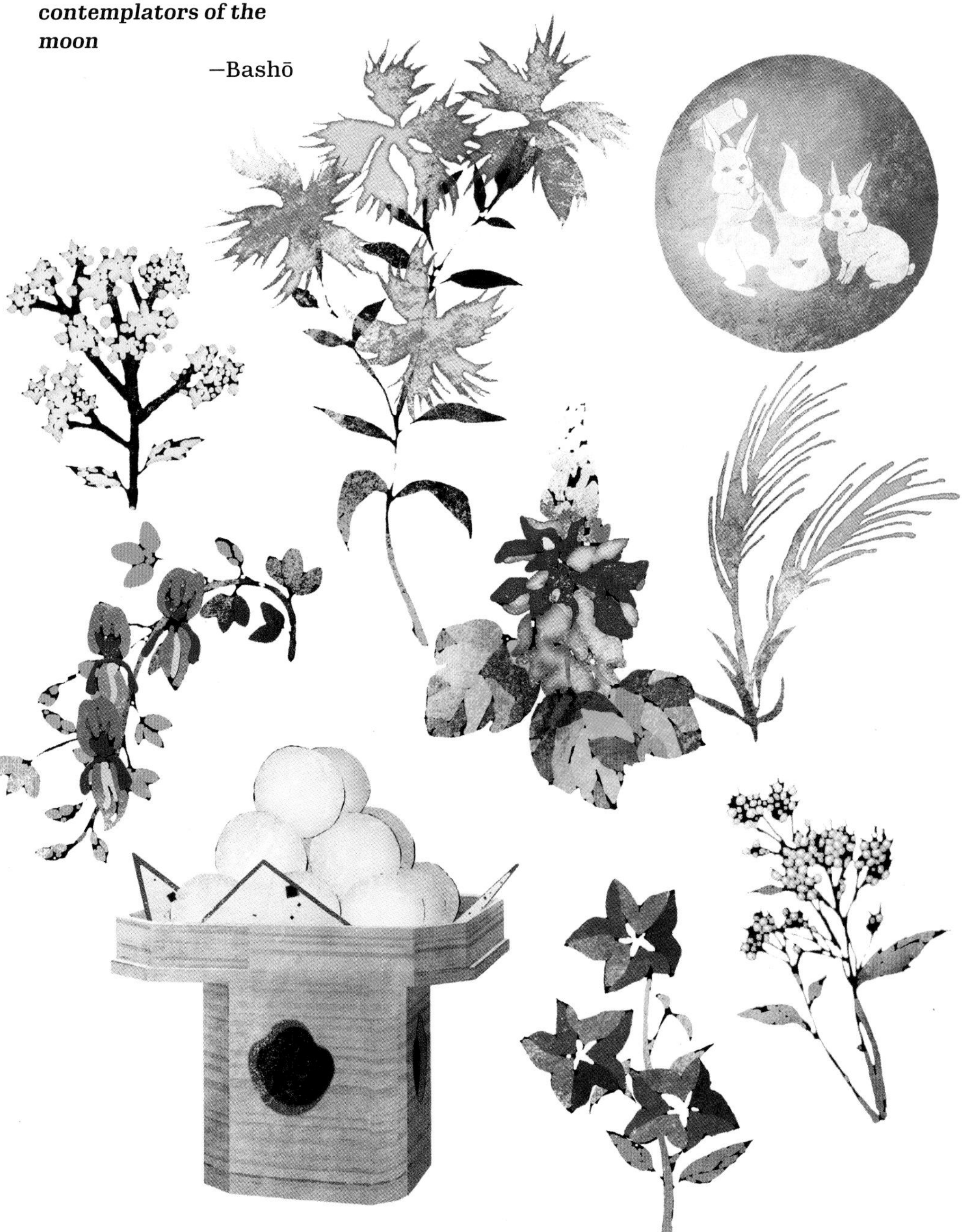

津波
Tsunami

Tidal Waves

Lying at the convergence of four tectonic plates, Japan experiences as many as 100,000 earthquakes a year, of which 1,500 are noticeable by people, and account for about 20 percent of all the tremors that occur around the globe. This seismic activity is also the reason Japan is home to an active 100 volcanoes, though deadly eruptions are rare.

Jishin, as they are known, are a part of life in Japan, where even young children are well drilled in what to do when an earthquake strikes. Some people point to the prevalence of such natural disasters as one of the forces that has shaped Japanese culture, forcing people to cooperate, look out for each other and stay calm in the face of adversity.

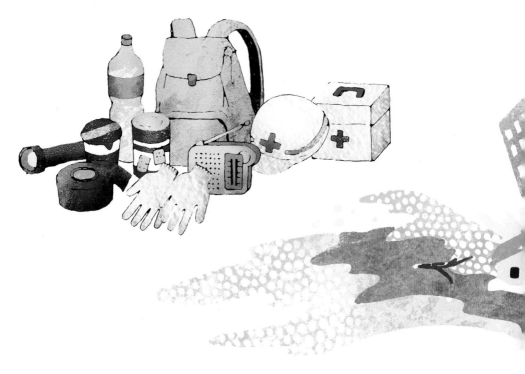

After the Kobe earthquake of 1995, building codes were made even stricter, and earthquake resistant engineering improved further. Earthquakes of magnitudes that are fatal in many countries often result in no serious injuries in Japan because buildings are designed to absorb the seismic waves and rarely collapse. Even the immensely powerful magnitude 9 offshore quake in March 2011 destroyed surprisingly few buildings and other structures. Similarly, the earthquake detection system safely brought the *shinkansen* bullet trains to a halt before the worst of the shaking struck, preventing any serious injuries. It was the enormous *tsunami* that the earthquake triggered, reaching heights of almost 40 m (130 ft) in some places and traveling 10 km (6 mi) inland, which took the vast majority of the nearly 20,000 lives that were lost. The nation has since further strengthened its disaster preparation and mitigation measures, with warnings now sent direct to mobile phones. However, the prediction of earthquakes and *tsunamis* remains a very imprecise science. A major earthquake and *tsunami* in the Nankai Trough, which runs along the Pacific coast, was said to have a 70–80 percent chance of occurring in the next three decades, but authorities now concede they have little chance of accurately predicting it.

浮世絵
Ukiyo-e

Japanese Woodblock Prints

Who does not know Hokusai's *Wave*? That simple and definitive image that permanently imprints itself on one's memory has the power of a masterpiece. Nonetheless, it was not conceived as a work for a museum, but as something resembling an illustrated tourist guide. It is one of many prints that circulated on a daily basis in Edo in the 18th and 19th centuries thanks to a sensational new artistic trend, *ukiyo-e*. The peaceful era that

followed centuries of war saw the emergence of *chōnin,* a new urban middle class comprised of merchants and artisans eager to enjoy their newly amassed wealth on light diversions, such as those of the table or brothel, the theater, boat trips on the river and popular festivals. Artists, too, were commissioned to create carefree works, reflecting the reality and interests of the newly rich, works comparable to today's fashion

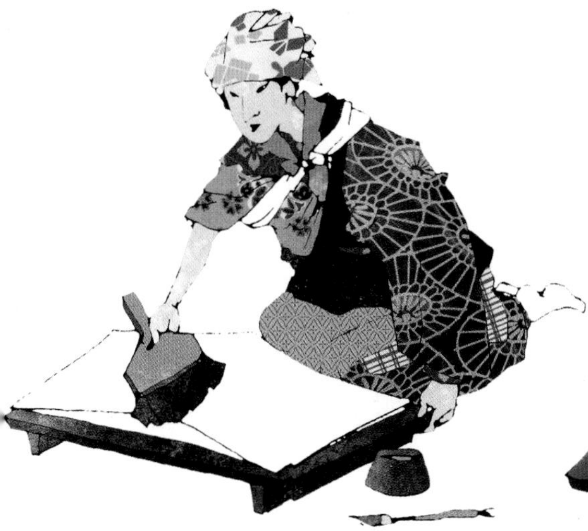

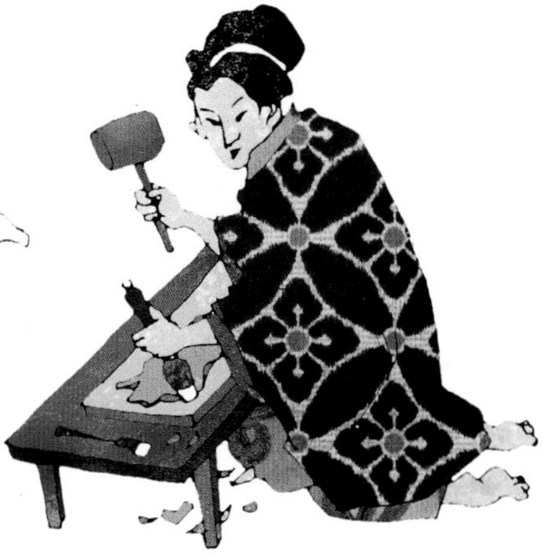

and popular magazines, calendars and posters. *Ukiyo-e* means “art of the floating world,” in which “floating” signifies frivolous and ephemeral as opposed to solid values like frugality and moral rigor upheld by the samurai. Xylography, that is, woodcuts, made it possible to produce multiple prints at affordable prices. This was also the technique used to churn out almanacs with images of historical and legendary heroes; albums with portraits of *Kabuki* actors, for example, Sharaku’s powerful modern ones; Utamaro’s polished catalogs of “celebrated beauties” (*bijin*); Harunobu’s snapshots of everyday life; and Hiroshige’s lyrical landscapes. Last but not least are Hokusai’s series of iconic views, almost violent in their immediacy, which, upon reaching the West, inspired artists such as Van Gogh, Monet, Degas and Klimt, and revolutionized the art of the 12th century.

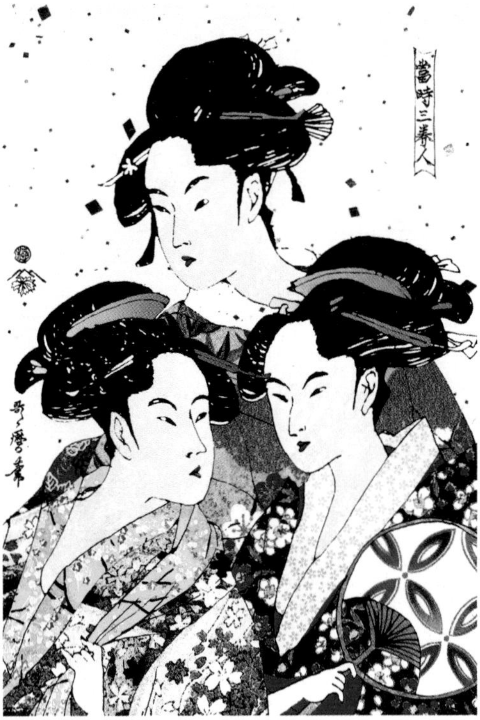
當時三美人

漆

Urushi

Exquisite Japanese Lacquerware

Lacquer is to Japan what porcelain is to China. It is nearly impossible to imagine a Japanese table without elegant black bowls lined in vermilion or glossy square boxes with *bentō* compartments. Lacquer makes wooden containers waterproof and durable, impervious to corrosion even by sea salt and acids. Combined, wood and lacquer can be shaped into veritable masterpieces.

It took thousands of years for Japanese craftsmen to realize that the sticky resin of *Rhus vernicifera*, excellent for gluing arrowheads to shafts, could be used to cover objects and turn them into jewels. By the 9th century, however, sumptuous furniture, utensils, vases and combs coated with this material began to be displayed in homes, naturally those of the aristocracy, because then, as now, lacquer was a valuable material few could afford.

A tree produces no more than one cup of resin per year, at which point this already precious raw material must undergo a series of long and laborious processes that require infinite skill. "Raw lacquer," as the collected liquid is called, must be applied in super thin layers, each of which must dry before the next one is applied. If pigments or decorative inserts are added, the number of layers can rise to several dozen. In the case of certain ancient lacquered objects, 200–300 layers were applied.

Other societies also use lacquer, but the Japanese, who have access to the purest and strongest resin in Asia, have learned how to turn it into a unique art, so much so that when called upon to present an object representing the culture of Yamato to the country hosting the 1939 World's Fair, they chose a lacquer screen.

Maki-e

Although there are many techniques for decorating lacquer, the costliest, *maki-e,* is also one exclusive to Japan. It involves sprinkling gold, silver or mother-of-pearl dust over a still-damp lacquer base to create a pattern that is then fixed with a fresh layer of lacquer. By repeating the process multiple times, one can create a pattern with an amazing sense of three dimensions.

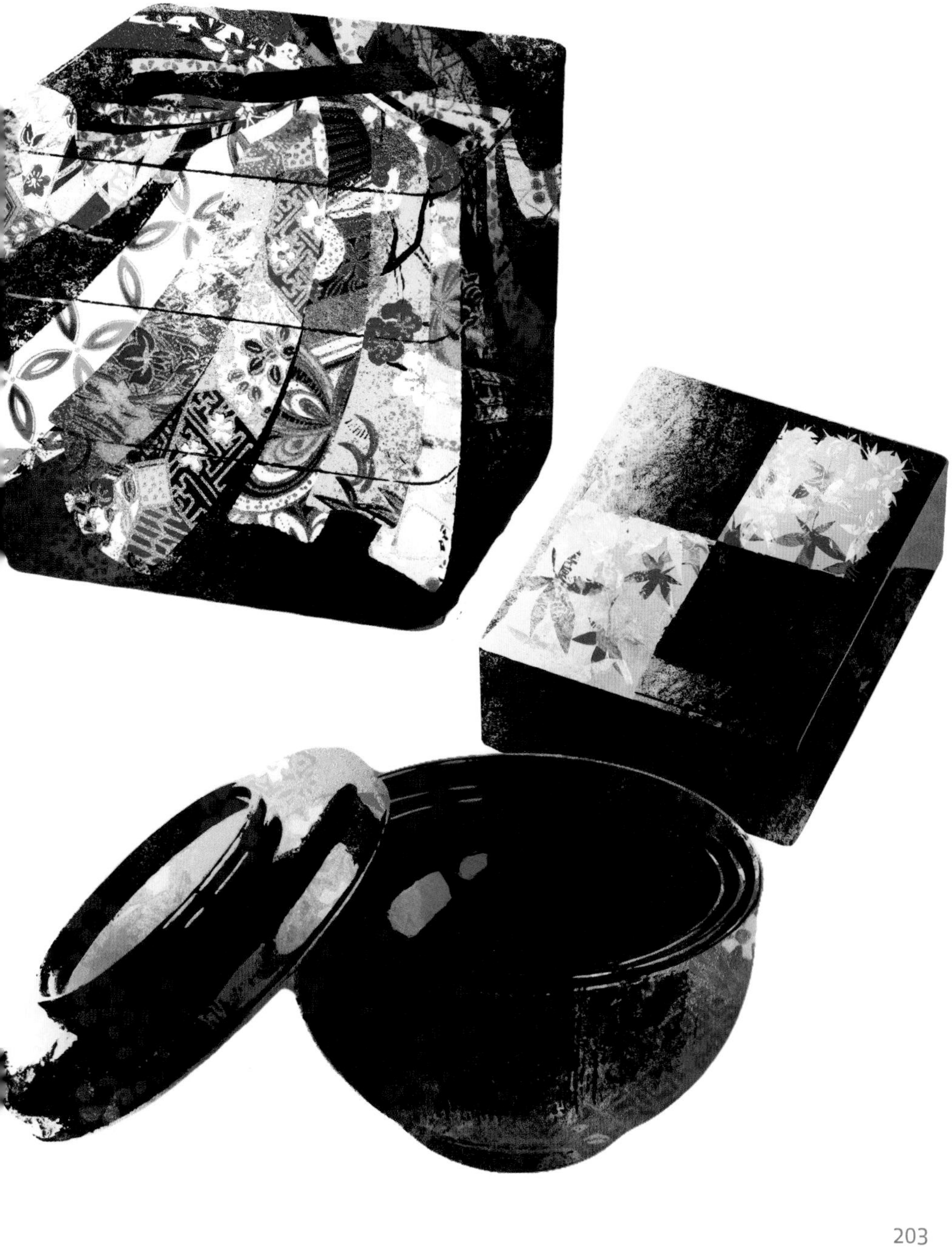

和
Wa

The Japanese Concept of Harmony

This may be the most emblematic and multifarious word in the Japanese vocabulary. The word *wa* symbolizes Japan, and at the same time refers to the way in which Japan represents itself both within the country and to the world, and how it speaks about its ideals and about the social model it intends to pursue. Its secondary meaning is "harmony."

Everything pertaining to Japan, its traditions, its culture, is *wa*. Handmade paper, once commonly known as "rice paper," is *washi*; a room with a *tatami* floor is a *washitsu*; the desserts served at a tea ceremony are *wagashi*, etc. The simple reason is that Yamato, the ancient word for Japan, is written as 大和, or "great *wa*," or, if one prefers, "great harmony."

The *kanji* of *wa* evokes nature's friendly face, the one that is orderly and tractable, tamed by human labor, as opposed to the threatening and uncontrollable universe of the wild (*ara*). Above all, *wa* is the harmony of a community living in peaceful and respectful coexistence, in which individual egos merge without being stifled and instead discover fulfill-ment in the common good. In short, *wa* is the symbol of a people who have worked throughout the country's history to accommodate and integrate that which is different, wisely and gently promoting the coexistence of multiple religions, styles and mindsets, and conscious of the fact that an open approach to "the other" does not necessarily signify submission or failure.

Reiwa

Due to its special meaning, the ideogram *wa* is often integrated into the names of Japanese historical eras. The current era, which began on May 1, 2019 with Prince Naruhito's accession to the throne, is called *reiwa*, a term that can be translated as "propitious harmony." It was inspired by an ancient collection of poetry, in which *rei* appears in the word *reigetsu* ("propitious month," the first month of spring) while *wa* appears in the verb *yawaragu* ("to soften," "calm down," as in the case of the wind). The term *reiwa* thus conveys Japan's wish for a new spring, in which the winter of the previous, difficult years turns into a gentle, mild breeze.

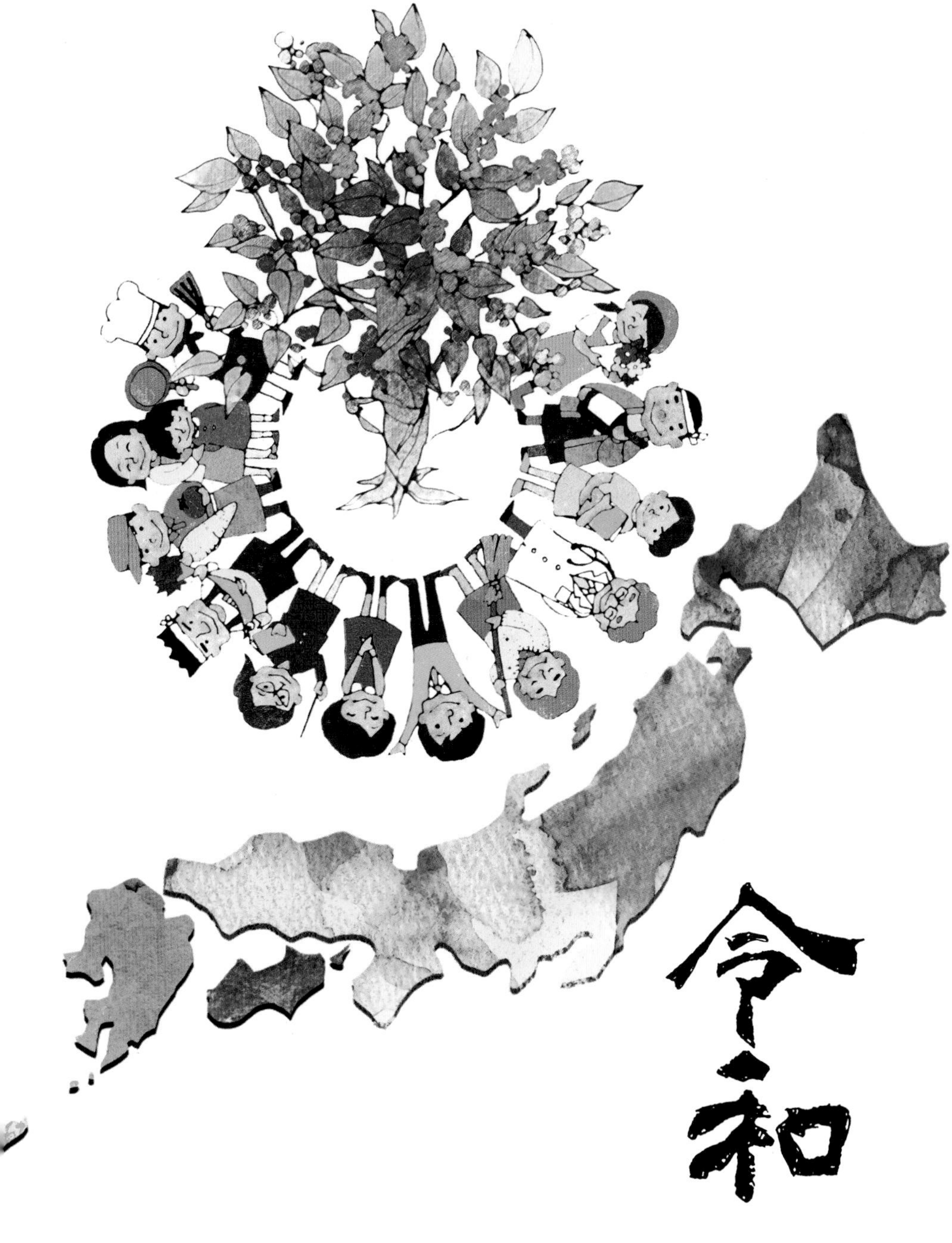
令和

侘寂
Wabi sabi

Finding Beauty in Simplicity and Imperfection

Sen no Rikyū, unrivaled master of the tea ceremony, had a precise notion of the essence of beauty. He saw it in certain types of surfaces that were rough and coarse to the touch, in the irregular rims of bowls, in opaque, earthen shades, in artifacts in which the craftsman's labor was so sophisticated that it remained imperceptible, as if born of nature, in the discoloration, oxidation and cracks that recounted the life of an object. This view of beauty, so alien to that of the West, has a name dating back to ancient history: *wabi sabi*.

Originally *wabi* connoted the spirit, the solitary and meditative attitude of the ascetic who lives a secluded life in tune with nature. *Sabi*, in turn, referred to the quality of a poor and worn object, ruined by use. In around the 14th century, Zen joined the two terms to indicate a single concept: a simple, rustic, time-worn, deliberately imperfect beauty that can only spring from an inner journey that is willing to touch on the idea of transience. *Wabi sabi* expressions reflect awareness that things arise out of nothing and are destined to sink back into nothingness, absorbed into the cycle of nature that creates and destroys everything.

This ideal is not embodied in the moment of maximum splendor or lush flowering, but rather in not yet fully shaped forms or in the subtle process of decline, when what lies before us is inexorably sliding back into non-existence. Far from monumentality and immobility, from any hope of eternity, *wabi sabi* beauty is evanescent and evocative; through imperfection it reveals that germ of non-being that marks the beginning of all becoming. Silver that has oxidized and gradually lost its shine, a stone lantern corroded by moss, a pine trunk twisted by age, a kimono made of raw silk in muted hues, a hand-molded and unfinished piece of pottery—all these are images that whisper the beauty of transience, that is, *wabi sabi*.

やくざ
Yakuza

Japanese Organized Crime Gangs

Although *yakuza* membership is a fraction of its 1960s peak of 180,000, Japan still has more organized crime members than any other country in the world. *Ya-ku-za* can be read as "8-9-3," the worst hand in an old gambling game, signifying a loser. Some mobsters prefer *ninkyo-dantai* or "chivalrous group," while others call their world *goku-dō*, literally "extreme path." The precise origins of *yakuza* are unclear, but during the 18th century *bakuto* gambling groups and *teki-ya* peddlers emerged, the forerunners of today's gangs, which the police call *bōryoku-dan* (violent groups).

At the core of a strict hierarchical, familial structure is the *oyabun-kobun* father–son relationship within the groups. Membership is legal and gangs' offices display their crests.

The *yakuza* flourished in the 20th century, even during the postwar US occupation, when they ran black markets and won sympathy from ordinary citizens for battling criminal gangs formed by Chinese and Koreans left in Japan after the war. Korean-Japanese and *burakumin* would go on to be over-represented in the *yakuza* as they provided a haven for outsiders. The *yakuza* grew in tandem with the Japanese economy, moving into finance, property, construction and other fields. The crash of the bubble economy created opportunities for the ever-adaptable *yakuza*, with company liquidations and debt recovery becoming lucrative sources of revenue.

The traditional police approach was that organized crime was better than disorganized crime, and cooperation was common. This tacit understanding began to unravel in the 1990s and a fatal shooting of the mayor of Nagasaki in 2007 by a *yakuza* boss led to an unprecedented clampdown that has weakened the gangs.

Along with missing fingers, the *yakuza* are most obviously defined by their *irezumi* tattoos. Literally meaning "inserting ink," the intricate designs depict scenes from Japanese myths or history. Poked by hand in a painstaking and painful process, a full-body *irezumi* signifies money spent and pain endured.

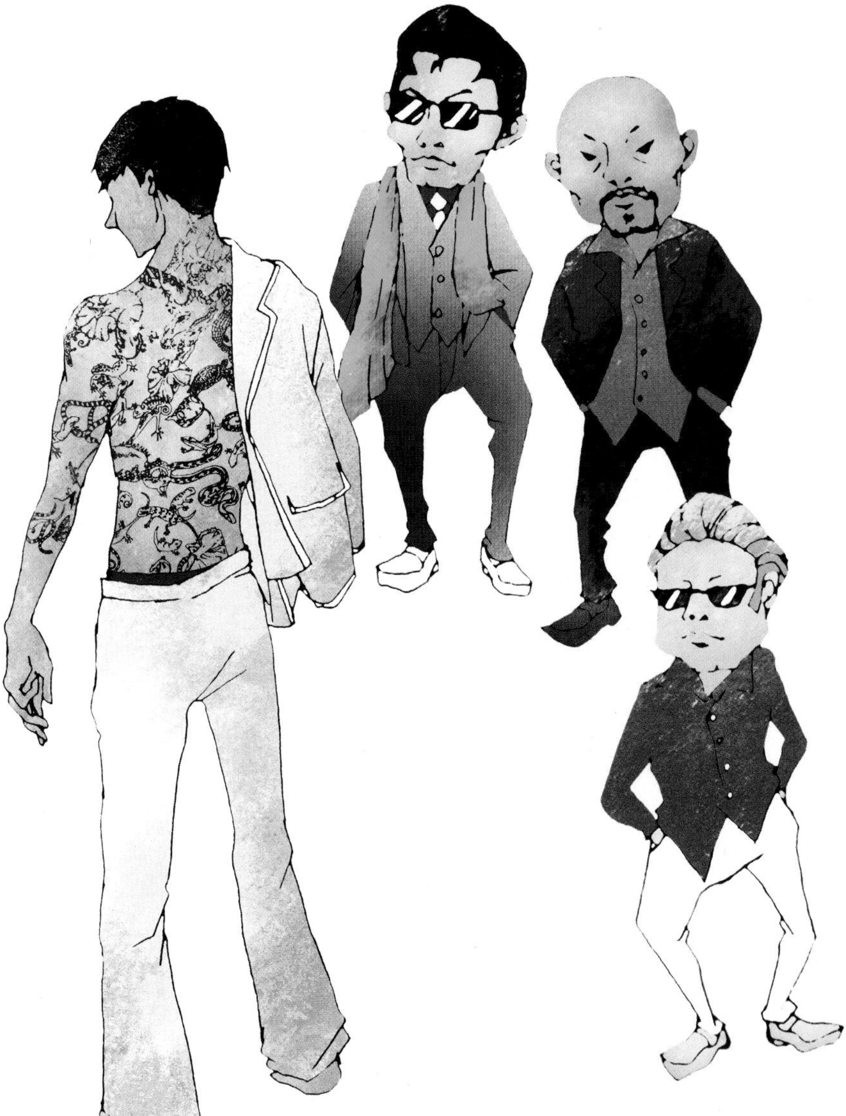

山伏
Yamabushi

Ascetic Mountain Monks

These monks are known as *yamabushi* or "mountain men" because they choose the forest or mountains rather than temples as the sites of spiritual practice. They leave the village community or monastery and climb in solitude through wild and treacherous nature to the sacred heart of the mountain in order to absorb the supernatural powers with which they will heal the bodies and souls of those in need.

Yamabushi must undergo harsh initiation practices in order to develop physical and psychic faculties beyond those of the average person. The first of these is fasting, next comes abstaining from drink, then a series of hypnotic exercises accompanied by ritualized hand movements along with the repetition of prayers and magic formulas.

But the two most terrible trials are putting up with extreme heat and extreme cold: *misogi*, or meditation, beneath a waterfall in icy winter, and *gomasai*, a walk over burning coals.

According to legend, the *yamabushi's* guide and master is the *tengu*, the mythical mountain goblin who grants the hermit the power

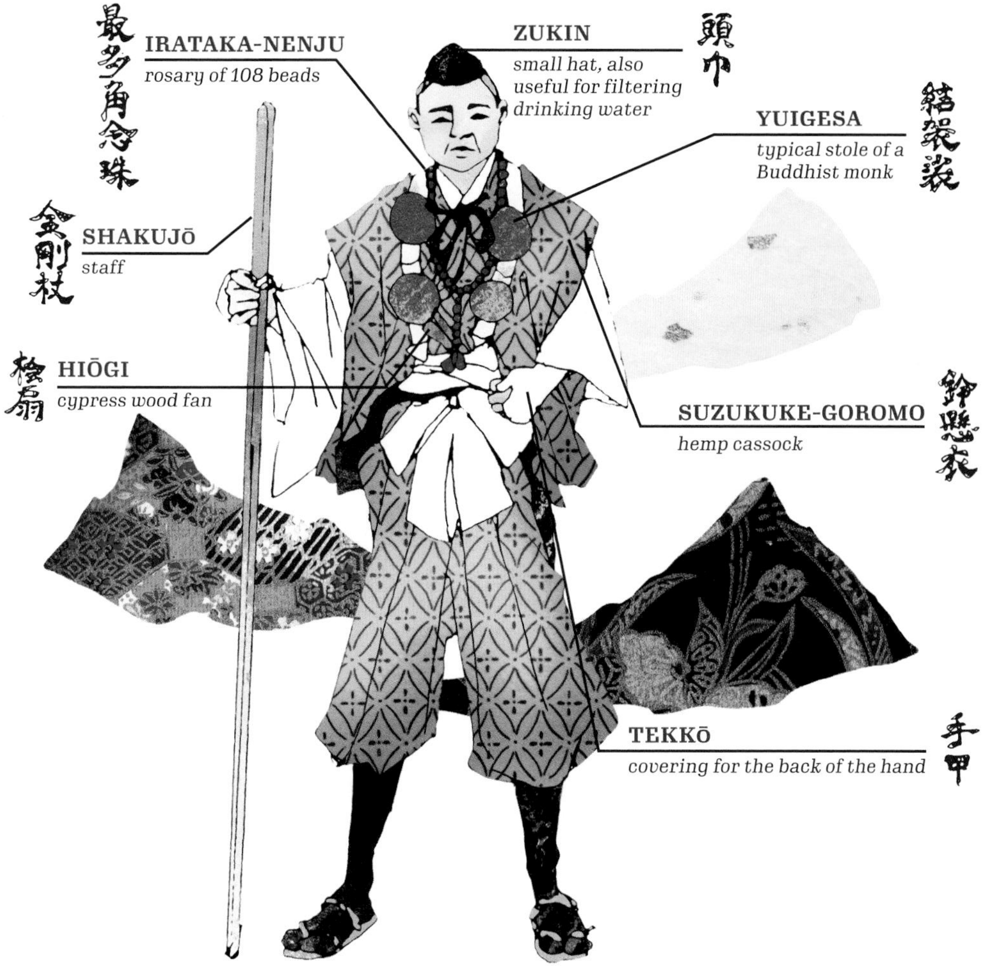
最多角念珠
IRATAKA-NENJU
rosary of 108 beads
ZUKIN
small hat, also useful for filtering drinking water
頭巾
YUIGESA
typical stole of a Buddhist monk
結袈裟
金剛杖
SHAKUJŌ
staff
檜扇
HIŌGI
cypress wood fan
SUZUKUKE-GOROMO
hemp cassock
鈴懸衣
TEKKŌ
covering for the back of the hand
手甲

to change shape, transport himself through contemplation, heal others and master the arts of combat so that he can become an invincible warrior.

The religion of the *yamabushi* is called Shugendo, a fascinating syncretic cult that combines shamanism, Shintoism, esoteric Buddhism and Taoist magic. Tradition dates it back to the 8th-century monk En no Gyōja, but most likely its origins lie in the ancient cult of the mountain, the sacred abode of the *kami* and ancestral spirits. The practices and teachings of the sect, which are kept secret and transmitted orally from master to disciple, have survived to the present day. The rituals and gatherings of the *yamabushi* are celebrated annually, for example, on the night of the summer solstice or the autumn equinox, in Kumano, Yoshino and the Three Holy Mountains of Dewa, within the prefecture of Yamagata.

大和
Yamato

The Spirit of the Nation

Many Japanese people consider themselves, at least to some extent, to be a uniquely distinct and homogeneous ethnic group. The truth is more complicated, but that belief remains a powerful force nonetheless. Although Japan is commonly referred to as *Nihon* or more formally *Nippon*, the more evocative *Yamato* is used when emphasizing the historical and cultural roots of the nation. The component characters, "great/big" and "harmony," don't read as *Yamato*, leading to a number of theories as to its origin. They read as *Daiwa*, also widely used, including for a major financial company. The *wa* character likely originates from China, where it was used to describe the inhabitants of ancient Japan. Yamato Province, in today's Nara Prefecture near Kyoto, was the location of an early imperial court and may have been the first place the *Yamato* people settled. The Yamato court was established sometime between the 4th and 6th centuries and the imperial family is still on occasion referred to as the Yamato

Dynasty. The *Yamato* are believed to be descended from both the indigenous *Jōmon* and the immigrant *Yayoi* peoples, though they were also joined by numerous Chinese and Koreans during the centuries of the Yamato court. The myth of racial purity largely prevails despite the recently abdicated Emperor Akihito once publicly acknowledging his family's Korean ancestry.

Undoubtedly linked to the ethnocentric beliefs is the notion of *Yamato damashii*, which translates as "Japanese spirit or soul," though that fails to capture all the nuances of the original. It invokes the idea of a pure, practical, indomitable and wise culture and tribe that traces its roots back to ancient times. The notion was propagandized by nationalists leading up to and during World War II, when the battleship *Yamato*, one of the largest naval ships ever built, was deployed. It sank in 1945. The phrase has come back into use in recent decades to describe the ideal, if romanticized, Japanese spirit.

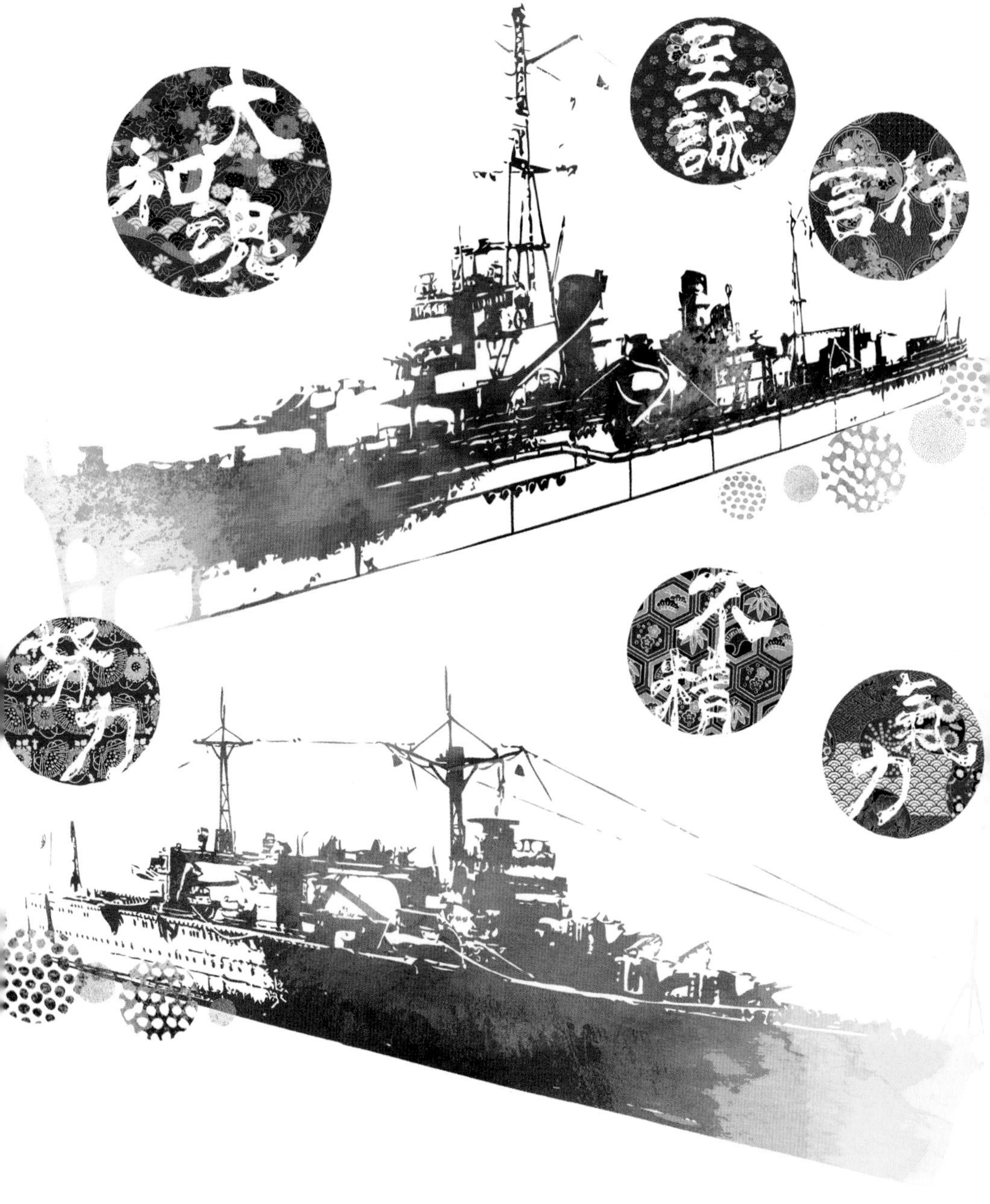
至誠
言行
大和魂
氣力
努力

妖怪
Yōkai

Demons with Supernatural Powers

Japanese folktales are chock-full of monsters: huge terrifying monsters as well as tiny, almost likable and unpretentious ones. *Anime*, *manga* and horror movies have dusted these off and brought them back to life, offering them new settings in which to perform. Nearly all of them have a good and bad side, both because this is the nature of the human character but also because over the centuries they have been somewhat "tamed." *Kappa* (the water sprite) and *tengu* (the bird-man of the forest), for example, who embody the fear of nature in all its violence, have gradually become man's powerful allies as he has learned to harness natural forces. The crude *oni*, at times a sadistic tormentor of the damned, at other times a benevolent protector against evil, is likewise an ambiguous character.

The elusive feminine "other" seems to have been equally threatening and, assimilated into the wilderness, generated a substantial legion of "orcas" from Yamanaba, the filthy and dishevelled mountain witch, to Yuki-onna, the pale and lovely snow woman, murderess of travelers, to Futakuchi-onna, endowed with a second, ravenous mouth hidden beneath her hair. The reassuring objects of everyday life, the umbrella, the *sake* wine-skin, the teapot, can likewise become monstrous after a hundred years by coming to life and transforming themselves into *tsukumogami*. One such case is Karakasa, the disturbing, one-eyed parasol with a single leg in place of a handle. Many *yōkai* are mutants, lying somewhere between a beast, a human being and a supernatural spirit. Among these is Nekomata, the cat with a forked tail and magic powers, Ōkami, the majestic divine wolf, and Kitsune, the fox who assumes the guise of a woman in order to seduce and ruin her unfortunate victims.

Tanuki

The prize for sympathy goes to the racoon-like *tanuki,* who, with his jokes about mankind, takes center stage in an infinite number of anecdotes. With his large testicles, his most distinctive trait, thrown over his shoulder like a sack or turned into a drum, he can often be found on good luck charms.

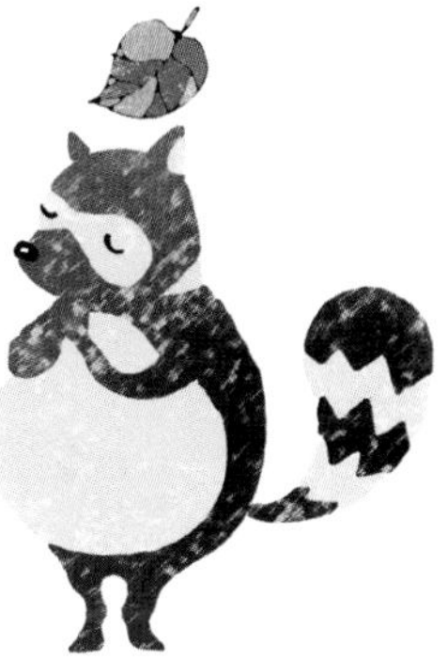

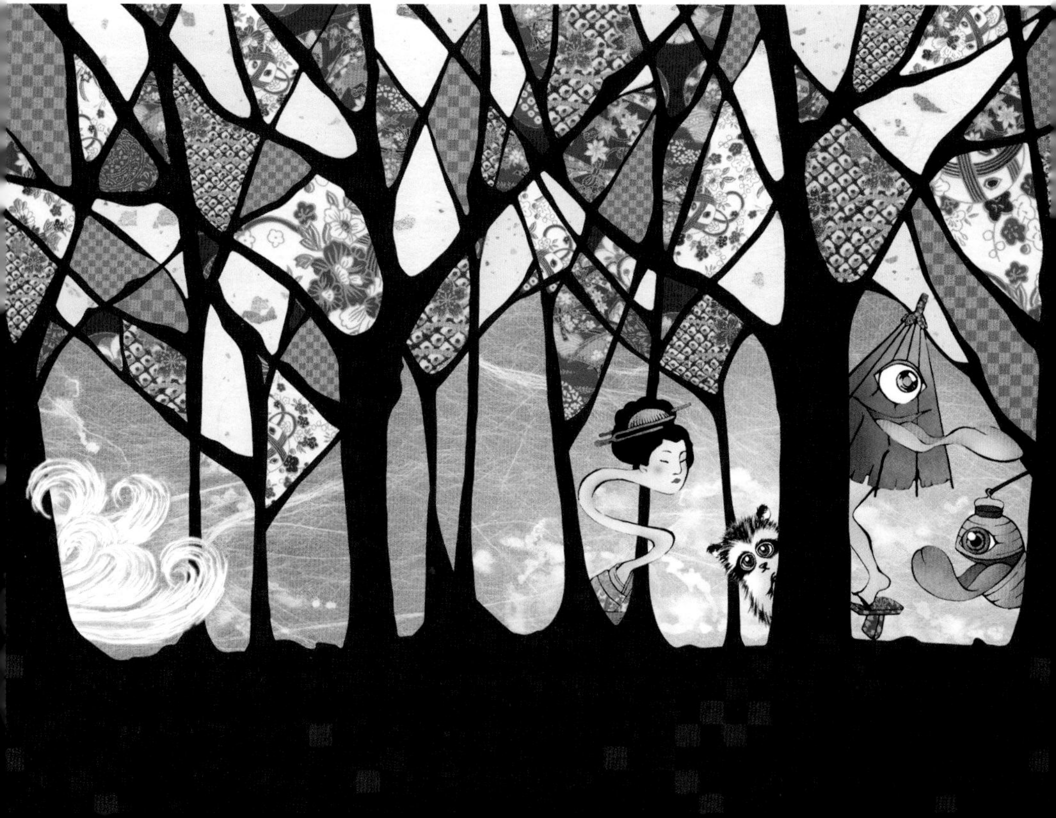

幽玄
Yūgen

An Elusive, Ethereal Beauty

Of all the aesthetic concepts that run through Japanese culture, the most elusive and complex is undoubtedly *yūgen*, which refers to an impalpable beauty sustained by mystery. The term is comprised of two ideograms, the first meaning "diaphanous and indistinct," the second "profound and murky."

Perhaps the fullest theoretical definition is that offered in the 15th century by Zeami Motokiyo, a renowned author of *Nō* dramas. In technical instructions regarding the staging of a spectacle, the famous playwright calls for a small, unadorned stage that will be transformed by the viewers' imagination into a vast beach or battlefield. In this anti-realist, symbolic art form, each movement responds to a codified sign, accompanied by a rhythm with no melody, in which each pause plays an essential part. All the instruments work together to call forth *yūgen*, a suggestive impression that does not reveal the full truth, but merely allows it to shine through. As Zeami notes, the flower of *Nō* blooms if the actor, after submitting himself to rigorous self-reflection, is able to transcend technical perfection in order to express the ineffable. In the theater, in the arts, in poetry, *yūgen* is an experience that is somewhat similar to Zen enlightenment in that it leads to a glimpse of the silent abyss lurking behind forms.

It is for this reason that the images which best capture *yūgen* are ink drawings depicting rocky mountain peaks barely visible behind an autumn haze. No line made by a brush is capable of describing the depth suggested to the imagination by the indistinct grayness of that fog.

Beneath the reality visible to us and that can be perceived by the senses, lies another that is deeper and more mysterious, which can only be reached through intuition. *Yūgen* is the quality of that which can subtly and allusively evoke the most intimate essence of things.

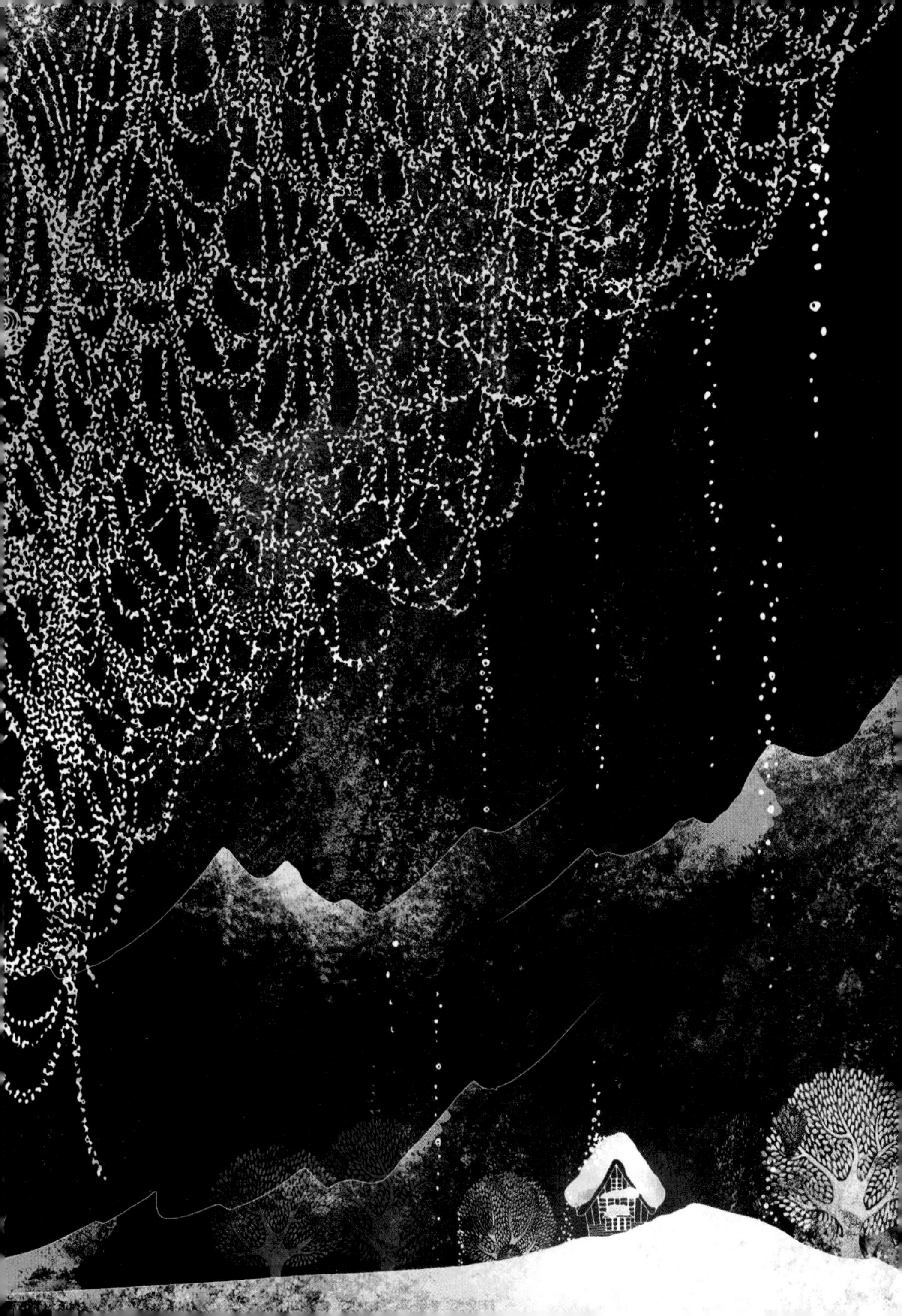

友禅
Yūzen

Fabric Dyeing Techniques

Techniques for dyeing clothes similar to those used in Indonesian batik existed in Japan as far back as the 8th century. But it was around 1,000 years later that the *yūzen* technique, most famously used for creating the vivid colors and patterns of the kimono, is said to have been developed by the Kyoto craftsman Miyazaki Yuzensai, who gave his name to the new method. Substituting the more flexible rice paste for the wax used in batik, stencils and the paste are used to create patterns and to stop the individual colors running into each other on the fabric. The method, which contains around 20 separate steps, is associated most closely with Kyoto, and the work of kimono dyers in the ancient capital is usually referred to as *kyo-yūzen*. Other branches of the method include *kaga-yūzen*, named for the province on the Sea of Japan coast, and *edo-yūzen*, which developed in the current capital, both known for using more subdued colors than *kyo-yūzen*. The techniques are often passed down through generations of the same families, and the artisans will spend long days working on the designs of a single kimono.

Another collection of silk dyeing techniques is known as *shibori*, meaning "to tie," "to squeeze" and "to tie-dye." There are around 50 such techniques, some dating back more than 1,300 years, including a number known as *kyo-kanoko-shibori*, which again originated in Kyoto and are close to tie-dyeing. Material is bound in certain parts using silk or cotton thread to isolate those areas to be dyed in a wooden bucket. The most commonly used dye is indigo as it creates the best effects with the techniques and fabric. Variations include *take-kawa-shibori*, tying with a bamboo leaf; *maki-age-shibori*, using stitching; and *oke-shibori*, tying directly into the bucket. Yūzen and *shibori* have influenced contemporary Japanese fashion designers, including Yohji Yamamoto, who has employed both techniques in his collections.

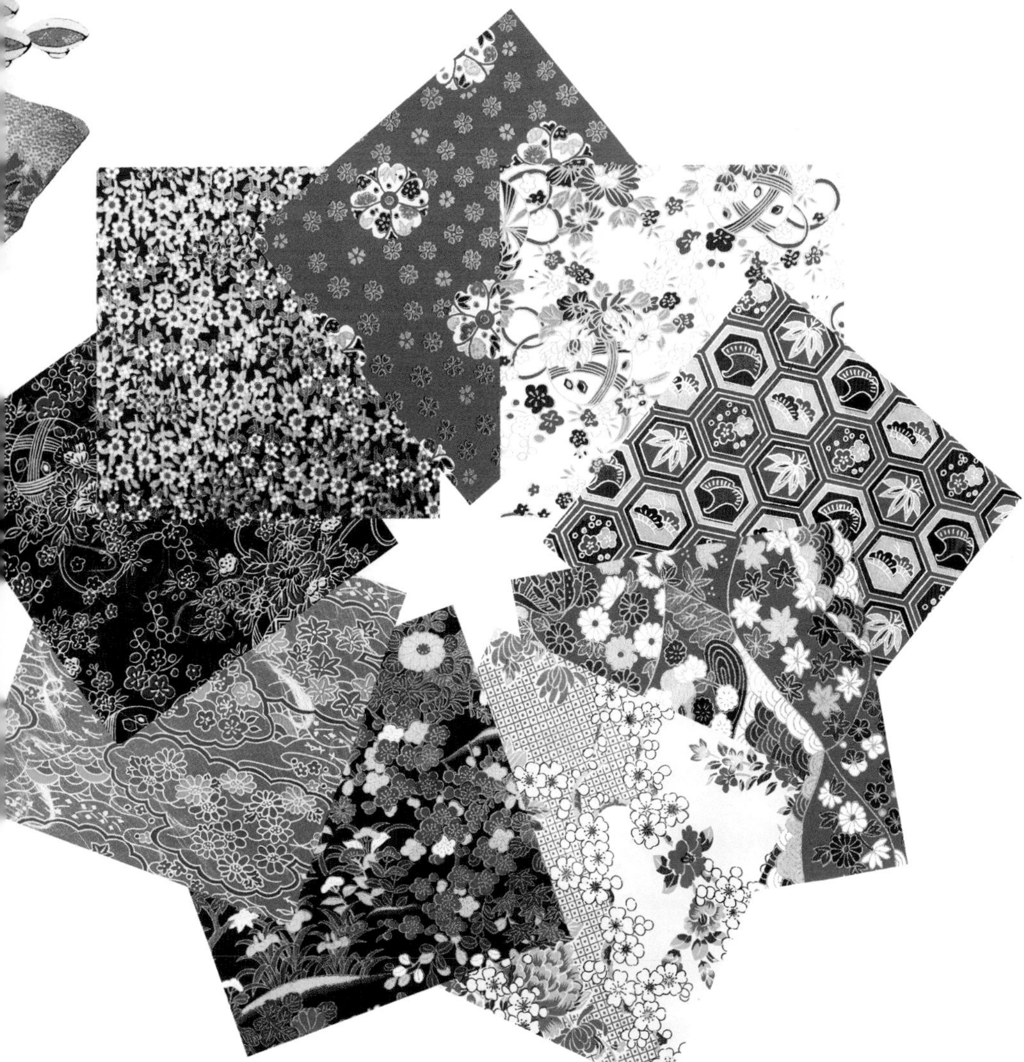

禅

Zen

The Teachings of Zen Buddhism

If there is one force that has shaped the culture of Japan above all others, it is Zen Buddhism. Other Buddhist schools were already established when a monk named Eisai returned to Japan in the late 12th century after studying Chan Buddhism in China. Eisai and a younger monk, Dōgen, who made the same journey with one of Eisai's disciples, were instrumental in spreading the new philosophy of Zen, which evolved from Chan, in Japan. Eisai established the Rinzai school, currently the largest in Japan, while Dōgen started the Sōtō school, whose foundational practice is meditation. An austere school of thought, Zen's emphasis on self-discipline, simplicity and the importance of direct experience and action over thought held much appeal for Japan's warrior class, many of whom became keen adherents. In the first half of the 20th century, Zen was co-opted by ultra-nationalists as a tool of Japanese militarism. The notions of respect, etiquette and harmony that help define Japanese society to this day owe much to Zen teachings.

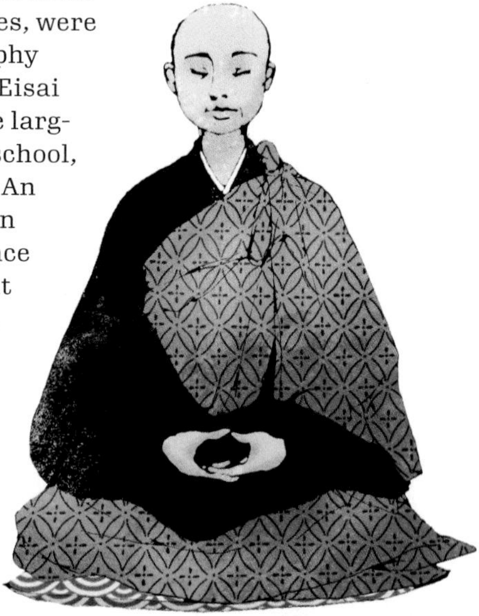

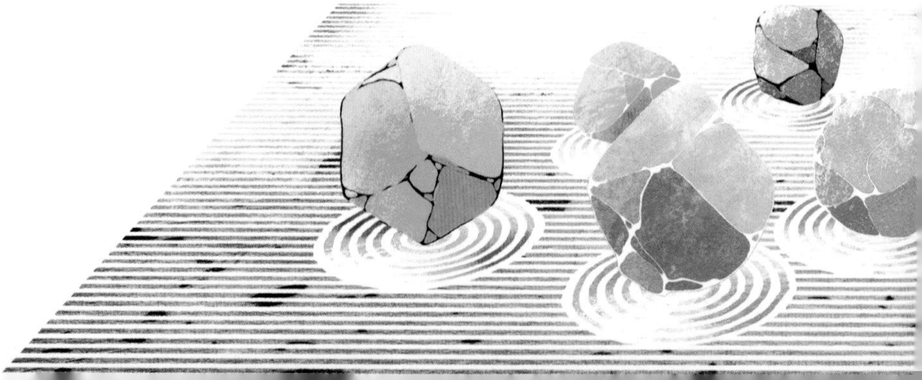

From Zen also comes the Japanese taste for minimalism, the irregular, the patina of time that occurs so much in the traditional Japanese arts, from calligraphy to ceramics and *ikebana*. Despite having experienced alternate phases over the centuries, this discipline has never ceased to exert its subliminal influence on numerous aspects of Japanese culture.

Zazen

Zazen, literally "seated Zen," is a meditative tradition based on sitting in the lotus (*kekkafuza*) or half-lotus (*hankafuza*) position, cultivating an awareness of breathing and quietening the mind. Interpretation of *zazen*'s exact methods and purpose varies between Zen schools, but for all, enlightenment is achieved by renouncing the ego and coming to a fusion with the world outside us. The awareness that Everything is One, however, is not a rational acquisition, but an all-encompassing experience, both of the body and of the spirit.

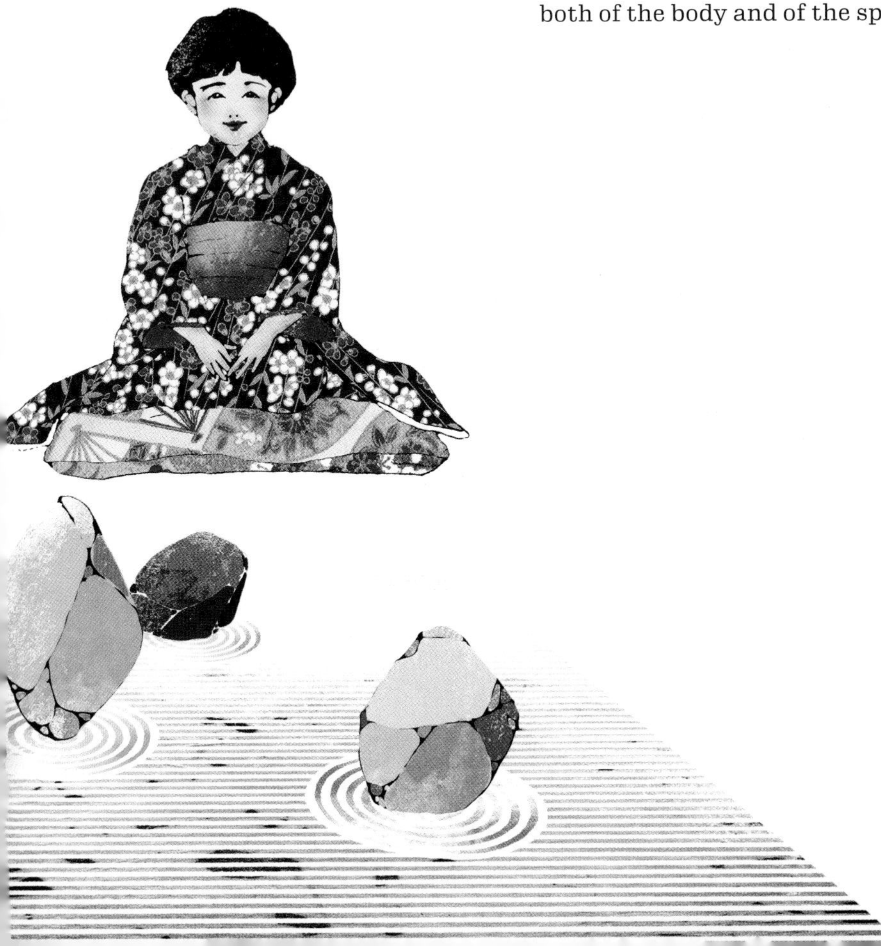

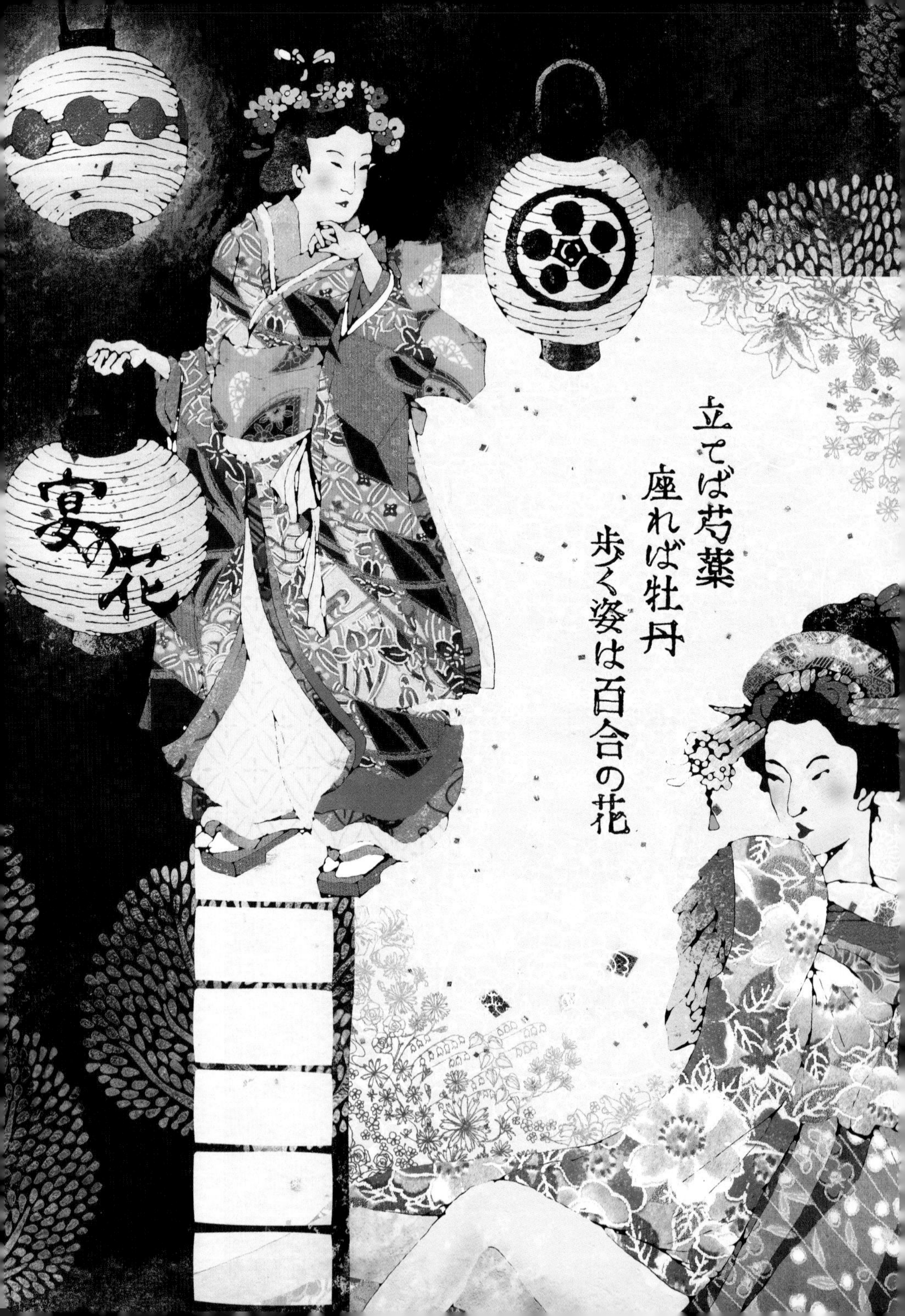
立てば芍薬
座れば牡丹
歩く姿は百合の花
宴の花

AYANO OTANI is a Japanese artist whose sensitivity is expressed through various forms of visual art. She draws inspiration both from natural forms, with works of an absolute simplicity, all built on lively monochrome tones, and from the urban environment. She has exhibited her works in pencil and watercolor and her paper creations throughout Asia and Europe. She has also collaborated with some European fashion designers.

ORNELLA CIVARDI has a degree in Oriental Languages and Literature and has translated and edited the works of many celebrated Japanese writers, including Yukio Mishima, Yasunari Kawabata, Junzaburō Nishiwaki, Yōko Ogawa, Ōgai Mori and Ikkyū Sōjun. She has also written and edited works on Zen and on Japanese culture and art history. In 2005, she won the Alcantara Prize for her translation of Kawabata's *Palm-of-the-Hand Stories*.

GAVIN BLAIR has spent nearly two decades in Japan as a writer and journalist. He covers the Japanese entertainment industry for *The Christian Science Monitor* and *The Hollywood Reporter*, and reports on Japan for France 24 TV, CBC/Radio-Canada, Al Jazeera, Radio France Internationale and BBC Radio, as well as writing for other publications in Asia, Europe and the United States. He is fascinated by Japan's complex culture, including its martial arts.

"Books to Span the East and West"

Tuttle Publishing was founded in 1832 in the small New England town of Rutland, Vermont [USA]. Our core values remain as strong today as they were then—to publish best-in-class books which bring people together one page at a time. In 1948, we established a publishing office in Japan—and Tuttle is now a leader in publishing English-language books about the arts, languages and cultures of Asia. The world has become a much smaller place today and Asia's economic and cultural influence has grown. Yet the need for meaningful dialogue and information about this diverse region has never been greater. Over the past seven decades, Tuttle has published thousands of books on subjects ranging from martial arts and paper crafts to language learning and literature—and our talented authors, illustrators, designers and photographers have won many prestigious awards. We welcome you to explore the wealth of information available on Asia at **www.tuttlepublishing.com**.

Published by Tuttle Publishing, an imprint of Periplus Editions (HK) Ltd.

www.tuttlepublishing.com

First published as *Il Giappone in 100 Parole*
© 2019 Snake SA by NuiNui
This English edition © 2020 Tuttle Publishing

Engiish translator: Irina Oryshkevich

ISBN: 978-4-8053-1621-4

25 24 23 22   6 5 4 3 2
Printed in Malaysia   2205TO

TUTTLE PUBLISHING® is a registered trademark of Tuttle Publishing, a division of Periplus Editions (HK) Ltd.

Distributed by

**North America, Latin America & Europe
Tuttle Publishing**
364 Innovation Drive,
North Clarendon,
VT 05759-9436, USA
Tel: 1 (802) 773 8930; Fax: 1 (802) 773 6993
info@tuttlepublishing.com
www.tuttlepublishing.com

Japan
Tuttle Publishing
Yaekari Bldg., 3rd Floor
5-4-12 Osaki, Shinagawa-ku
Tokyo 141 0032
Tel: (81) 3 5437 0171; Fax: (81) 3 5437 0755
sales@tuttle.co.jp
www.tuttle.co.jp

Asia Pacific
Berkeley Books Pte Ltd
3 Kallang Sector #04-01
Singapore 349278
Tel: (65) 6741 2178; Fax: (65) 6741 2179
inquiries@periplus.com.sg
www.tuttlepublishing.com

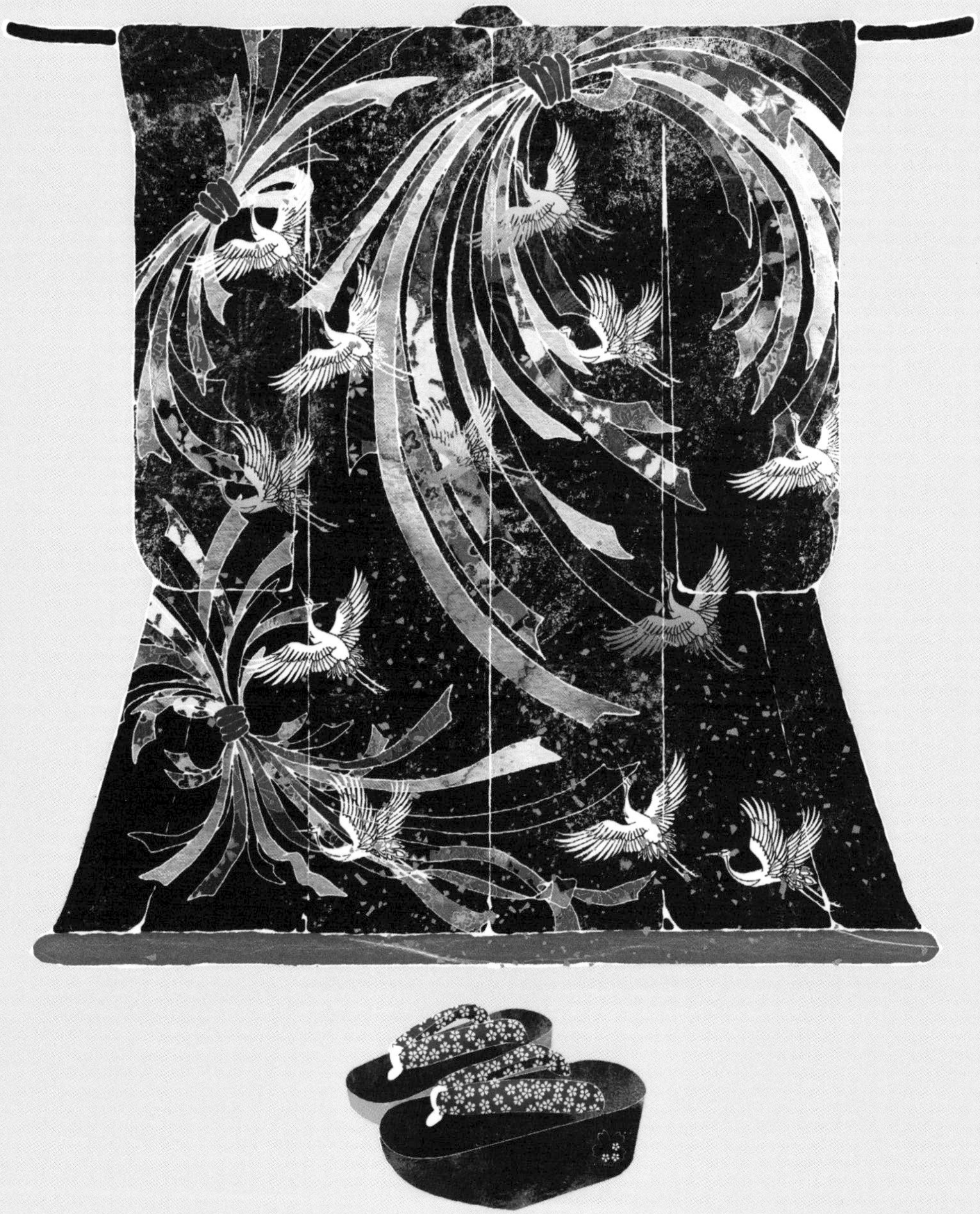

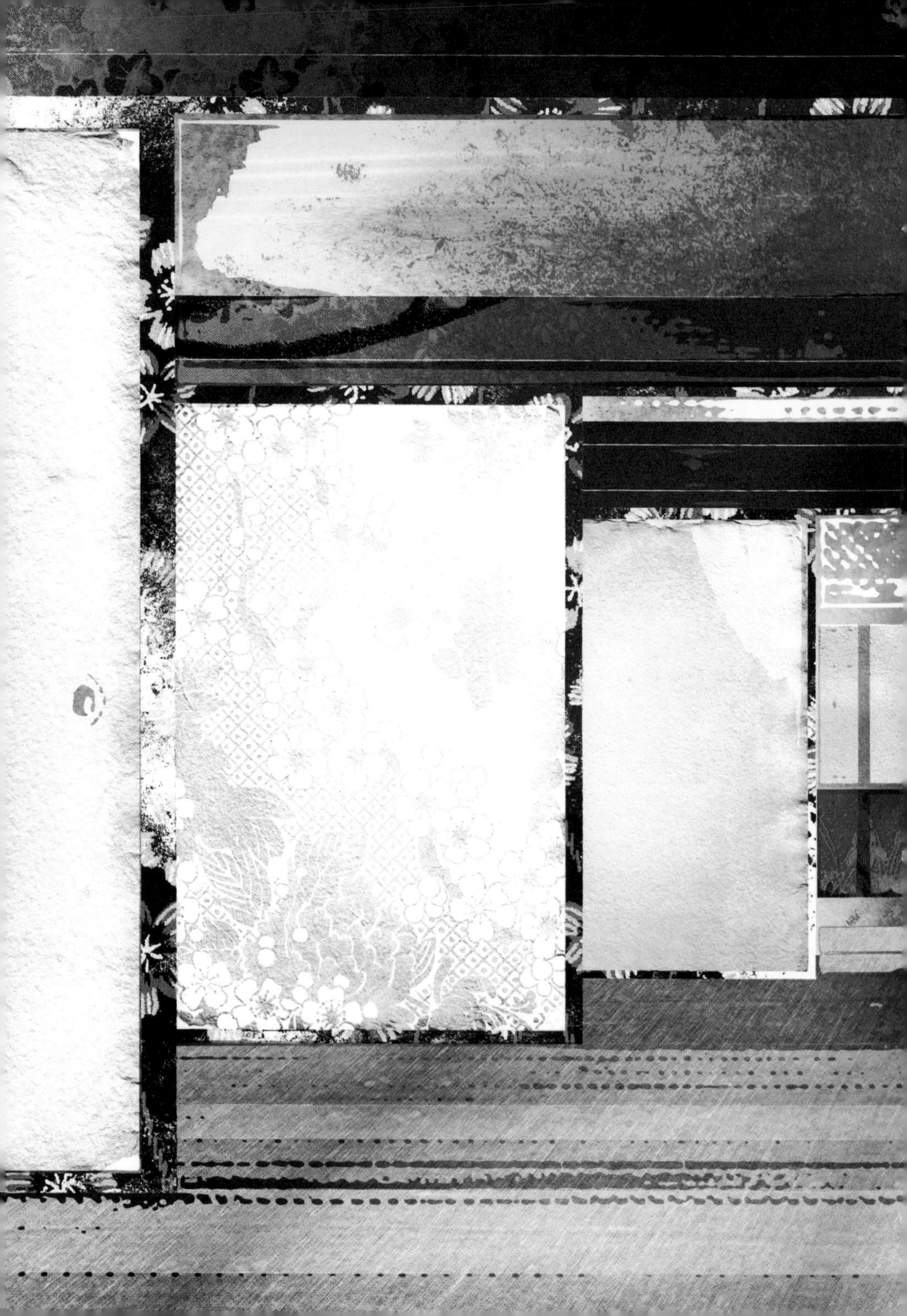